Economics and Managem[ent of] the Food Industry

The food industry is a vast and complex network of processors, wholesalers, importers/exporters, retailers, restaurateurs, and more, which spans the entire globe. *The Economics and Management of the Food Industry* analyzes both the economic principles at work and the management challenges facing people working in the industry at every stage between the farm gate and the kitchen counter.

Central to the book is the principle of equilibrium – the balancing of economic forces – which is the key to understanding the economics of the food industry and addressing such problems as allocating production between competing products, spatial competition, interregional trade, optimal storage, and price discrimination. Real world applications are emphasised throughout to demonstrate the ideas and models in practice with examples drawn from each section of the industry. This book is ideally suited to students taking agricultural marketing, food industry management, agribusiness, and applied microeconomics courses as well as anyone working towards a management career in the food industry.

Jeffrey H. Dorfman is Professor in the Department of Agricultural and Applied Economics at the University of Georgia, USA.

Routledge textbooks in environmental and agricultural economics

1. **The Economics of Agricultural Development**
   Second edition
   George W. Norton, Jeffrey Alwang and William A. Masters

2. **Agricultural Marketing**
   Structural models for price analysis
   James Vercammen

3. **Forestry Economics**
   A managerial approach
   John E. Wagner

4. **Agribusiness Management**
   Fourth edition
   Freddie Barnard, Jay Akridge, Frank Dooley and John Foltz

5. **Sustainability Economics**
   An introduction
   Peter Bartelmus

6. **Food Economics**
   Industry and markets
   Henning Otto Hansen

7. **Economic Growth and Sustainable Development**
   Peter N. Hess

8. **The World of Agricultural Economics**
   An introduction
   Carin Martiin

9. **Agricultural Finance**
   Charles B. Moss

10. **Economics and Management of the Food Industry**
    Jeffrey H. Dorfman

Economics and Management of the Food Industry

Jeffrey H. Dorfman

LONDON AND NEW YORK

First published 2014
by Routledge
2 Park Square, Milton Park, Abingdon, Oxon OX14 4RN

Simultaneously published in the USA and Canada
by Routledge
711 Third Avenue, New York, NY 10017

Routledge is an imprint of the Taylor & Francis Group, an informa business

© 2014 Jeffrey H. Dorfman

The right of Jeffrey H. Dorfman to be identified as author of this work has been asserted by him in accordance with the Copyright, Designs and Patent Act 1988.

All rights reserved. No part of this book may be reprinted or reproduced or utilised in any form or by any electronic, mechanical, or other means, now known or hereafter invented, including photocopying and recording, or in any information storage or retrieval system, without permission in writing from the publishers.

Trademark notice: Product or corporate names may be trademarks or registered trademarks, and are used only for identification and explanation without intent to infringe.

British Library Cataloguing in Publication Data
A catalogue record for this book is available from the British Library

Library of Congress Cataloging-in-Publication Data
Dorfman, Jeffrey H.
Economics and management of the food industry / Jeffrey Dorfman.
   pages cm
Includes bibliographical references and index.
1. Food industry and trade–United States. 2. Food industry and trade–United States–Management. 3. Competition–United States. I. Title.
HD9000.5.D625 2013
338.1'973–dc23   2013007130

ISBN: 978-0-415-53991-3 (hbk)
ISBN: 978-0-415-53992-0 (pbk)
ISBN: 978-0-203-79573-6 (ebk)

Typeset in Times New Roman
by Cenveo Publisher Services

Printed and bound in Great Britain by
TJ International Ltd, Padstow, Cornwall

To my wife, Melody

Contents

List of figures and tables ix
Preface xi
Acknowledgements xiii

1 The basics of the food industry 1

2 Cost economics for processing plants 4

3 Pricing economics for food processors 21

4 Trade among regions 34

5 The economics of storage 47

6 Plant location and size decisions 58

7 Risk management 70

8 The economics of the marketing sector 78

9 Price discrimination 91

10 Imperfect competition and game theory 105

11 Spatial competition 122

12 The food service industry 132

13 Food retailers 153

14	Launching a new product	164
15	Special organizational features in the food industry	175
	Notes	192
	Index	195

Figures and tables

Figures

2.1	A fruit packing operation	6
2.2	The fruit packing operation with minimum and maximum station crews	7
2.3	Labor requirements table for a fruit packing operation	9
2.4	Hourly labor cost function	10
2.5	The shape of the hourly labor cost function	10
2.6	The variable cost function and its component parts	12
2.7	Average variable cost function for a step-shaped total variable cost function	14
2.8	Finding the minimum average variable cost	15
4.1	An opportunity for trade	35
4.2	The three-panel trade diagram	36
4.3	Adding the import supply curve to the trade panel	37
4.4	The three-panel trade model equilibrium	38
5.1	One-period production, two-period sales	49
6.1	Components of transportation costs	60
6.2	Possible combinations of plant numbers and locations	61
6.3	An example of a net value surface	62
6.4	Net value surfaces for two ingredients shipping to one plant	63
6.5	Net value surfaces for two competing plants	63
6.6	Site rent for farms two distances from the same plant	65
8.1	Farm, wholesale, and retail supply curves	83
8.2	Market equilibrium at all levels	84
10.1	Basic 2×2 game	107
10.2	The prisoner's dilemma	109
10.3	Cournot reaction functions and Nash equilibrium	111
10.4	Bertrand duopoly, reaction functions in different shapes, and Nash equilibriums	113
10.5	Kinked demand curve with marginal revenue curves	115
10.6	Stackelberg Cournot with isoprofit and collusive lens	116
11.1	A kinked demand curve	128
13.1	Market share pie chart	154

Tables

4.1	Algebraic supply and demand equations for analyzing trade	39
5.1	Initial equations for the two-period storage model	50
12.1	Franchise terms and details for some common chains	145

Preface

Audience

This book is designed to be used in a class at the senior undergraduate or Master's level. A basic knowledge of microeconomics is assumed. Students should be familiar with the concepts of elasticity, opportunity cost, discounting, cost minimization, profit maximization, marginal, average, total, variable, and fixed costs, marginal revenue, perfect competition, monopoly, and oligopoly. An introductory microeconomics course should have covered all these topics, and students who have taken intermediate-level microeconomics would definitely have all the necessary tools to succeed in a course using this book.

The book uses a limited amount of calculus, so it would be helpful if students had at least one class in differential calculus. However, it is not essential as an instructor can work around most of these instances and instead use subtraction to motivate the marginal concepts. Further, the calculus is employed mostly for instructional purposes. If students are familiar with the concept of derivatives, they can follow the math in the book; the students do not actually need to take derivatives to use the book. A few of the practice problems (such as in chapter 10) and occasional application boxes do require derivatives, but an instructor who wants to teach without calculus can avoid those.

The book provides lots of intuition and tries to balance that economic intuition with mathematics and graphs; thus, the book is very appropriate for a course in an MBA or similar non-economics graduate program. The book would fit well in courses of study in agribusiness, business, or retailing and marketing programs.

Book organization

This book is organized in several different ways. First, the chapters move in some sense from food processing, to areas that fall in the realm of wholesaling and marketing, concluding with retail-level topics such as food retailing and restaurant management. In a second sense, the chapter organization makes sense (to me, at least) in that the chapter topics build on earlier chapters. There are certainly breaks in this chain, so that a professor need not use every chapter in this book. Here are some possible subsets of the book that could be used for part or all of a course.

Chapters 2 and 3 present the optimal management of food processing plants and the economics behind the setting of prices for both products sold and inputs purchased. These chapters could stand alone as a unit on those topics in an agribusiness class. Chapters 2 and 3 also could be combined with chapters 6, 7, 8, and 9 on business location decisions, risk management, marketing margins, and price discrimination, respectively, to make a fuller unit or course on the economics and management of a business in the manufacturing sector. Such a course might also utilize chapter 14 on new product development and even chapter 10 on game theory, which can apply to management of large companies in the food manufacturing sector. Such a set of chapters would certainly fill a quarter or, with a little augmentation by the instructor, a full semester course.

Chapters 4 and 5 cover economic models of trade and storage. These can be incorporated with the other chapters from 2 through 9 to comprise a traditional course in agricultural marketing. Once such a sequence is completed, it can then be extended as the instructor wishes. One possible direction would be to add chapters 10 and 11 (covering game theory and spatial competition) for a more advanced and modern course. Another (or an additional) extension would be to include chapter 14 on new product development. Such a course would be an excellent syllabus for an economics of agricultural markets course.

Instructors who wish to broaden their course to cover the entire food industry beyond the farm gate (food manufacturing, wholesaling, retailing, and food service) can include all 15 chapters, which means including chapter 12 on food retailing and chapter 13 on the food service industry. These two chapters both include aspects of the economics of those industries along with aspects of management. Adding these chapters to the course adds coverage of the food retailing and food service industries, which together represent an enormous share of the modern food industry in developed countries. Chapter 15 covers a set of topics involving special features of the food industry: government regulations and programs, cooperatives, marketing orders and commodity associations, vertical integration, and franchises. If 15 chapters are too many to fit into a course, but the chapters on the food service and retail sectors are priorities for inclusion, chapters 7, 10, 11, and 15 are possible candidates for skipping as those topics are not essential in order to follow the other chapters, and they are also topics that may be covered by other courses.

Instructors can choose chapters that focus more on economics or, with different selections, make a course that is a management class. The economics-heavy course might include chapters 2, 3, 4, 5, 8, 9, 10, 11, and 15. To take a management focus, choose chapters 2, 3, 6, 7, 8, 9, 10, 11, 12, 13, and 14.

Really, there are many possibilities for different courses that can be constructed. Many of the chapters can be covered without material from other chapters. Chapters 2 and 3 are connected; chapter 5 builds on chapter 4, and then those themes reappear in chapter 8. A few concepts from chapter 10 are mentioned in chapter 11, but they could be defined quickly by the instructor if chapter 10 is skipped.

Acknowledgements

This book is an outgrowth of over 20 years of teaching a class on the economics and management of the food industry. My interest in the topic started even before my teaching career, while still a student at the University of California, Davis. There I took classes covering many of the topics in this book from two professors who were very influential for my career: Ben French and Richard Sexton.

I took a class on agricultural marketing (the old traditional name for most of the topics in this book) from Ben French while I was an undergraduate and then served as a teaching assistant for that class in my first year as a graduate student. This class was taught using the classic book by Raymond Bressler and Richard King, *Markets, Prices, and Interregional Trade* (1978). This book has long been out of print, but it inspired my approach to the topics in the early chapters of this book, especially chapters 2 and 3. Then Richard Sexton was the professor for my graduate class in agricultural marketing, laying the foundation for how I think about imperfect markets, game theory, and spatial competition. His influence continues to this day as he graciously provided guidance on chapter 11 when I hit an impasse. Essentially, this book is my attempt to bring Bressler and King's book up to the current day, making their approach modern, augmenting what they did with what I have learned studying and teaching these topics, and broadening the topic coverage to include more on risk management, food retailing, and restaurants because those subjects are much larger parts of the food industry today than when Bressler and King wrote their book.

Besides Ben French and Richard Sexton, other professors and colleagues who have influenced me in terms of teaching style, writing style, and just generally how to present and explain things to students include Art Havenner, my dissertation advisor, who taught me much about being an economist; Thomas Hazlett, who has taught me most of what I know about being an economist outside the confines of the university; and Dale Heien, the first professor who taught me about economics research and with whom I wrote my first few papers. I have also learned about the subjects in this book from Barry Barnett, Wade Brorsen, Greg Colson, Jim Epperson, Robert Feenstra, Randy Fortenberry, Philip Garcia, Berna Karali, Scott Irwin, Mark Manfredo, Chris McIntosh, Matt Roberts, Dwight Sanders, Wally Thurman, Steve Turner, and Carl Zulauf. I have benefited much from pleasant and enlightening conversations with all of them through the years.

Over 20 years of my students have also contributed to the refinement of my knowledge and the ability to explain the topics in this book. My fall 2012 class used a draft of this book as their text and provided some feedback on it. Guest speakers to my class have also taught me while they were teaching my students. In particular, Tom Johnson, Shona Johnson, Mack Guest, and Casey Jones helped me learn about restaurant management, new product development, logistics, and supply chain management, respectively.

I thank Beth Nielsen and Clay Carswell for careful editing and proofreading. Beth Nielsen also did work helping with market research for the book proposal. Jennie Allison and Anne Karner chipped in as things were getting rolling. Mary Alice Jasperse helped with research on restaurants and food retailing; Clay Carswell, in addition to proofreading, did research on marketing order features and other subjects as needed. Zeke Baxter worked diligently on the figures and also performed some general research for the book. Greg Colson kindly read through the game theory chapter and provided some suggestions for improvement, and Rich Sexton did the same for the chapter on spatial competition. I thank all of these individuals for their valuable help on this project. If the book falls short anywhere, it is probably because I did not listen to them enough or follow through on their advice.

My daughter Jennifer contributed to this book by being a budding economist in her own right, which challenged me to increase the clarity of my explanations and economics thinking. Finally, my wife deserves special thanks and unlimited appreciation for allowing me so many evenings to write this book. I have been blessed to have her as a wife for even longer than I have been a professor. This book would have been impossible without the support, love, and patience of my family. I am grateful to them for all they do to brighten my life.

1 The basics of the food industry

The food industry is an incredibly diverse sector of the world economy, ranging from farming to food processing, wholesaling, retailing, and food service. Some parts of it are very local, but international trade is a large component. Some parts of the food industry are very well documented, such as food processing and the major commodity markets in developed countries; other parts lack comprehensive data, such as sales of farm production and small-scale food processing in less developed countries. Certainly, the world food industry represents at least $4 trillion in value.

In this book, the focus will be on the food industry from the farm gate to the dinner table. Discussion will cover the economics and management of food processing firms, wholesalers (including exporters and importers), and retailers. The book will specifically cover grocery retailers (supermarkets) and also restaurants. Many of the topics covered apply to firms at all three of those stages, and interregional trade, risk management, and game theory will be covered in the chapters to come. Some topics apply to just two of the three stages: optimal storage, for example, really applies mostly to food processors and wholesalers.

Size, scope, and value of the industry

The food and fiber sector consists of farms, input suppliers, food processors, wholesalers, retailers, restaurants, natural fiber textiles, paper products, wood manufacturing, tobacco product manufacturing, small and large food markets, restaurants, caterers, and food service facilities. This is an enormous economic sector. In the United States, the food and fiber sector represents about 16 percent of the economy, or about $2.5 trillion per year, and supports roughly 20 million jobs.[1] Actual farm-level production of agricultural commodities represents only 14 percent of the food and fiber sector, totaling around $350 billion or a little over 2 percent of the total gross domestic product (GDP). The next stage, food processing, adds $750 billion in value or about 5 percent of the total GDP. Tobacco and wood manufacturing add an additional $120 billion. Restaurants, bars, and other food service establishments produce approximately $575 billion of the United State's total gross domestic product, or almost 4 percent of the

2   *The basics of the food industry*

total economy. The remaining $700 billion of the food and fiber sector comprises the food wholesaling and food retailing (supermarkets, etc.) industries.

The food industry is based on the transformation of raw products into food products. The food industry takes farm commodities and prepares them for retail according to consumers' tastes and preferences. Sometimes, the transformation is trivial: a peach on the farm turned into a peach in the grocery store by basically washing it and transporting it to the grocery store; while other times the transformation is significant: rice fermented into saké (a Japanese rice wine), bottled, labeled, and shipped to a foreign country for sale. The food industry gets basic ingredients to markets for people to purchase such as meat, fish, fruits, and vegetables. The food industry also produces highly processed, complex foods with many ingredients for the convenience of the consumer who does not want to cook (or cook from scratch); examples here include items such as frozen dinners, canned soups, instant pasta bowls, and to-go dishes now widely available in developed-country markets. At the other extreme, restaurants and caterers take the food all the way to the plate and only require that the consumer do the eating. All these activities take place for one simple reason: the companies involved hope to make a profit through their efforts and by selling their products. What guides all the companies that populate the food industry in this profit-seeking quest is opportunities for arbitrage.

Arbitrage—a central concept for our analysis

Arbitrage is the most important concept in economics. The most popular definition in this era of advanced financial engineering is that arbitrage is the process of profiting from price differentials in different markets for the same product. For example, a gold trader might buy gold in London and sell it in New York after spotting that gold is $0.01 per ounce less expensive in London. While making one cent per ounce may not seem exciting, if the trader buys and sells 10,000 ounces, the profit is $100. Even $100 may not seem exciting, but since the transaction takes only seconds the hourly profit (or annualized return on investment) can be very high.

In a more general, economic sense, arbitrage is the taking advantage of price differences in linked markets to earn profits. Within the context of the food industry, arbitrage is why a company decides to store a product for later sale rather than selling it now; it expects to profit from a higher price later. When a juice processor sees higher prices for juice than the price of the fresh fruit plus processing cost, it arbitrages between those two markets by buying fruit and making juice. Companies that buy a product in one country in order to resell it in another country at a price that is higher by more than the transportation cost are arbitraging between the product markets in the two different countries. Essentially, this broader view of arbitrage includes all profits earned from recognizing differences in a product's potential net value between markets that can be linked by some physical, spatial, or temporal transformation.

Arbitrage defined in this broader manner is an extremely valuable process. When a price difference (adjusted for transformation costs) exists between markets that can be linked, the arbitrager is helping the consumer by moving resources from markets where their value is lower to higher-valued uses. The persons or companies doing the arbitrage are rewarded with profits, but they also serve society by allocating resources efficiently among markets according to the relative strength of demand in those markets. In the food industry, markets can be linked by

- physical transformation: tomatoes into spaghetti sauce,
- spatial transformation: Georgia shrimp shipped to New York City, or
- temporal transformation: apples harvested in the fall, stored, and sold months later.

In terms of the economics and the mathematics, all of these transformations function in an identical manner. The transformation is the link between two otherwise unrelated markets. The opportunity to arbitrage and earn the resulting profits is the incentive that causes firms in the food industry to transform products and link the markets together. This transformation of products and the subsequent linking of markets leads to increased consumer and producer surplus, economic-speak for a world that is better off.

A trip through the food industry

In the chapters to follow, I will attempt to lay out for the reader the economic principles that apply to the proper management of companies in all facets of the food industry after food leaves the farm. In the realm of food processing, you will learn how to manage a food processing factory, how to be a buyer or a salesperson for a food processing company, and how to determine which products are the most profitable to make. In the marketing (or wholesaling) sector, you will learn the economic rules that govern decisions about storage, trade between regions or countries, and price discrimination. Price markup rules and the economics that help a person derive them will be covered for food processors, wholesalers, and retailers. Most of the book covers the economic principles underlying profit-maximizing management of food industry companies; however, some parts focus more on management, such as how companies use risk management tools and common rules of restaurant management.

While this book is focused on the food industry, the economic principles that apply to the management of a food company apply to virtually all other industries. The things you will learn from this book could be used to run a department store, a jewelry store, any manufacturing facility, and almost any company that sells a product or service. The lessons of running a company in the food industry easily can be applied to the management of businesses in all sorts of industries. Hopefully, whatever career you end up in, you will find the lessons and principles contained here useful for success in that career.

2 Cost economics for processing plants

Standard microeconomic theory tends to present cost analysis using nice smooth curves so that students can find where tangencies occur and the optimal point at which to operate. Unfortunately, in the real world, not all inputs are infinitely divisible. You cannot use one half of an assembly line; it is all or nothing. As we will see in this chapter, the fact that inputs such as workers and assembly lines come in discrete (not continuous) amounts mean that the familiar cost curves transform from their normal, smooth shapes into new shapes that resemble shoddy staircases.

Economists like to call such discretely adjustable inputs lumpy inputs. Working with lumpy inputs also means that rather than being able to use calculus to solve mathematical problems, we need to resort to more basic math and some careful thinking. So, at least for the remainder of this chapter, solving economic problems will rely on the ability to determine the minimum of a set of numbers and the basic operations of addition, subtraction, multiplication, and division. If you can temporarily forget all that you learned about taking derivatives and setting them equal to zero, let's do some real-world economics the old-fashioned way.

Fixed versus variable costs in the real world

In our introductory microeconomics class, the concepts of fixed and variable costs are quite straightforward: fixed costs are costs that don't change when the quantity produced changes, whereas variable costs are costs that do change as the quantity of output changes. This dichotomy is simple and neat. However, in the real world it gets a little bit more complicated. First, you must define the time period to be able to identify which costs are fixed and which are variable. Are you analyzing costs for a day, a week, a month, a year, or a decade? A lot of costs are fixed when you look at production over short periods of time, but become variable costs when you are analyzing a longer time period. Second, some costs vary only when the quantity produced changes from 0 to 1. An example is the costs to start up (or shutdown) a plant or an assembly line. If we are thinking about a peach packing plant, these start-up and shutdown costs are variable costs when looking at the costs for a season, but would be fixed costs if we are looking at a week in the middle of July. Another example is depreciation. The depreciation for a building is a fixed cost in virtually all circumstances, but depreciation on a piece of equipment might be a variable cost if the depreciation schedule is based on hours of use.

Variable costs can also be more confusing or subtle than they are made out to be in the standard micro class. Some costs vary with the quantity produced; that fits our traditional definition of a variable cost. But there are also costs that vary with hours of operation (say heating and cooling costs) or the rate of production (running an assembly line faster may use more electricity) that do not strictly vary with output, but are somewhat tied to the level of production. In general, we will consider all such costs to be variable costs but we will need to be careful that we handle such costs properly when choosing the optimal manner in which to operate a plant.

Building a cost function through economic engineering

To build a cost function for the sort of real-world situation that one typically encounters in food processing plants as well as almost any other factory or assembly-line-style operation, the best way is what I call the economic engineering approach. I learned this method from a classic book by Bressler and King (1978).[1] Much of what is presented here follows or is modified from their presentation on this topic.

To begin your analysis of the firm's costs, draw a picture of their operation, representing the process as a line and showing each step in the process from start to finish. Figure 2.1 below provides an example for a simple fruit packing operation. In the diagram, you can see where the fruit enters the packing shed (called the receiving/dumping station), moves through a washing operation, and then gets labeled. The next stop is the sorting station, where fruit are separated by grade as necessary and removed if damaged. The fruit is then packed into boxes, and the final station on our diagram is where the boxes are closed and taken to storage until a truck comes to pick them up.

The second step in building a cost curve is to establish the minimum and maximum work crews at each station. To find these, you ask the plant foreman or other person familiar with the operation. If nobody is sure, the easiest way to determine the minimum and maximum crews is to conduct a little experiment. If a station is completely automated, then the minimum and maximum crews are simply zero. It is not complicated to establish the minimum number of people to accomplish a task. For example, the fruit usually comes in from the field in very large bins that take two people to lift onto the dumping station, so the minimum crew at that first station is two. The maximum number of workers per station is usually based on the amount of space available. When more people will just be in the way and lower productivity, you have found the maximum for that station. These minimum and maximum crews for each step can be added to our diagram by simply writing them in the arrows representing each station. This is done below in Figure 2.2.

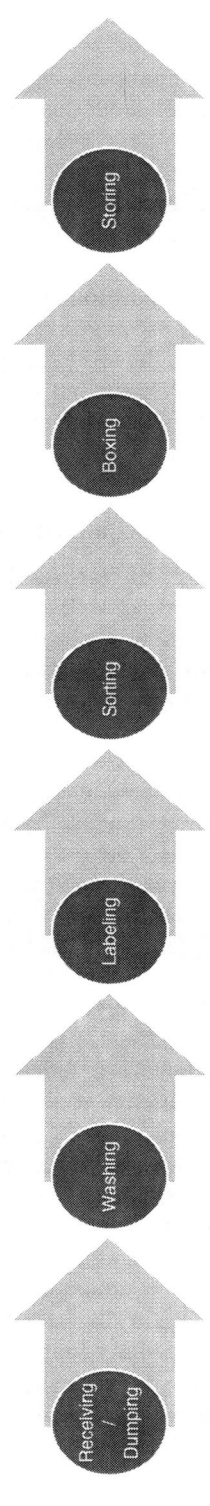

Figure 2.1 A fruit packing operation.

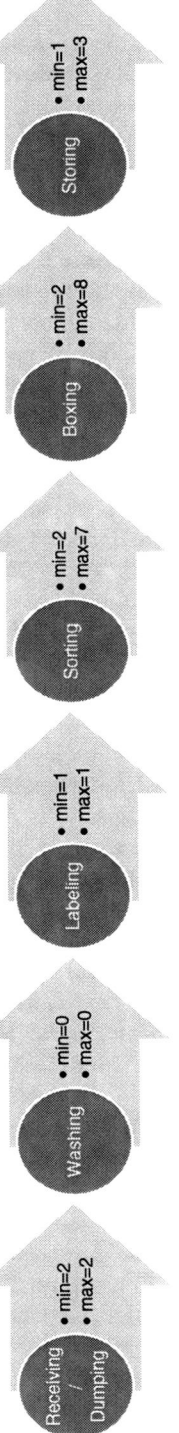

Figure 2.2 The fruit packing operation with minimum and maximum station crews.

After completing the drawing of the operation, you must collect additional information before you can work out a cost function. You need to know the labor standard for each station, the maximum work capacity per station, and the wage rate paid at each station.

Starting to bring in economics

The labor standard is the most work per unit of time a worker can accomplish. This is measured in some type of output/time units that make sense for the plant being studied. In a fruit packing plant, the labor standard would normally be in pounds-per-hour (lb/hr). Sometimes this is governed by a union contract or federal or state labor regulations. Other times it is simply based on how much work can be done. For example, at the sorting station a worker can only manage to sort through a certain number of pounds per hour of fruit. If you ask for any higher productivity, the worker will fall behind and start missing things. If the plant manager does not know the labor standard for each station, then experiments should be conducted to establish them. The experiment can be as simple as measuring the workflow when a good (but not the best) worker is going as fast a speed as can be maintained for a shift.

The maximum work capacity is determined either by the physical capacity of the machinery at a particular station or by the combination of the labor standard and the maximum work crew. For example, the labeling machine might only be able to stick labels on 5,000 lb/hr of fruit. Taking the labor standard and multiplying it by the maximum number of workers at a station gives you an alternative figure. Whichever of the two approaches yields the smaller number, that number is the maximum work capacity for that station. The plant capacity is the minimum of all the machine capacities of the different stations. While it might be surprising to see all the different capacities in a single plant, it is actually quite common as machinery is purchased from separate suppliers and is not necessarily made for just one specific use.

Finally, the wage rates paid to workers at each station should be collected from the plant foreman or somebody in the firm management. The rates are likely to vary across the stations, with workers paid more at stations involving more technology or more dangerous equipment. So the storage station workers get paid more than workers at the dumping station because the storage workers drive a forklift, which takes some training.

Once all this information is collected, it can be organized into a table along the lines shown below in Figure 2.3. Note that in Figure 2.3 each station from the earlier diagrams shown in Figures 2.1 and 2.2 is represented by a row and that we have added one more station: administration. Administration represents receptionists, accountants, salespeople, the plant foreman, and anyone not part of the production process but still working within the operation. They appear in the table to ensure that they are included in the labor costs when you construct the cost function. With this labor requirements table completed, you can begin to construct the hourly labor cost function, which shows the hourly labor cost as a function of the pounds per hour of fruit being processed.

Station	Min-Crew	Max-Crew	Labor Standard	Machine Capacity	Wage Rate
Receiving/Dumping	2	2	3,000 lb/hr	6,000 lb/hr	8.00 $/hr
Washing	0	0	n/a	8,000	n/a
Labeling	1	1	7,000	7,000	8.00
Sorting	2	7	900	6,300	8.50
Boxing	2	8	900	7,200	8.50
Storage	1	3	2,000	6,000	10.00
Administration	2	2	n/a	n/a	20.00

Figure 2.3 Labor requirements table for a fruit packing operation.

As foreshadowed in our earlier discussion of variable costs, you can consider the fruit packing operating costs for a variety of time periods (hour, day, week, or month) and units (pounds, tons, or cases). Because it is going to be important later to learn how to choose the optimal speed at which to operate our packing plant (in terms of pounds/hour), we choose here to analyze costs on a per-hour basis first, so our quantity produced will be measured in pounds per hour (lb/hr).

The hourly labor cost function

To turn the information in Figures 2.2 and 2.3 into an hourly labor cost function, the trick is to start with an output rate of 1 lb/hr and then increase the output while identifying the output levels at which the plant would need to hire an additional worker at each station. How do you find the points when workers must be hired? To begin, the plant must have a minimum crew at each station as soon as the quantity per hour equals one. Those workers can continue until the plant speed (in lb/hr) reaches a value equal to the product of the station's labor standard and the minimum crew number. For example, for the sorting station, the labor standard is 900 lb/hr and the minimum crew is 2. Thus, the plant does not need to add another worker at the sorting station until the plant speed reaches 900 × 2 = 1800 lb/hr. From that point, the sorting station will need an additional worker every time the plant speed increases by another 900 lb/hr; so workers will be hired for the sorting station at output levels of 1,800; 2,700; 3,600; 4,500; and 5,400 lb/hr. We stop at 5,400 lb/hr because that is seven workers at the sorting station, the maximum for that station, and because the plant capacity is 6,000 lb/hr, so an eighth worker is never needed (that worker would have been needed at 6,300 lb/hr).

Following the procedure outlined above, the labor cost function is built station by station as shown in Figure 2.4. Each row represents a range of plant speeds (hourly production levels) requiring the same number of workers. The beginning of the range for each new row represents the point at which one or more workers are hired. In each box of the figure, the number of workers is in the top row of

10 *Cost economics for processing plants*

Quantity (lb/hr)	Receiving/ Dumping	Labeling	Sorting	Boxing	Storing	Admin.	Total Labor Cost
1–1800	2 $16.00/hr	1 $8.00/hr	2 $17.00/hr	2 $17.00/hr	1 $10.00/hr	2 $40.00/hr	$108.00/hr
1801–2000	2 $16.00/hr	1 $8.00/hr	3 $25.50/hr	3 $25.50/hr	1 $10.00/hr	2 $40.00/hr	$125.00/hr
2001–2700	2 $16.00/hr	1 $8.00/hr	3 $25.50/hr	3 $25.50/hr	2 $20.00/hr	2 $40.00/hr	$135.00/hr
2701–3600	2 $16.00/hr	1 $8.00/hr	4 $34.00/hr	4 $34.00/hr	2 $20.00/hr	2 $40.00/hr	$152.00/hr
3601–4000	2 $16.00/hr	1 $8.00/hr	5 $42.50/hr	5 $42.50/hr	2 $20.00/hr	2 $40.00/hr	$169.00/hr
4001–4500	2 $16.00/hr	1 $8.00/hr	5 $42.50/hr	5 $42.50/hr	3 $30.00/hr	2 $40.00/hr	$179.00/hr
4501–5400	2 $16.00/hr	1 $8.00/hr	6 $51.00/hr	6 $51.00/hr	3 $30.00/hr	2 $40.00/hr	$196.00/hr
5401–6000	2 $16.00/hr	1 $8.00/hr	7 $59.50/hr	7 $59.50/hr	3 $30.00/hr	2 $40.00/hr	$213.00/hr

Figure 2.4 Hourly labor cost function.

the box, and the hourly cost of those workers is in the bottom row of the box. Stations that have just added a worker are denoted by shading. The labor cost function is found by matching the first and last columns, which tells you what your labor cost will be for any plant speed.

Note in Figure 2.4 that several of the stations never change their work crew (this is consistent with the fact that in Figure 2.3 these stations have matching minimum and maximum crews). Also, note that since the washing station is fully automated, it does not appear in the table that constructs the hourly labor cost function. The quantity ranges and discrete jumps in labor costs shown in Figure 2.4 mean that the labor cost function is not a smooth, continuous function, but instead it is a step function with a discontinuity at each point where a new worker is hired. The shape of the function is shown in Figure 2.5.

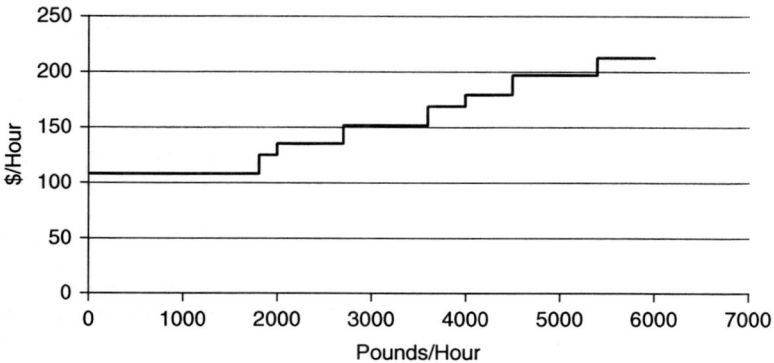

Figure 2.5 The shape of the hourly labor cost function.

Adding in the other variable costs

At this point, you have moved from the basic engineering information of the fruit packing plant to a labor cost function. To arrive at the complete variable cost function, you need to add in the non-labor costs. Generally, these are the ingredient and packaging costs (input costs) and utility costs.

For simplicity, packaging costs will be included in with other ingredient costs as they are just as much a part of the product; after all, a jar of spaghetti sauce clearly includes the jar. Ingredient costs are almost always a constant cost per unit of production. For a fruit packing plant, the ingredient costs are as follows: the fruit, the labels, the boxes the fruit gets packed in, and the pallets those boxes get stacked on. These are all well represented as constant marginal cost items, so that all the ingredient costs can be said to be r/lb, where the plant speed has no effect on the cost of ingredients. In the variable cost function, these ingredient costs will be represented by the variable r. To present the costs on a $/hr basis to equate with the labor costs of Figure 2.4, we multiply them by the plant speed, q (where q is the number of pounds per hour processed through our fruit packing plant). Thus, the ingredient costs per hour are given by rq/hr.

Utility costs are items such as electricity, gas (if used for heat, power, or to run forklifts), phone lines, Internet connections, and the like. Some of these costs (such as phone lines) seem unlikely to vary with the production level or plant speed, but are more likely to be a set price per month. Electricity and gas may actually be used at higher rates when the plant runs at higher speeds, but may well be reasonably approximated by a constant cost per pound produced (like the ingredients). However, as long as some of the utility costs vary with time (so much per month), they would change as the plant speed changes when presented on a $/lb basis. In most cases, the best approximation is probably to treat these costs as constant on a daily or hourly basis. For now, denote the utility costs by the variable u, and assume that they are constant on an hourly basis. In other words, assume that all the plant utilities cost a total of u/hr.

The labor costs found in Figure 2.4 can be represented by the function c(q), where q is the plant speed in lb/hr. For any given value of q within the range of our plant's capacity, denote the hourly labor cost as c(q) = c_i, where c_i is the value of the labor costs on one step of the labor cost function. With all these definitions out of the way, the variable cost function for the fruit packing plant (with all parts in $/hr) can be written as

$$\text{VC}(q) = \text{c}(q) + rq + u. \tag{2.1}$$

Figure 2.6 shows an example of the shape of each part of the variable costs and the shape of the combined function obtained by summing the three parts together. It ends up looking like a set of steps built by someone with no carpentry skills at all, but it will prove very useful in managing the fruit packing plant in an optimal manner.

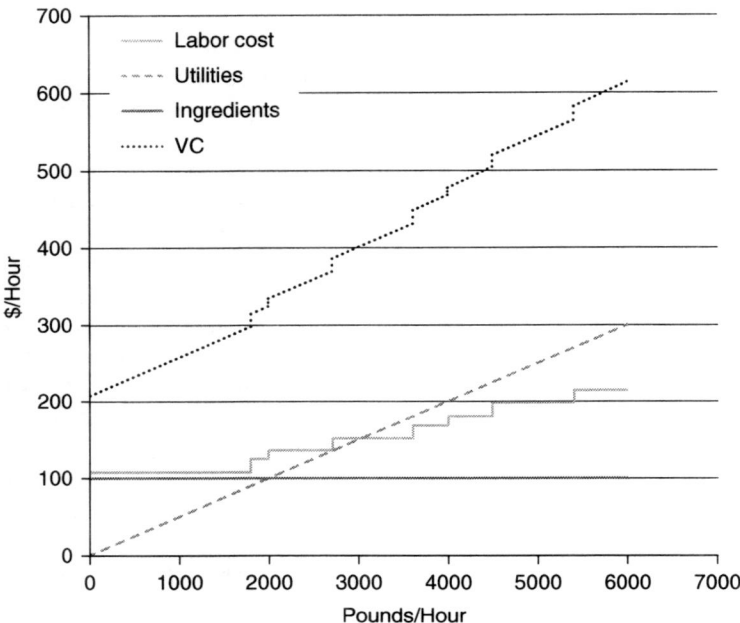

Figure 2.6 The variable cost function and its component parts.

Using the cost function to optimize plant operations

The economic engineering approach is a great way to build the cost function for a food processing plant or general manufacturing facility. However, finding the optimal way to manage the plant is the province of economics, not engineering. From this point forward, the approach is much more in line with traditional economics as you have learned it in previous classes. The big difference is that we have to operate without the benefit of calculus since the cost function is not differentiable.

Plant operation under cost minimization

The most common situation in a fruit packing plant (or most other food processing and even general manufacturing operations) is that the company has a contract to deliver a set quantity of output on a specific date in exchange for a fixed price. This is exactly the set of assumptions that apply to cost minimization. The company is not in a profit-maximizing world because quantity and price are already chosen—by the contract. Further assume that the quality of the product is specified in the contract, so the company cannot lower costs by providing an inferior quality product. All that is left within the manager's control is to produce the output at the minimum cost possible.

In the fruit packing plant, technology is already fixed in place (at least between now and when any contract is due), wages are set, and input costs are also generally known and fixed when the contract is signed. Thus, the manager can control costs primarily by adjusting the plant speed: how many pounds per hour the line processes. So the goal is to find the plant speed—the q—that would allow the firm to satisfy the contract at the lowest possible production cost. If variable costs were a smooth, continuous function, you would find the minimum average variable cost by taking the derivative of the average variable cost function and setting it equal to zero. You cannot do that here, but you can compute the average variable cost and then find its minimum the old-fashioned way: by simple comparison.

First, make sure you understand why minimizing the average variable cost is equivalent to minimizing the total variable cost. Since the quantity if fixed by the contract, dividing by the quantity is the same as dividing by any constant number: it just changes the scale of the objective function. Whatever plant speed produces the lowest average variable cost (the lowest cost in $/lb) will be the same plant speed that has the lowest total variable cost for producing the quantity specified in the contract. If the plant will only be run at a single speed for the entire time that it takes to fulfill the contract, then the relationship between the quantity in the contract (denoted here by Q), the plant speed (q), and the hours of plant operation it takes to finish the contract (denoted by H) is given by

$$Q = qH. \qquad (2.2)$$

The total variable cost for the contracted quantity is simply the product of the hourly variable cost function found in equation (2.1), VC(q), and the hours it takes to complete the contract. Mathematically, the total variable cost for the contract is

$$\text{VC}_c(Q) = \text{VC}(q)H = \left[c(q) + rq + u\right]H. \qquad (2.3)$$

The reader should note that since Q is fixed by the contract, when the plant manager chooses the optimal plant speed (let us denote that by q^*), the hours of operation can be immediately found by simple division:

$$H^* = Q/q^*. \qquad (2.4)$$

That is, the plant manager can choose the plant speed or the hours of operation, but not both independently. The plant speed is the one to focus on since you already have a cost function that shows how costs vary as you change the plant speed. If you substitute the formula for hours from equation (2.4) into equation (2.3) and then divide by the contracted quantity, Q, you arrive at the formula for the average variable cost in $/lb:

$$\text{AVC}(q) = \left[(c(q) + rq + u)(Q/q)\right]/Q = (c(q) + rq + u)/q = c(q)/q + r + u/q. \qquad (2.5)$$

Note that dividing the hourly variable cost in $/hr by the plant speed in lb/hr converts the units to $/lb. To check this, note that ($/hr)/(lb/hr) = ($/hr)(hr/lb) = $/lb. When the units are consistent, the calculation is usually correct.

Checking the average variable cost computed as in the above equation (equation 2.5) for every possible plant speed from $q = 1$ all the way to whatever the plant capacity is (which was $q = 6{,}000$ lb/hr in the above example) would be tedious work, although it would allow for finding the minimum average variable cost. However, the following insight can save us a lot of trouble. Because the hourly labor cost function $c(q)$ is a step function, the average variable cost function will have a series of local minima with the average variable cost function, $AVC(q)$, reaching one of these local low spots just prior to each plant speed at which a worker needs to be hired. This occurs because the labor cost remains constant along each step while the output per hour is increasing. So the numerator of the fraction is constant while the denominator is increasing, which implies that the fraction must be decreasing. Then when a new step begins, the numerator increases while the denominator remains virtually constant, and the average variable cost jumps up. Figure 2.7 shows what the average variable cost function derived from Figure 2.5 looks like.

So instead of needing to check every possible plant speed, we need only investigate the average variable cost at the end of each step in the labor cost function. How to do this is made clear in Figure 2.8. Below, we assume $u = \$100$/hr and $r = \$1.50$/lb. (Note that the ingredient cost used in Figure 2.8 does not match that of Figures 2.5 and 2.6.)

The numbers in Figure 2.8 show the steps to finding the minimum average variable cost. In the example of Figure 2.8, this minimum occurs at $q = 6{,}000$ lb/hr. This is q^*, the plant speed that minimizes the total variable cost of fulfilling the contract. Having found this, you can simply use equation (2.4) to find the number

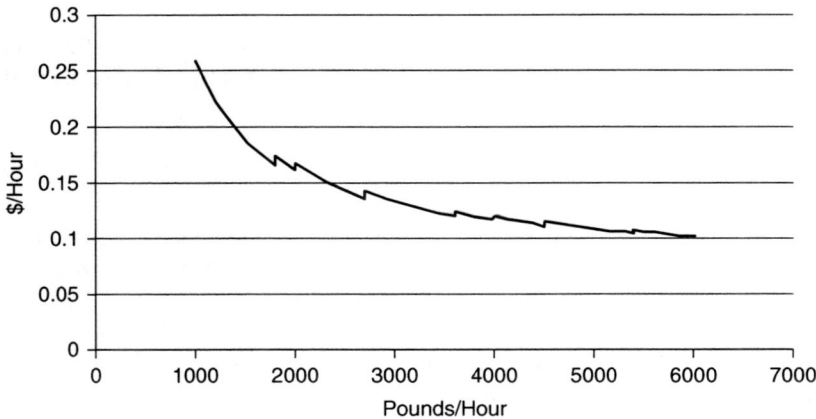

Figure 2.7 Average variable cost function for a step-shaped total variable cost function.

Quantity (lb/hr) (A)	Max Quantity (B)	Total Labor Cost (C)	Average Labor Cost (D) = (C)/(B)	Average Utility Cost (E) = u/(B)	Average Variable Cost (F) = (D) + r + (E)
1–1800	1800 lb/hr	$108.00/hr	$0.0600/lb	$0.0555/lb	$1.6155/lb
1801–2000	2000 lb/hr	$125.00/hr	$0.0625/lb	$0.0500/lb	$1.6125/lb
2001–2700	2700 lb/hr	$135.00/hr	$0.0500/lb	$0.0370/lb	$1.5870/lb
2701–3600	3600 lb/hr	$152.00/hr	$0.0422/lb	$0.0278/lb	$1.5700/lb
3601–4000	4000 lb/hr	$169.00/hr	$0.0425/lb	$0.0250/lb	$1.5675/lb
4001–4500	4500 lb/hr	$179.00/hr	$0.0398/lb	$0.0222/lb	$1.5620/lb
4501–5400	5400 lb/hr	$196.00/hr	$0.0363/lb	$0.0185/lb	$1.5548/lb
5401–6000	6000 lb/hr	$213.00/hr	$0.0355/lb	$0.0167/lb	($1.5522/lb) ← Minimum value

Figure 2.8 Finding the minimum average variable cost.

of hours that the plant needs to run at that optimal speed in order to complete the contract. If the contract is for $Q = 100{,}000$ lb of fruit, then $H^* = Q/q^* = 100{,}000$ lb/6,000 lb/hr = 16.67 hr.

After arriving at a solution for the optimal plant speed and the number of hours it will take to fulfill a contract, the next step always is to check that the solution will work. The contract will have a delivery date (usually a specific date, time, and location; the location might be the plant itself, a distribution center, or the buyer's store). You must check that the number of hours of operation it will take to fulfill the contract at the optimal plant speed will allow you to finish the order in time. If not, then you will have to run the plant faster (if possible; in our example the plant is already running at its capacity).

A final step is to check for compliance with any pay rules for workers. Many union contracts have minimum pay rules in them such that a worker must be paid for a minimum number of hours in any day for which he reports to work (often this is 4 or 5 hours). Other plants may not have a union contract that specifies such a rule, but still may operate under such a *de facto* rule based on tradition. Going back to the above example, if the only job to be done in a particular week is the contract discussed above and the plant has a rule that means workers are paid for a minimum of 4 hours per day, you would not want to schedule the work for two 8 hour days followed by a 40-minute work day on the third day. That would incur unnecessary labor costs. Instead, you would schedule something like work days of 6, 6, and 4.67 hr to complete the job. Obviously, when a plant is busy moving from one contract to the next without downtime in between, this step becomes unnecessary. However, when the facility is not very busy, accidentally falling afoul of a minimum daily pay rule is definitely something to be avoided.

Supply chain management

At the most basic level, supply chain management is about making sure that ingredients and labor are on-site and ready for use when they are needed. People have written entire textbooks and teach whole classes on supply chain management, so this section will only provide a very basic overview of what goes into supply chain management. Also, unlike a book or course on supply chain management, we will focus less on the actual logistics and more on the economics that should be involved in supply chain decisions.

A food processing facility must ensure that it has a steady supply of raw food ingredients, otherwise the entire process has to shut down. They might be able to operate at some level with fewer than an optimal number of workers, but if you run out of chicken you cannot make any more chicken soup. Having a larger inventory on hand at the processing facility provides more safety against running out of ingredients, but it costs more money. Storing ingredients costs money, both to buy the products and to build, operate, and maintain the storage facilities. The optimal amount to store should be found according to the standard economic rule: equate the marginal cost of more storage against the marginal benefit of having a larger safety margin provided by the larger inventory. The rule is simple; determining the marginal benefit of safety from inventory is not so straightforward.

One way to approach the task of valuing the safety provided by inventory is to estimate the economic losses that would be suffered from a production stoppage. Those losses have two parts. First, the company will suffer direct economic losses from a production stoppage equal to the lost profits that would have been earned from the product not produced. Second, the company could suffer longer-term losses if they fail to fulfill a contract and buyers decide they are an unreliable supplier. A production stoppage long enough to affect deliveries of the company's product could have economic consequences in terms of lost customers or reduced selling prices that are likely much larger than the immediate losses incurred during the production stoppage.

The marginal cost of storage is likely to be fairly constant as on-hand inventory is increased while the marginal benefit of additional ingredient storage will be decreasing. The marginal benefits of having a few hours' or a day's worth of ingredients would usually be quite large since even a simple traffic accident or road closure could delay supplies for a short period. However, since many food processing ingredients are fresh and do not store without quality deterioration, too large an inventory will not make sense. Given a company's supply chain (the system of suppliers and delivery methods used to obtain inputs), you should be able to assess the probability of supply interruptions of different durations. For example, a company might believe that within a year the probability of having a one-day shortage of at least one ingredient is 100 percent, the probability of a two-day shortage is 40 percent, the probability of a three-day shortage is 10 percent, the probability of a four-day shortage is 1 percent, and no interruption longer than that is considered likely to occur. Taking these probabilities in combination with the estimated losses from the production stoppages of these lengths, you can work out the marginal benefits of one, two, three, or four days' inventory on hand. These marginal benefits would be the estimated loss multiplied by the probability of its occurring. Then by comparing these marginal benefits to the marginal cost of storage, the company can choose the optimal inventory to hold.

An additional wrinkle in this situation is that for many food processing companies, the inputs are fresh products, and the output is processed into a much more stable form (such as chicken versus cans of chicken soup or peaches versus jars of peach jam). That means it is often less expensive to store finished products than the raw ingredients. Therefore, a company should consider whether storing enough finished product to avoid any delivery interruptions is the most cost-effective strategy. That would leave the lost profit from the production stoppage as the only economic loss, which is both smaller and easier to estimate.

Similar marginal cost versus marginal benefit arguments apply when deciding if the company should outsource an operation or keep it in-house. In the supply chain context, for example, a firm must decide if it wants to operate its own fleet of trucks or contract that transportation out to an independent company. In some cases, there is also the option of your buyer providing the transportation. Outsourcing is often less expensive, but one must analyze the possible risk involved in depending on an outside company for distribution.

Another important supply chain management issue today is the risk of a disruption in the entire transportation network, generally as a result of either terrorism or a major natural disaster. After the September 11 attack, air traffic was grounded for a period of time. Many large companies, particularly auto manufacturers, now require their major suppliers to locate within a specified distance of their plant. In fact, new auto plants are now usually built with enough on-site acreage for suppliers to co-locate right next to the auto plant. By the same reasoning, how close your food processing facility is to the source of your supply of ingredients has an impact on the risk of a supply interruption and therefore the optimal amount of inventory of ingredients to hold.

Summary

This chapter has explained how to manage an assembly line style factory such as is common in food processing facilities. Because inputs cannot be treated as infinitely divisible (half an assembly line makes no sense), we have to recast traditional economic rules for optimizations to work in this discrete setting. That means abandoning calculus and returning to simple arithmetic as our means of analysis. Using these simple tools, we learned how to run such a plant in order to minimize the total cost of completing fixed-quantity contracts. This is the most common way such plants are managed in the real world because pricing of the product is usually handled separately by a team of salespeople who make deals without worrying about the actual manufacturing process. In the next chapter, we will learn some rules for how those salespeople and their related fellow employees, the buyers, decide the prices at which to buy ingredients to use in the plant or to sell the product made at the plant. Those rules will move us from the cost minimization of this chapter into profit maximization.

18 *Cost economics for processing plants*

Chapter highlights

In this chapter, you should have learned:

- How to diagram the steps to a manufacturing process, including the order of the stations and details about the workers, needed to accomplish different levels of production.
- How to take that information and build a cost function for a food processing facility that can be used to analyze variable costs as the speed of production changes.
- How ingredient costs and overhead costs (such as utilities) should be combined with labor costs to form total variable costs. The formula is $VC(q) = c(q) + rq + u$.
- How the cost function can be used to compute the total variable cost per pound, the total variable cost per hour, the average variable cost per pound, or the average variable cost per hour.
- That the variable cost function converted to an average variable cost function looks like $AVC(q) = c(q)/q + r + u/q$.
- That the optimal speed at which to operate a food processing plant is where the average variable cost is at a minimum. Because the AVC function has a jagged shape, the minimum is at one of the local low spots, which are all at plant speeds right before a new worker is added.
- That once we know the optimal plant speed, the hours of operation are also fixed by the rule $H^* = Q/q^*$.
- How to check that we are fulfilling contracts at the minimum cost given the time constraints.
- Some considerations about supply chain management that need to be considered for the efficient and minimum cost operation of a food processing facility.

Box 2.1

To give students not familiar with food processing facilities a feel of a very simple such plant, the pictures here show a peach packing plant in Georgia. The photos show several stations of the assembly line. In this plant, peaches enter directly from the field in large plastic bins that are dumped onto the line. They are then washed, cleaned, and labeled, all by machine. Workers enter for the first time at the sorting station where any remaining debris are removed along with any damaged fruit. Fruit are also sorted by quality, separating those for fresh fruit consumption from the lower-quality fruit that goes into processed foods such as peach preserves and peach ice cream. After sorting, the fruit is placed in boxes for either retail sale or shipment to supermarkets. Those boxes are then closed, stacked on pallets, and stored in a cold room until the truck arrives to take them to a supermarket chain's distribution center.

Practice problems

You are the foreperson of a processing plant that produces Vidalia onion relish. The relish is produced in an assembly line plant with stations with the following characteristics:

20 Cost economics for processing plants

Station	Min crew	Station capacity	Max crew	Wage rate	Labor standard
Receiving	2	5,000 lb/hr	4	$8.00/hr	1,500 lb/hr
Sorting	2	6,000	5	7.50	1,000
Chopping	1	6,000	2	8.00	3,000
Mixing	2	5,000	4	8.50	1,500
Bottling	1	5,000	2	9.50	2,500
Boxing/Shipping	2	9,000	4	7.00	1,500
Administration	2	—	2	20.00	—

Utilities at the plant run at $50/hr regardless of the line speed.

1. Construct the total labor cost curve for this plant using the economic engineering approach outlined in class. Report the costs in a table and on a graph (it does not need to be perfectly to scale) for quantities from 0 to 5,000 lb/hr.
2. Assume that your relish has two ingredients, onion and spices. The onion costs $0.50 per pound, the spices cost $0.25 per jar, the jar costs $0.05, and the case for 12 jars costs $0.25. Each jar holds one pound of relish which requires 2 pounds of onion. Use your answer from problem 1 (remember to factor in utility costs) to find the total variable cost per hour and average variable cost per pound for the relish when q = 5,000lb/hr.
3. Now calculate the optimal quantity per hour at which to operate your plant if you are given an order for 75,000 lb that must be filled in one week. Assume that overtime and doubleshifting are impossible, so that the maximum hours of operation are 40.
4. Assume that the relish plant is operating at $q = 3,500$ lb/hr. Calculate the average variable cost per hour and the average operating cost per pound.

For the following problems, use the following information. A plant making cases of canned soup has total labor costs of:

Quantity range	Total labor cost
1–1000 cases/hr	$100/hr
1000–2000	$150/hr
2001–3000	$200/hr
3001–4000	$300/hr

The plants utility cost is $50/hr regardless of the plant speed. Ingredients for the soup (including the cans and case boxes) cost $15.00/case. The factory can operate for 8 hours per day, 5 days per week.

5. Find the optimal speed at which to operate the soup factory (in cases/hour).
6. If the plant has a contract to deliver 100,000 cases of soup for a supermarket chain in one week, what speed should they operate at to minimize production costs and how many hours will it take?
7. What if the contract in Problem 6 was for 150,000 cases?

3 Pricing economics for food processors

The last chapter covered how to optimally manage a food processing plant in order to minimize the cost of producing a set quantity of its product. Now, this chapter covers how the salespeople and ingredient buyers for a food processing plant go about the buying and selling of the ingredients and finished products. The basic assumption made in this chapter is that the buyers and sellers are motivated by profit maximization: they want to buy ingredients for as little as possible and sell the finished product for as much as possible so as to maximize the company's profits.

Profit maximization is not quite enough, however, to fully understand the behavior of the ingredient buyers and salespeople. After all, that just means that in each negotiation they try to get the best deal possible. So does everybody else. In some cases, the best deal possible would still leave the company losing money (after all, profit maximization does not mean that profit is positive, only that it is as large as possible). The buyers and sellers need more guidance than "go and sell the product for as high a price as possible."

Companies provide that guidance through target pricing formulas. Each day, ingredient buyers are provided with a list showing the price for each ingredient or item that they purchase that they should stay below ("buy for this price or less"). Sometimes they receive a list of price ranges to stay within, or several prices that they can aim at. Salespeople get a list of all the products they are selling with target prices to aim at or above. In reality, the lists are somewhat more detailed than this, and later in this chapter you will learn how the company computes the price targets provided to its employees.

The break-even pricing formula

To begin, consider the prices at which a company sells its product. Clearly, the first thing you want to know is the price at which your company will break even: earn a profit equal to zero. After all, if you sell your product for less than the break-even price, very often you will go out of business.

By definition, profit = total revenue − total costs. Total revenue = price × quantity sold and total costs = average costs × quantity produced. If we assume that the quantity produced and the quantity sold are the same, then we can rewrite the definition of profit as

$$profit = (price - average\ cost) \times quantity. \tag{3.1}$$

Expressed like this, it is easy to see that the profit will equal zero when the price is equal to the average cost. Thus, the break-even price is the average cost of producing the product.

Now, the average cost could be the average total cost or the average variable cost (remember that the average total cost is the average variable cost plus the average fixed cost). Given that fixed costs are sunk and should not affect short-term decisions, the best approach here is to use the average variable cost in the break-even pricing rule. If all of the product a company produces is sold at the break-even price, the company will eventually go out of business, because it is only covering its variable costs, not total costs. However, although the company is not going to sell all its products at the break-even price, it still wants to know what it is because sometimes it makes sense to sell products at or near that break-even price.

Chapter 2 provided us with a formula for the average variable cost of a product from a food processing plant. The formula is repeated here:

$$AVC(q) = c(q)/q + r + u/q. \tag{3.2}$$

Recall that all the units in equation (3.2) are in $/lb (or another unit that the product is sold in), so we can set this average variable cost equal to the price to arrive at the break-even pricing rule:

$$p^{BE} = c(q)/q + r + u/q. \tag{3.3}$$

This break-even price, p^{BE}, is just the cost of producing the firm's product. It serves as the minimum price a salesperson should ever accept in making a deal. Agreeing to sell the product at a loss hurts the company's profit and could lead to the salesperson being fired. Although the break-even price provides a lower bound price for the sales force, more guidance would certainly be helpful to them.

The target profit margin pricing rule

Most companies also provide their salespeople with at least one target price. The computation of these target prices, which are higher than the break-even price, is based on trying to achieve a particular profit margin. The definition of profit margin used here is the percentage of the total revenue that is profit, and is sometimes also called the gross profit margin. That is,

$$profit\ margin = (total\ revenue - total\ variable\ cost)/total\ revenue. \tag{3.4}$$

Companies, with an eye both to covering fixed costs and earning a desired amount of profit, often set a target for the gross profit margin. If we divide equation (3.4) by the quantity, we can express the relationship on a per-unit, or average, basis:

$$\text{unit profit margin} = (\text{price} - \text{average variable cost})/\text{price}. \quad (3.5)$$

Then, solving equation (3.5) for the price, we arrive at the target price needed to achieve a specified unit profit margin. To do this, first separate the terms on the right-hand side:

$$\text{unit profit margin} = 1 - (\text{average variable cost}/\text{price}). \quad (3.6)$$

Next, solve for (average variable cost/price):

$$(\text{average variable cost} / \text{price}) = 1 - \text{unit profit margin}. \quad (3.7)$$

Now invert both sides:

$$(\text{price} / \text{average variable cost}) = 1/(1 - \text{unit profit margin}). \quad (3.8)$$

Finally, multiply both sides by the average variable cost:

$$\text{target price} = [1/(1 - \text{unit profit margin})] \times \text{average variable cost}. \quad (3.9)$$

If we now denote the target gross profit margin by *gm* and express it in decimal form, so that a 20 percent gross margin would be 0.20, our gross margin target price (p^{GM}) expression becomes

$$\begin{aligned} p^{GM} &= [1/(1-gm)]\,\text{average variable cost} \\ &= [1/(1-gm)][c(q)/q + r + u/q] \\ &= [1/(1-gm)]\,p^{BE} \end{aligned} \quad (3.10)$$

You can see from equation (3.10) that the gross margin pricing rule is simply the break-even price from equation (3.3) inflated by a function of the target gross profit margin. To achieve a 20 percent gross profit margin, the company must charge 25 percent more than the break-even price (because 1/(1 − 0.20) = 1.25). That is because the profit margin is measured relative to the total revenue, not to the total cost.

By using the pricing rules in equations (3.3) and (3.10), companies can provide their sales force with a set of target prices: the desired price that achieves the company's target profit margin, perhaps a lower profit margin price to offer to

> **Box 3.1**
>
> Within the food industry, one can find companies with a wide array of gross profit margins and final (after taxes and all expenses) profit margins. At the high end, Coca-Cola has averaged a gross profit margin of 68.4 percent over the last five years and a post-tax profit margin of 23.5 percent. Its main competitor, Pepsi, has been nearly as impressive with an average gross profit margin of 57.5 percent and a post-tax margin of 13.1 percent.
>
> Nearly as good as been Campbell's Soup. Campbell's has a five year average gross profit margin of 44.5 percent and a five-year average post-tax profit margin of 9.9 percent.
>
> At the lower end, you can find companies involved in processing more basic, less branded and differentiated food products. Archer Daniels Midland, which does lots of processing of raw ingredients into processed ingredients for other firms to use (as well as some finished, ready-for-retail products), has averaged a gross profit margin of 7.7 percent and a post-tax profit margin of 3.2 percent over the past five years. Sanderson Farms, a large poultry processor, has averaged a gross profit margin of 12.0 percent and a post-tax margin of 3.0 percent for the past five years.
>
> Clearly, if you are managing a food processing company, there is no one-size-fits-all gross profit margin target to use. Many new firms start with a 20 percent gross profit margin target and then adjust from that as they learn and grow.

particularly high-volume or long-standing customers, and a break-even price that salespeople should never drop below.

Pricing rules for ingredient buyers

Similar rules can be developed for buyers. If a company has a contract for its product, then the price is set for the quantity in the contract. Given that price, the pricing formulas above in equations (3.3) and (3.10) can be solved for ingredient prices so that buyers have guidance for the prices they should try to pay for what they are buying.

Single-ingredient pricing rules

If a company manufactured a product with only one ingredient, reversing the pricing rule would be very simple. Using the break-even pricing rule for an example and solving for the ingredient cost r, we get

$$r^{BE} = p - c(q)/q - u/q. \tag{3.11}$$

This rule would be the maximum price a buyer should pay for the ingredient in order for the company to break even on the contract. Using the target margin pricing rule and solving for r would give us

$$r^{GM} = (1-gm)p - c(q)/q - u/q. \tag{3.12}$$

The target margin pricing rule above would provide a buyer with the price to pay for an ingredient in order to achieve the target profit margin, conditional on the output price already set in a contract.

Multiple-ingredient pricing rules

The above section showed some pricing rules for buyers in a setting where a product only has a single ingredient. Unfortunately, the world is rarely that simple. Even the fruit packing shed example in the previous chapter, where the food processing involves taking peaches from the field and turning them into peaches for sale in the supermarket, involves multiple ingredients: peaches, labels, and boxes. To work with multiple-ingredient products, first you need a formula for combining the costs of all those ingredients into the combined input cost variable r.

Denote the price of each ingredient by r_j and the amount of each ingredient in one unit of the processed product by n_j (where n_j will be referred to as the recipe factor), where the subscript j is used to identify the different ingredients. If the price of the finished product we are using is in $/lb, then n_j shows the amount of each ingredient needed to produce one pound of peaches for sale. If the price of the finished product we are using is in $/case (such as for a case of 24 cans of chicken soup), then n_j shows the amount of each ingredient needed to produce one case of canned chicken soup for sale. The recipe factor, n_j, tells people the units of the ingredients per unit of product, including the units themselves. So if you are producing cans of chicken soup and selling them by the case (24 cans per case), then the recipe factor for chicken might be (3 lb of chicken)/(1 case of chicken soup), and for the box the case of cans goes into, the recipe factor is (1 box)/(1 case of chicken soup). With these definitions in mind, the aggregate ingredient cost can be disaggregated as

$$r = \sum_{j=1}^{J} r_j n_j \tag{3.13}$$

To derive the pricing rules for a single of these J different ingredients, we simply need to substitute the formula for r in equation (3.13) into the pricing rule (either equation (3.11) or (3.12) from above), and then move all the parts to the right-hand side except the price of the one ingredient whose pricing rule you want to derive. For example, for ingredient 1, we would get breakeven and target margin pricing rules of

$$r_1^{BE} = [p - c(q)/q - u/q - \sum_{j=2}^{J} r_j n_j]/n_1 \tag{3.14}$$

Box 3.2

We can stick with the canned soup theme to see what might go into combining all the different ingredient costs into the single, composite r. For this example, we will make cream of asparagus soup. The soup contains three ingredients: asparagus, condensed milk, and spices. While spices may sound like multiple ingredients, our soup factory can buy them premixed to their specifications from a supplier. In each 15-ounce can of soup, the company uses 3 ounces of asparagus, 12 ounces of condensed milk, and 0.3 ounces of spices. The company also needs a can, a label for each can, and a case box for every 24 cans. We can display all these ingredients and costs in a simple table.

Ingredient	Cost per unit	Units per case = n_j	Cost per case
Asparagus	$2.00/lb	(3 oz/can)(1 lb/16 oz)(24 cans/case) = 4.5 lb/case	$9.00/case
Condensed milk	$2.00/lb	(12oz/can)(1 lb/16 oz)(24 cans/case) = 18 lb/case	$36.00/case
Spice mix	$0.25/oz	(0.3 oz/can)(24 cans/case) = 7.2 oz/case	$1.80/case
Can	$0.20 each	(1 can/can)(24 cans/case) = 24 cans/case	$4.80/case
Label	$0.02 each	(1 label/can)(24 cans/case) = 24 labels/case	$0.48/case
Case box	$1.00 each	1 box/case	$1.00/case

The table shows how to convert the units from what is listed in the recipe into the same units as the price of the ingredient per unit of product as it is sold. Since our soup is sold by the case, everything is converted to units per case. These numbers, in column three, are the ingredient factors, the n_j's. Then you can multiply the cost per unit times the ingredient factors to arrive at the cost per case for each ingredient. Summing the items in column four, as in equation (3.13), gives us r. Here, r = $53.08/case. That is some very expensive soup!

and

$$r_1^{GM} = [(1-gm)p - c(q)/q - u/q - \sum_{j=2}^{J} r_j n_j]/n_1. \quad (3.15)$$

These ingredient-buying rules take the revenue from selling the product and then subtract the processing cost, overhead cost, and the cost of all the other ingredients to determine how much is left over to spend on the first ingredient.

Pricing economics for food processors

Equation (3.14) provides the break-even ingredient-buying price, the highest amount the buyer can pay without causing the company to lose money. Equation (3.15) provides the target margin ingredient buying price, the amount the buyer can pay for ingredient 1 while allowing the company to achieve its target gross profit margin. Similar math leaving the prices of ingredients 2, 3, ..., J on the left-hand side one-by-one will allow the company to find the full set of ingredient prices its buyers should use as their goals in negotiations.

Combining the pricing rules

All the pricing rules derived so far in this chapter treat the prices and costs of all the other parts of the food manufacturing process as fixed. In reality, the salespeople are out making deals to sell the product at different prices at the same time that the buyers are out making deals to buy various ingredients at changing prices, so these target prices are in constant need of updating.

When a company commences operations, it finds the cost of ingredients in the market and uses the average, or expected, ingredient prices to derive the break-even and target margin prices for their products. The company can then either set prices for all buyers or use the pricing rules as guidance for its sales people.

Each ingredient price depends on all the other ingredient prices used in a product and the price of the product. The pricing rules all need to be recomputed each time any of the other prices changes. That is, each time a buyer buys a batch of ingredients or a salesperson sells a quantity of a product, that new price is plugged into the rules for calculating everything else. In the modern world, this is accomplished electronically. The pricing rules are pre-programmed in a spreadsheet or other program. Each time ingredients are purchased or product is sold, the buyer or salesperson reports the price back to headquarters, these days usually by e-mail or by logging into a database system and entering the new price. The company can recompute all the pricing rules using either the most recent price, or some blended average of recent prices, perhaps weighted by the quantities of each of the purchases or sales. Other buyers and salespeople will be advised of the new prices by e-mail or by logging into the secure database.

The only remaining difficulty is when an ingredient is used in more than one product made by the same company. In such cases, we might derive two differing sets of pricing rules for the same ingredient. Here, a company can choose one of the two sets of prices, or use an average of the prices. If, for example, 40 percent of the purchases of a particular ingredient go into product one and the other 60 percent go into product two, then a company might reconcile the two pricing rules with a weighted average, with weights of 0.4 for the ingredient price rules using product one's price and 0.6 for the price rules using product two's price. Denoting the different price rules for the same ingredient with superscripts 1 and 2 and suppressing the subscript for the ingredient number for simplicity, such a weighted average is simply

$$r_{avg} = w^1 r^1 + w^2 r^2, \qquad (3.16)$$

Box 3.3

An example of how to compute buying prices for an ingredient will help make these concepts more concrete. First, recall the two ingredient-buying rules:

The break-even price buying rule is $r_1^{BE} = [p - c(q)/q - u/q - \sum_{j=2}^{J} r_j n_j] n_1$

and the target profit margin buying rule is

$r_1^{GM} = [(1-gm)p - c(q)/q - u/q - \sum_{j=2}^{J} r_j n_j] n_1.$

For the example, continue with the canned cream of asparagus soup example from before, but add information on the product price so we can compute the pricing rules. Repeating the ingredient information from above:

Ingredient	Cost per unit	Units per case = n_j	Cost per case
Asparagus	$2.00/lb	(3 oz/can)(1 lb/16 oz)(24 cans/case)=4.5 lb/case	$9.00/case
Condensed milk	$2.00/lb	(12 oz/can)(1 lb/16 oz)(24 cans/case) = 18 lb/case	$36.00/case
Spice mix	$0.25/oz	(0.3 oz/can)(24 cans/case) = 7.2 oz/case	$1.80/case
Can	$0.20 each	(1 can/can)(24 cans/case) = 24 cans/case	$4.80/case
Label	$0.02 each	(1 label/can)(24 cans/case) = 24 labels/case	$0.48/case
Case box	$1.00 each	1 box/case	$1.00/case

Now also assume that the last sale of our cream of asparagus soup was for $60.00/case, the labor processing cost is $2.00/case, and utilities and overhead add another $0.50/case. The target gross profit margin is 20 percent.

Focusing on buying rules for asparagus, the two buying rules give us

r_1^{BE} =$60.00/case − $2.00/case − $0.50/case − $44.08/case = $13.42/case (where the $44.08/case is the cost of all the ingredients other than asparagus), and

r_1^{GM} =(1− 0.20)($60.00/case) − $2.00/case − $0.50/case − $44.08/case = $1.42/case.

Converting these two prices from per case to per pound, we need to use the fact that there are 4.5 lb of asparagus per case, so if we divide the per-case prices by the ingredient factor, we will get per-pound prices. Thus,

r_1^{BE} = ($13.42/case)/(4.5 lb/case) = $2.982/lb, and
r_1^{GM} = ($1.42/case)/(4.5 lb/case) = $0.316/lb.

Given that the current price of asparagus in our table above is $2.00/lb, it appears the company has been buying asparagus for a price below our break-even price. That means it is making money. However, it is not even close to the target margin buying price, and it does not appear obtainable. If the company is to reach its gross profit margin target, it should either sell the product for a higher price or buy the other ingredients (the condensed milk contributes most to the cost) for less.

where the weights w^1 and w^2 should sum to one. In the example mentioned above, the two weights would be 0.4 and 0.6.

Using pricing rules for decision making

Choosing ingredients

The above ingredient-buying rules can be used by a food processing company to decide between two possible ingredients if there are options in the "recipe." For example, some baked goods can use any of a variety of different oils in their recipes. Although the oils will all serve the same purpose, the recipe factor may be slightly different for the different oils (because their properties are not identical). By comparing the current market prices of the oils to their target margin buying rules, the company can choose to buy the ingredient that will be the best buy in the sense of helping to make the company as profitable as possible.

Choosing products

Similar comparisons can help a company decide which products to produce. If a company makes tomato sauce and tomato paste, but only has the capacity to make one at a time, it can use the pricing rules to find which is more profitable. If the company knows the likely price it can sell each product for, it can find each product's gross profit margin at the current ingredient prices. Using the target margin pricing rule of equation (3.10) with the summation for multiple ingredients included, we have a target gross margin pricing rule of

$$p^{GM} = [1/(1-gm)][c(q)/q + \sum_{j=1}^{J} r_j n_j + u/q]. \tag{3.17}$$

Producing the higher-profit-margin product does not necessarily lead to higher profit (since a lower profit margin on a higher-priced good might be a larger profit), but we can modify equation (3.17) to give us the per-unit profit and then convert that to the total profit. The per-unit gross profit for a product i, denoted below by π_i, will be given by

$$\pi_i = p_i - [c(q)/q + \sum_{j=1}^{J} r_j n_j + u/q]. \tag{3.18}$$

Now the company simply needs to multiply each π_i by the quantity it expects to produce to get the total expected gross profit from making each product. Given production constraints, the company can choose to use its time (and plant capacity) to make the product that will yield the most profit for the company.

Factoring in fixed costs

Most of what has preceded this section of the book has focused on variable costs. The pricing rules focused on gross profit margins, which do not include fixed costs (or taxes). Yet, at some point the company must deal with fixed costs. Ensuring that revenues exceed variable costs is not enough in the long run; the company must cover fixed costs at least over some longer time period.

How can a manager factor in such fixed costs as start-up and shut-down costs for a factory, annual depreciation, and interest expenses? Equation (3.18) above allows the company to estimate the gross profit per unit for a product that the company is considering producing. The manager can plug in the current market prices for the needed ingredients and an expected average price for selling the product and get an estimated gross profit margin for the product under consideration. Multiplying that gross profit per unit (the π_i from equation (3.18)) by the expected total production for some time period (a season, a month, or a year) provides the company with the expected gross profit from the production of the product. Then the manager can compare that gross profit to the fixed costs of operation. If the estimated gross profit exceeds the sum of the fixed costs, the decision to go into production is clear; make the product, and the company will make money.

If the gross profit is sufficient only to cover some of the fixed costs, but not all, then the manager needs to consider a breakdown of the fixed costs and how "fixed" they are. Start-up and shut-down costs are common in plants such as fruit or vegetable packing sheds and even some large processing plants such as tomato sauce and ketchup factories that only operate during part of the year when the fruit or vegetable is being harvested. These costs are only incurred if the company enters production that season, so they must be covered by the gross margin, otherwise production should not be undertaken. In terms of a season-long time period, those costs are variable; and if the company cannot cover them, it is better off staying shut down. Depreciation, insurance, and interest costs may be the same (or nearly constant) whether or not the plant operates. Thus, if the estimated gross margin cannot cover all of these fixed costs, it is still likely worth beginning production. Perhaps the company can sell the product for higher-than-expected prices or buy ingredients for less than it thinks. Certainly, a company would expect to be better off in operation than shut down in such a situation, so the manager should give it her best shot.

Using pricing rules for new products

When a company creates a new product, one aspect of that process is determining the price of the new product. Depending on the business, the company may need to set the precise sale price, or it may just need an expected price for planning and to use as a guide for its sales force to begin selling the new product. The pricing rules of this chapter can be used in new product development in two distinct ways.

The first approach is to set the product (expected or target) price. Once the recipe for the new product is established, the company can use the current market prices for the needed ingredients along with the estimated production costs to establish what selling price would be necessary to hit a target gross profit margin. If the target price seems unreachable, the company will likely choose not to launch the product.

The second approach is to work in reverse. When wholesale food manufacturers and restaurants develop new products, they often begin with the product idea and a target price, for example, a new fruit pie for their dessert menu that they can serve for $4.50 per serving. From that point, the product development team works backward to create the product while ensuring that the ingredients chosen and the processing cost necessary are such that they can meet their price target while earning the hoped-for profit margin.

This gets quite constraining at the lower-cost end. A dessert sold for $0.99 in a fast food restaurant will be sold to the restaurant by the wholesale food manufacturer for about $0.50 and will have a target ingredient cost of around $0.30. As the price point changes, so do the quality of ingredients, the selection of ingredients, and the amount of labor that can be involved in the processing. In many cases, the same food manufacturer makes multiple products in the same food category for different price points in the retail market (inexpensive for sale as a supermarket brand, mid-priced for sale under a name brand, and expensive for sale under another brand or in restaurants). In this manner, a company can make very similar gross profit margins on similar products sold at three quite distinct price levels.

Summary

In this chapter, we covered how to compute ingredient costs for products with multiple ingredients. We derived formulas that are used to calculate break-even and target profit margin pricing rules for both buying ingredients and selling the processed products. These rules are used in the real world to provide guidance to buyers and salespeople so that they know how to negotiate contracts that help their company to reach its profit goal.

Because the pricing rules for each ingredient and for the processed products all depend on each other, every time an ingredient is purchased or a product is sold, those latest prices should be used to update the pricing rules for all the other ingredients and products. With modern technology, the buyers and salespeople of a company use the Internet to enter new prices into a company database that updates all the pricing rules and alerts the other buyers and salespeople of those new prices by e-mail or text message. Small companies can make do with a spreadsheet and updates that are called or e-mailed in, entered by hand into the spreadsheet, and the new prices can then be e-mailed or texted out.

When a firm makes multiple products that share some common ingredients, the pricing rules for those ingredients may disagree, suggesting two different price ranges to buyers. Companies can take the average of the two pricing rules, perhaps weighting the differing prices by the share of the ingredient used in each product. Using this method, or other approaches such as taking the lowest price from different products, the company can resolve these differences and provide their buyers with a single set of price guidance rules.

Companies can also use the pricing rules to make decisions. Buying rules can help a manager decide between competing ingredients. Pricing rules and the closely related formula for the estimated gross margin per unit can aid managers in deciding which products would be best to produce. The same gross margin estimates also allow managers to make operation decisions that factor in fixed costs. Finally, we saw how the pricing rules could be used to set a price for a new product.

Chapter highlights

- The product break-even pricing rule is $p^{BE} = c(q)/q + r + u/q$.
- The product target gross profit margin pricing rule is $r^{GM} = (1 - gm)p - c(q)/q - u/q$.
- The ingredient break-even pricing rule is

$$r_1^{BE} = \left[p - c(q)/q - u/q - \sum_{j=2}^{J} rn_j \right] / n_1.$$

- The ingredient gross profit margin pricing rule is

$$r_1^{GM} = \left[(1-gm)p - c(q)/q - u/q - \sum_{j=2}^{J} rn_j \right] / n_1.$$

- Companies resolve these rules when new prices are known for either ingredient purchases or product sales.
- When a single ingredient is used in multiple products, the ingredient pricing rule can be solved separately using the product prices for each product in which the ingredient is used.
- The different resulting buying price rules can then be resolved either by using the one that provides the lowest prices to the buyers or by taking a weighted average where the weights are the proportion of the total ingredient purchases used in each different product.
- The gross margin formula, $\pi_i = p_i - \left[c(q)/q + \sum_{i=1}^{J} r_i n_i + u/q \right]$, can be used to compare profitability among products and to factor fixed costs into production decisions.
- The gross margin pricing rule can also be used to set starting prices for new products, or in the development of those products when reverse-engineering the ingredients.

Practice problems

1. Assume that you are making an onion relish. The relish has two ingredients, onion and spices. Each jar of relish holds one pound of relish which requires 2 pounds of onion and one "unit" of premixed spices. The onion costs $0.50 per pound, the spices cost $0.25 per unit, the jar costs $0.05, and the case for 12 jars costs $0.25. Using that information, find the total ingredient cost, r, for the onion relish.
2. Using the below information find:
   a. The break-even price for Quinn's Quince jelly in $/case.
   b. The target margin price if the Quinn's Quince Jelly Company wants to achieve a 40 percent gross profit margin (again in $/case).

Each jar of jelly needs as ingredients 1 pound of quinces, 1 pound of sugar, and 2 dashes of spices. The quinces cost $0.80/lb, the sugar costs $0.12/lb, and the spices cost $0.10/dash. The processing cost for the jelly is $0.25/jar for labor at minimum cost and $1,000/hr for utilities and overhead. The plant runs at minimum average cost at 1,000 cases per hour. There are 24 jars of jelly per case. Jars cost $0.10 each and the box for a case costs $0.25.

4 Trade among regions

One of the central features of modern society is trade. We no longer personally make most or even more than a few of the items that we consume. Instead, people specialize in the production of a few goods or services in which they can acquire training and skill and then trade either their produced goods or money for what they want to consume. This is a very good thing as trade benefits society in two important ways: through productivity gains derived from specialization of labor and through increased consumer utility from the greater variety in consumption. This chapter will examine the economics of interregional trade in a manner that makes clear how the possibility of extraordinary profits serve as the incentive to bring separate markets into a trading equilibrium that benefits both regions (although not all parties involved). Arbitrage opportunities between regions is the driving force behind interregional trade.

Why trade exists

The short answer to why trade exists is because profits and gains in happiness can be captured through trade, so people are motivated to increase trade between regions until such opportunities are exhausted. The longer answer is a little more complicated.

Economists refer to the natural resources of an area as its factor endowment. A country's factor endowment consists of its land area, its minerals and natural resources, natural transportation networks such as rivers, and its labor. Different countries and different regions within countries have been blessed with different factor endowments. In most cases, these factors cannot easily be moved among countries or regions in order to even things out; labor can move if countries let it, but land is pretty much fixed in place. The differences in factor endowments make some regions better suited to the production of certain goods: a region with lots of labor will have an advantage in labor-intensive goods, a region with lots of timber will have an advantage in products processed from wood, etc.

Over time, regions and countries have also created different levels of capital stocks, both physical capital (such as factories) and human capital (education and training). These differences also lead to different comparative advantages in production, so that regions will have an advantage in the production of goods that more intensively use the resources that they have in abundance. The theory of comparative advantage was developed by economists to prove that in cases where factor endowments or capital stocks vary, two countries or regions can both gain by specializing in the production of goods and services that more intensively use the resources they have in relative abundance. That is, even if a country has less of every type of input, it will have a comparative advantage in producing the good that most heavily relies on the input of which it is the least deprived. By specializing in production, the total production of the two regions can be increased, and then trade can be utilized to allow each region to consume its desired combination of goods.

This is the basic theory of trade, which is developed in great detail in general economics textbooks. For our purposes, the above discussion is enough to motivate trade and to allow the beginning of an economic analysis of trade between two regions. Because this chapter analyzes trade in a partial equilibrium setting (one good at a time), it will not demonstrate the overall gains from trade. The chapter will, however, make clear the gains from trade in a single good, as well as how different parties in each country or region may gain or lose from trade.

The single-good two-region trade model

In agricultural marketing, it is usually sufficient to analyze single goods. Begin with the demand and supply for a good (say, kiwi fruit) that can be produced in both regions with equal quality. Assume that initially there is no trade in that good. Figure 4.1 shows the supply and demand for kiwi fruit in each region in this initial state, called *autarky* (from the Greek, meaning "no trade").

In Figure 4.1, you can see that one region (region 1 in this case) has a higher equilibrium price. Thus, if a resident of region 1 visits region 2, she will be surprised at the affordability of the kiwi fruit there. If she has good business instincts, she will also see a profitable business opportunity: she can buy kiwi

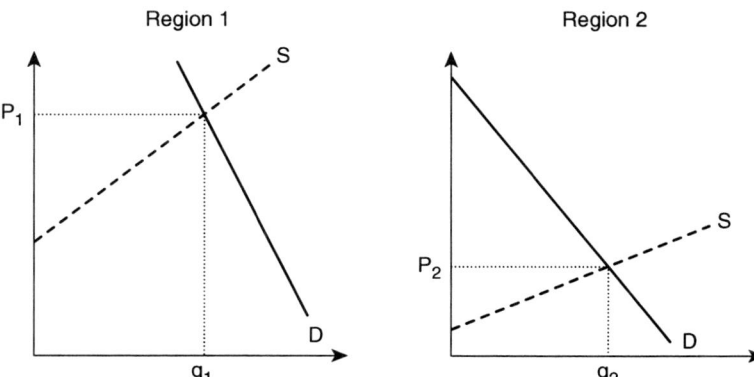

Figure 4.1 An opportunity for trade.

in region 2 at a low price, pay to transport them to region 1, and sell the kiwi for a profit.

Graphically, our businesswoman can analyze this opportunity by deriving what are commonly referred to as the export supply and import demand curves. The export supply curve represents the potential surplus in region 2 at any given price that the businesswoman can purchase for export; it is the horizontal distance between the region 2 supply curve and demand curve at each price above the autarky (pre-trade) equilibrium price. The export supply curve only exists above the current price in region 2 because the region is already in equilibrium. To gain supply for export, the businesswoman must outbid existing buyers, so she must offer a price higher than the prevailing market price. The import demand curve represents the potential demand in region 1 at any given price that the businesswoman could fill by selling her imported kiwis. It is the horizontal distance between the region 1 demand curve and supply curve at each price below the autarky price. The import demand curve lies below the current market price in region 1 because to enter this market, the businesswoman will need to gain new buyers by offering a more attractive (that is, lower) price. Figure 4.2 shows the original two markets from Figure 4.1 with a new trade sector market in the middle panel that displays the export supply and import demand curves.

Usually the crossing of supply and demand curves has great meaning in economics, but that is not the case in the middle panel of Figure 4.2. One curve in our middle panel is a supply curve of kiwis for export, and the other is a demand curve for imported kiwis. These are two different goods, in two different locations; where the curves cross is meaningless. What is needed is to factor in the cost of turning exported kiwis into imported kiwis.

The costs of the import/export business

The business of turning a product in one region or country into a product for sale in another region or country involves many costs. At the simplest level, labor costs are surely involved in buying up supply, arranging for transportation, and getting retailers in the importing region. Our businesswoman will also have to pay the transportation cost of getting the product from region 2 to region 1.

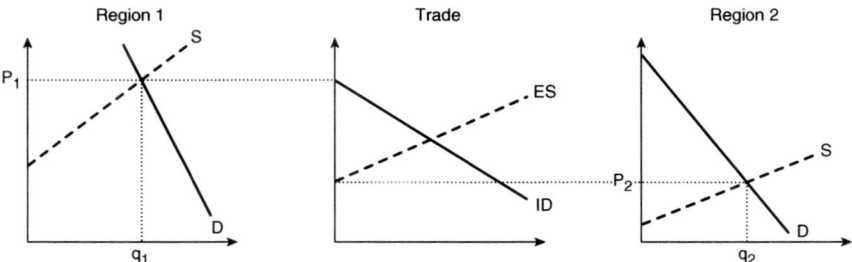

Figure 4.2 The three-panel trade diagram.

Then she will have to deal with all the regulatory issues imposed on the particular product by the two governments involved: safety inspections, labeling requirements, any packaging issues, and any required taxes or fees. Some of the taxes may be import tariffs: taxes that a country imposes on imported products, usually on an *ad valorem* basis, which means that they are levied as a percentage of the price. Finally, there are some miscellaneous costs such as insurance, carrying costs (the cost of borrowing or not having the money required to purchase the product until the time you sell it and get paid), and advertising if necessary. Overall, these marketing costs involved in exporting and importing a product are generally either constant per unit costs or can be well represented as a percentage of the price in the exporting region.

The best way to incorporate these marketing costs into the diagrams presented above is to think of the product in region 2 and in the export supply of the middle panel of Figure 4.2 as one product (kiwi for export) and then the product for sale in region 1 as a separate product (imported kiwi fruit). Think of these marketing costs as similar to the processing costs in a food processing plant similar to the one you studied in chapters 2 and 3. Then the export supply curve is a representation of the costs of the main input (kiwi). To derive the supply curve for the output—the imported kiwi ready for sale in region 1—one simply adds the marketing costs to the export supply function. Figure 4.3 below shows the middle panel from Figure 4.2 with the addition of the marketing cost and the new import supply curve that represents the sum of the export supply and the marketing cost functions. At each quantity in the figure, the import supply function is above the export supply curve by a vertical distance equal to the marketing costs of turning region 2's kiwi for export into imported kiwi in region 1.

Another way to think about the trade panel shown in Figure 4.3 is with a concept called the price-linkage equation. The export supply and import demand curves do not establish an equilibrium because they are for two different prices, p_1 and p_2. A price linkage equation establishes the relationship between the prices

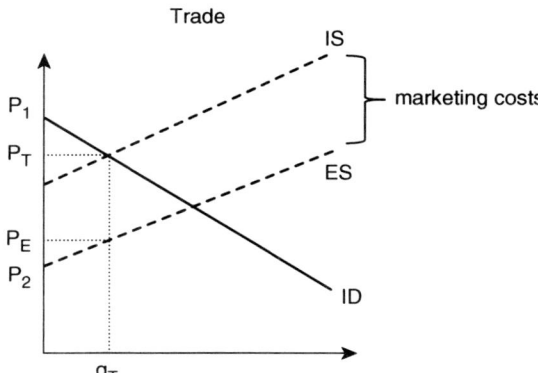

Figure 4.3 Adding the import supply curve to the trade panel.

38 *Trade among regions*

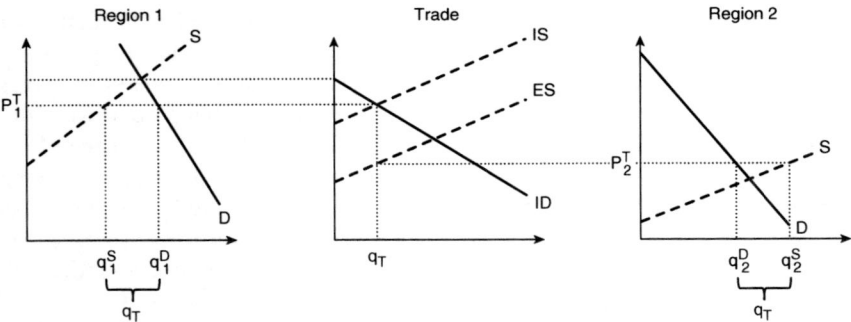

Figure 4.4 The three-panel trade model equilibrium.

in the two regions. Originally, before trade, there is no link between the two prices. However, after the commencement of trade, a price linkage will be established by the forces of free market economics. The price in the importing region (region 1) must exceed that of the price in the exporting region by at least the marketing costs of exporting and importing the product or the trade will not take place. If the price difference is greater than the marketing costs, other business people will see the profits being earned by the person who first thought of importing kiwis to region 1, and they will have an incentive to join in the trade (and take advantage of the arbitrage opportunity). This will cause the prices to eventually (that is, in equilibrium) differ by exactly those marketing costs. That difference is, in fact, the vertical distance between the export supply and the import supply curves. This concept will be developed further in the presentation of the mathematical analysis of this model later in this chapter.

The equilibrium in the export-import market can be found on Figure 4.3 at the point where the import supply function intersects the import demand curve. This intersection shows the price of the imported kiwis in region 1 and the quantity of kiwis imported. To find the price of the export kiwis (the price the exporter pays in region 2 to buy up the supply for export), go down on the figure from the intersection of the import demand and import supply to find the point on the export supply curve for that quantity. To trace these prices back into the market equilibria in each region, look at Figure 4.4, which contains all three panels. This figure allows you to see the quantities produced and consumed in each region and how the quantity traded fills the gap between domestic production and consumption. Also, the diagrams for each individual region should show offsetting domestic gaps; that is, the quantity traded between the two regions is equal to the difference between domestic supply and demand in both regions.

Mathematical analysis of the trade model

Having seen the trade model graphically, it is now time to analyze trade between regions mathematically. In this chapter and the several to follow, as we analyze

Trade among regions 39

multiple markets simultaneously, the key thing is to keep straight which variable needs to be on the left-hand side: quantity or price. If you can do this, the math is fairly straightforward.

To begin the analysis of two-region trade, write the supply and demand curves for each region as functions of price (that is, quantity on the left and price on the right):

Having done this, find the autarky (no trade) price in each region. This is easily done by setting the two equations for q_i equal. For example, in region 1, $f(p_1) = h(p_1)$. Solving this for price, one can determine which region is the exporter (the region with the lower autarky price) and which is the importer. Having established the direction of trade flows, the next step is to find the export supply and import demand curves. These represent quantities to be traded, so again it is important to have quantity on the left-hand side of the equations. The export supply function can be found by subtracting demand from supply at a fixed price. If we follow the diagrams and assume that region 2 is the exporter, the export supply curve is

$$\text{ES}(p_2) = q_{2T} = g(p_2) - k(p_2) = s(p_2). \tag{4.1}$$

Similarly, the import demand function is found by subtracting the importing region's supply from its demand. Using the curves given in Table 4.1, the import demand curve is

$$\text{ID}(p_1) = q_{1T} = h(p_1) - f(p_1) = d(p_1). \tag{4.2}$$

With the export supply and import demand curves, you have two of the three components needed to fill in the middle diagram of our trade problem. The next step is to add the marketing costs to the export supply curve to derive the import supply curve. However, this step must be done carefully because the marketing costs, $M(q_T)$, are like a price; they are in \$/unit or some similar type of unit, and they cannot be added to a quantity. Therefore, you must take the export supply curve and invert it by solving it for p_2 before you add in the marketing costs. Solving for the inverse export supply curve gives us

$$\text{IES}(q_T) = p_E = s^{-1}(q_T), \tag{4.3}$$

where p_E is the price of exports and the $s^{-1}(q_T)$ notation represents having solved whatever the equation $q = s(p)$ was so that it is now $p = s^{-1}(q)$. Once the inverse

Table 4.1 Algebraic supply and demand equations for analyzing trade

	Region 1	Region 2	Marketing costs
Supply:	$q_1 = f(p_1)$	$q_2 = g(p_2)$	$M(q_T) = c(q_T)$
Demand:	$q_1 = h(p_1)$	$q_2 = k(p_2)$	

export supply curve of equation (4.3) has been found, you can add in the marketing costs of turning those exports into imports, thereby arriving at the inverse import supply curve:

$$IIS(q_T) = p_1 = s^{-1}(q_T) + M(q_T) = s_I^{-1}(q_T). \tag{4.4}$$

Since we would prefer to work with the regular import supply curve rather than its inverse, you should next reverse equation (4.4) to solve for the quantity traded, yielding

$$IS(p_I) = q_T = s_I(p_I). \tag{4.5}$$

Now that you have found both the import supply and import demand functions, you can set them equal and solve for the equilibrium price in the importing region:

$$IS(p_I) = q_T = s_I(p_I) = d(p_I) = ID(p_I). \tag{4.6}$$

After solving equation (4.6) for the price in the importing region, you can then plug that price into either the import supply or the import demand equation to solve for the quantity traded. That same price will also allow you to find region 1's domestic production and consumption by substituting the price into the original demand and supply curves for region 1 given in table 4.1. Then you can substitute the quantity traded into equation (4.3), the inverse export supply function, to solve for the price in region 2, the exporting region. Plugging that price into the original supply and demand curves for region 2 will yield the domestic supply and demand for that region. If you have done the math correctly, the differences in each region's domestic production and consumption will exactly equal the quantity traded, and the two regions' prices will differ by the marketing costs of turning exports into imports.

A second way to solve the two-region trade model mathematically is with the price linkage equation. Once you have the export supply and import demand functions shown in equations (4.1) and (4.2), you have two equations in three unknowns (p_1, p_2, and q_T). If you can solve for those three unknown variables, you can easily solve for the remaining four unknowns (domestic consumption and production in each region) by using the original demand and supply curves. So what is needed is an additional equation to add to the system of export supply and import demand functions. That equation is the price linkage equation. Because region 1 is the importing region, the price linkage equation sets that price equal to the price in the exporting region (region 2) plus the marketing costs, $M(q_T)$:

$$p_1 = p_2 + M(q_T). \tag{4.7}$$

Solving equations (4.1), (4.2), and (4.7) is generally straightforward. The best approach is usually to substitute the price linkage equation (4.7) into the import demand function (4.2), turning it into an equation in p_2. Then you can set that equation equal to the export supply equation and solve for p_2. Once you have a solution for p_2, substitute that value back into the price linkage equation to get a value for p_1, and use either import supply or export demand to solve for the quantity traded. See the application box 4.1 for a numerical example of solving a two-region trade model.

Winners and losers from trade

From either the graphical or mathematical analysis of a two-region trade model, changes in prices and quantities produced and consumed in each region can be found. These changes let an analyst determine who wins and who loses from the new trade flows. If we measure consumer welfare by consumer surplus (the area under the demand curve and above the equilibrium price) and producer welfare by producer surplus (the area above the supply curve and below the equilibrium price), then finding the impacts of new trade flows or a trade policy change is quite simple. When trade between two regions increases, the price falls in the importing region and rises in the exporting region. Consumers in the importing region will consume a larger quantity at a lower price; their consumer surplus will increase, so they are winners. Producers in the importing region will produce less and sell it at a lower price. Their producer surplus will shrink, so they are losers from the increased trade. Producers in the exporting region will produce and sell more of the product and receive a higher price. Their producer surplus increases, so they win from the new trade. Consumers in the exporting region will consume less and pay a higher price, so they will have less consumer surplus and will be losers from the increased trade. When trade decreases, the winners and losers are reversed.

In all situations, more trade leads to higher total welfare for all parties involved if welfare is measured by the sum of the two consumer surpluses plus the two producer surpluses. That is why economists always favor free or freer trade. However, economists neglect to mention as often as they should that there are always some parties hurt by the increased trade. While the net change is positive, the losers are not likely to be consoled by the fact that the winners gained more than the losers lost.

Features of trade models in the real world

In the real world, many governments around the world intervene in the markets of international trade to distort the trade flows that would otherwise occur. Policies are employed to block imports, slow imports, tax imports, subsidize exports, and even rarely to stop or slow exports. The most common national policies are those that slow or block imports, so we will start there.

Tariffs

The most common—and simplest to model—national policy in the international trade arena is a tariff. A tariff is a tax levied on products at the border as they are imported and is generally expressed as a percentage of the product's value.

Box 4.1 A numerical example

To make the conceptual math of the above section clearer, here is a specific numerical example using the supply, demand, and marketing cost functions given below.

Example supply, demand, and marketing cost equations

	Region 1	Region 2	Marketing costs
Supply:	$q_1 = -5 + 2p_1$	$q_2 = -10 + 4p_2$	$M(q_T) = 3$
Demand:	$q_1 = 95 - 3p_1$	$q_2 = 60 - 3p_2$	

1. Solving the problem begins with finding the autarky prices to establish which region is the importer and which is the exporter. To do this, set each region's supply and demand equal.

   a. $-5 + 2p_1 = 95 - 3p_1 \Rightarrow 5p_1 = 100 \Rightarrow p_1 = 20 \Rightarrow$ importer ($p_1 > p_2$)
   b. $-10 + 4p_2 = 60 - 3p_2 \Rightarrow 7p_2 = 70 \Rightarrow p_2 = 10 \Rightarrow$ exporter ($p_2 < p_1$)

2. Now derive the export supply and import demand.

   a. $ID = 95 - 3p_1 - (-5 + 2p_1) = 100 - 5p_1 = q_T$
   b. $ES = -10 + 4p_2 - (60 - 3p_2) = -70 + 7p_2 = q_T$

3. Write the price linkage equation. Here, it is a very simple equation, just a constant cost.

   a. $p_1 = p_2 + 3$

4. Substitute the price linkage equation into the import demand equation to replace p_1.

   a. $ID = 100 - 5p_1 = 100 - 5(p_2 + 3) = 85 - 5p_2$

5. Set ID = ES, with both functions of p_2.

   a. $ES = ID \Rightarrow -70 + 7p_2 = 85 - 5p_2 \Rightarrow 12p_2 = 155 \Rightarrow p_2 = 12.917$

6. Solve for the remaining unknowns:

   a. $p_1 = p_2 + 3 = 12.917 + 3 = 15.917$
   b. $q_T = 100 - 5p_1 = 100 - 5(15.917) = 20.415$
   c. $q_1(\text{supply}) = -5 + 2p_1 = -5 + 2(15.917) = 26.834$
   d. $q_1(\text{demand}) = 95 - 3p_1 = 95 - 3(15.917) = 47.249$

e. $q_2(\text{supply}) = -10 + 4p_2 = -10 + 4(12.917) = 41.668$
f. $q_2(\text{demand}) = 60 - 3p_1 = 60 - 3(12.917) = 21.249$

7. Check the math by subtracting each region's domestic supply from the demand to see if the gap is equal to the quantity traded (within the error induced by rounding). This solution passes that check.

Thus, a particular tariff might be 10 percent, meaning that the importer must pay a tax equal to 10 percent of the value of the product (generally taken to be the cost of the goods paid by the importer), so it is roughly a wholesale price. A tariff is easy to introduce into our mathematical model through the price linkage equation. With a tariff incorporated, the price linkage equation becomes

$$p_1 = p_2 + c(q_T) + \tau p_2 = (1+\tau)p_2 + c(q_T) \qquad (4.8)$$

where τ is the tariff rate expressed in decimal form (that is, a 20 percent tariff would be $\tau = 0.20$). It makes no difference whether you want to think of the tariff as part of the marketing costs (by including it as part of $c(q_T)$ at the end of the price linkage equation) or treat it as a higher wholesale price. Either way, by increasing the gap between the two prices, the new equilibrium will be where import supply and import demand are farther apart, meaning that the quantity traded will be lower, the price in the importing country will be higher, and the price in the exporting country will be lower. Go back and look at Figure 4.4 to confirm this for yourself.

Non-tariff barriers

Non-tariff barriers are extremely common in international trade. Examples include customs inspections, safety regulations, labeling requirements, packaging rules, and quotas. In general, all of these non-tariff barriers except quotas can be thought of as additional costs added to marketing expenses associated with the import-export business. Thus, these are easily represented in the trade model by including them in $c(q_T)$ within the price linkage equation. More and higher non-tariff barriers increase $c(q_T)$ more, making the price gap between the two countries larger. Therefore, all these non-tariff barriers reduce the quantity traded, lower the price in the exporting country, and increase the price in the importing country. That is, they reduce trade, which is usually the point of putting the policies in place. These non-quota, non-tariff barriers are protectionist policies designed to protect domestic businesses from lower-priced imports without having to officially admit that is what you are doing. By hiding behind an alternative reason (safety inspections to protect consumers), the politicians can deny that they are simply doing favors to a particular industry at the expense of all their citizens who might wish to consume the less expensive imported product.

44 *Trade among regions*

Obviously, some such non-tariff barriers are reasonable; some amount of safety inspections, regulations, and labeling rules makes perfect sense and is beneficial. The situation becomes more problematic when countries create non-tariff barriers that go well beyond the reasonable and are clearly designed to reduce the flow of trade.

Quotas have to be handled differently. A quota is a restriction on the quantity of a product that can be imported into a country. For example, the United States has quotas that limit imports of cane sugar and of Japanese cars (technically, this is a voluntary agreement with Japan, but it still limits imports to 2 million cars per year). A quota can either be non-binding (the market chooses to import less than the maximum allowable amount) or binding (the market would like to have imports exceed the quota, but the quota limits imports to the quota level).

If you solve the standard trade model we have been using (graphically or mathematically) and get a value for the quantity traded, q_T, that is less than the quota amount, the solution is correct and you can simply ignore the quota. This is a case of a non-binding quota. If when you solve the model you find a solution for the quantity traded that exceeds the quota amount ($q_T > q_{quota}$), the solution is not valid, and the solution for the quantity traded should be reduced to the quota amount ($q_T = q_{quota}$). With the quantity traded set to the quota level, that quantity can be used to solve for prices in each country using the other equations in the model. For example, the export supply function can be used to solve for the export price, which can then be substituted into the price linkage equation to find the price in the importing country.

Finally, non-tariff barriers are often evaluated as to how tough they are in restricting trade by converting them to what is called a tariff-equivalent basis. This concept is actually quite simple to understand. For the non-quota, non-tariff barriers, the model is solved with the non-tariff barrier's cost included in the marketing cost function $c(q_T)$. The next step is to use the estimated prices in each country to find a tariff rate (as in equation (4.8)) that would yield the same estimated prices without the non-tariff barrier costs included in the marketing cost function $c(q_T)$. In other words, one solves for an imaginary tariff that would produce the same outcome as a non-tariff barrier of a certain cost. In the case of a quota, the process is similar. Simply find the tariff rate that when inserted into equation (4.8) yields an estimated quantity traded that is equal to the quota level.

Summary

This chapter has introduced two important concepts within the setting of a two-region trade model. The first is the concept of derived demand and supply. The exporter wants to buy the product from the exporting country, not for personal consumption but to sell it in the importing country; that is a derived demand. Similarly, the import supply curve is derived from the export supply through the addition of marketing costs. As we will see in later chapters, derived demand and supply curves play an important role in the economics of marketing and give us the ability to model all the different layers of a market (farm, wholesale, and retail, for example) as a product moves through various processing steps and marketing channels.

The second important concept is that of the price linkage equation. This concept—that prices in different layers of markets are linked by the marketing costs of transferring and transforming the product as it moves through the marketing channel—will be the key to understanding the economics of marketing as we will study them. When markets are not linked, the prices can vary randomly, but once the markets are linked by trade between them, the prices in the two markets cannot differ by more than the marketing costs that separate the markets, otherwise entrepreneurs will see a profit-making opportunity and enter the market seeking that profit. This additional business competition will drive the prices into equilibrium at a point where the prices differ only by the marketing costs. That is arbitrage at work.

Chapter highlights

- Trade benefits both partners, allowing specialization in production and both parties to consume more.
- While trade has overall net benefits, we should remember that some parties involved will suffer losses of consumer or producer surplus due to increases in trade.
- Graphically, trade can be represented as a market where exports and imports find equilibrium prices and quantities based on curves derived from the original supply and demand curves in the two countries or regions.
- Trade barriers, whether tariffs or non-tariff barriers, enter the model mathematically in the same manner as marketing costs that are incurred as part of the physical process of carrying out trade.
- Non-tariff barriers can be converted to tariff rate equivalents to ease comparison among different policies in terms of how severely they restrict trade.
- An important concept from this chapter is the price linkage equation (see equations (4.7) and (4.8)) which shows how arbitrage in free markets will bring prices in two markets into an equilibrium with a price difference equal to the cost of transferring the product from one market to the other.

Practice problems

The United States and Mexico have the following demand and supply curves for an imaginary vegetable (all prices are in cents, and quantities are 1000 lb).

	United States	Mexico
Demand	P = 100 − Q	P = 50 − 0.5Q
Supply	P = 40 + 2Q	P = 10 + 0.5Q

46 *Trade among regions*

1. Find the equilibrium price and quantity in each country in autarky (no trade between the countries).
2. Find the equilibrium price and quantity in each country given free trade, but with a transportation cost of 5 cents per 1000 lb.
3. Discuss, using a graph if you like, what will happen if the United States raises its minimum wage by 25 percent, assuming that at least some labor in vegetable production or processing is currently paid less than the new minimum wage. Who wins and who loses?
4. Discuss, using a graph, what will happen if the United States imposes a 10 percent tariff on imported vegetables from Mexico. Who wins and who loses?

5 The economics of storage

Chapters 2 and 3 covered transforming the physical form of a product (like turning oranges into orange juice), while chapter 4 explained the economics involved in interregional trade, which is the transformation of the physical location of a product. Now, we turn to the analysis of storage. Storage allows us to transform the timing of the sale and consumption of a product. As should become apparent as we move through this chapter, the mathematics and graphical representations of optimal storage policies are very similar to those earlier types of transformations. The possibility of storage simply presents the seller of a product with two possible markets to sell in: the market right now and the market at a later date.

Why storage makes sense

To analyze the economics of storage, the first question to be addressed is why a seller would want to delay the sale of a product (through storage) rather than selling the product now and collecting revenue. Clearly, a seller will only delay the sale of a product if he believes that storing the product for later sale will result in a higher profit. To arrive at such a conclusion, three factors need to be considered: the current price, the expected future price, and the storage costs incurred. When you are dealing with a relatively homogenous product with many sellers and buyers, this reduces to a simple price linkage equation very similar to that encountered in the trade case. Arbitrage opportunities will cause sellers to adjust their sales and storage plans to ensure that the price linkage equation holds. In forming this price linkage equation, let $E_t(p_{t+s})$ refer to the current expected price of the product at a future date; this is, the seller's best guess at time t for what the product will be able to be sold for when it comes out of storage at future time $t+s$. Also, represent the cost of storing one unit of the product from now until the next period by $SC_{t,t+1}$. Essentially, a firm will sell its product now if

$$E_t(p_{t+1}) - SC_{t,t+1} < p_t. \tag{5.1}$$

Alternatively, a firm will divert some product into storage until the next period whenever

$$E_t(p_{t+1}) - SC_{t,t+1} > p_t. \tag{5.2}$$

48 *The economics of storage*

In these two equations, a potential seller is making a simple comparison: is the expected net revenue higher if I sell now or if I sell later? Here, the net revenue is used to denote that the seller is adjusting her sales revenue for the storage cost that must be incurred in order to sell later.

As we move through this chapter, we will examine this simple decision in more depth, investigate the components of storage costs in order to understand the likely shape of the storage cost function, and see how storage economics changes when a monopoly controls the storage.

The components of storage costs

Storage costs can be broken down into subcategories. Some relate to the physical facilities (rental of space or debt payments and depreciation on owned space), others to labor (costs of placing the product into and later retrieving it from storage), protection of the product (insurance, fumigation, refrigeration or other climate control costs, loss of quality over time), and, lastly, the opportunity cost of deferred revenue. The opportunity cost is incurred because the seller has to wait to collect the sales price, meaning that the opportunity to collect interest on that revenue or otherwise invest it is lost. Physical costs, protection costs, and opportunity costs are all clearly functions of the amount of time the product is stored; the labor costs are generally constant on a per-unit stored basis; and protection costs and opportunity costs are also functions of the value of the product being stored (higher-valued products cost more to insure, suffer larger dollar losses from any deterioration of quality, and imply that a larger amount of revenue is being deferred). These relationships mean that a typical storage cost function is as follows:

$$SC_{t,t+k} = a + bk + ckp_t \tag{5.3}$$

where a, b, and c are numbers, and k represents the number of periods for which the product is stored. The a term models constant per-unit storage costs such as the handling costs of getting the product into and out of storage. The b term models costs that vary by the length of storage, such as physical facility costs and climate control costs. The c term accounts for costs that vary by product value, such as opportunity costs and insurance premia. The value of c would equal the interest rate foregone on the deferred revenue plus the insurance rate (on a per-unit per-period basis) plus any expected percentage loss in quality per period.

The storage equilibrium: two periods with production only in the first period

The simplest possible storage model involves two periods across which the seller can allocate product sales with all the production occurring in the first period. An example would be an agricultural crop with a single harvest but the ability to store some of the harvest for sale at a later date. To keep the model as simple as possible, we will analyze the storage decision at the time of harvest, so that the

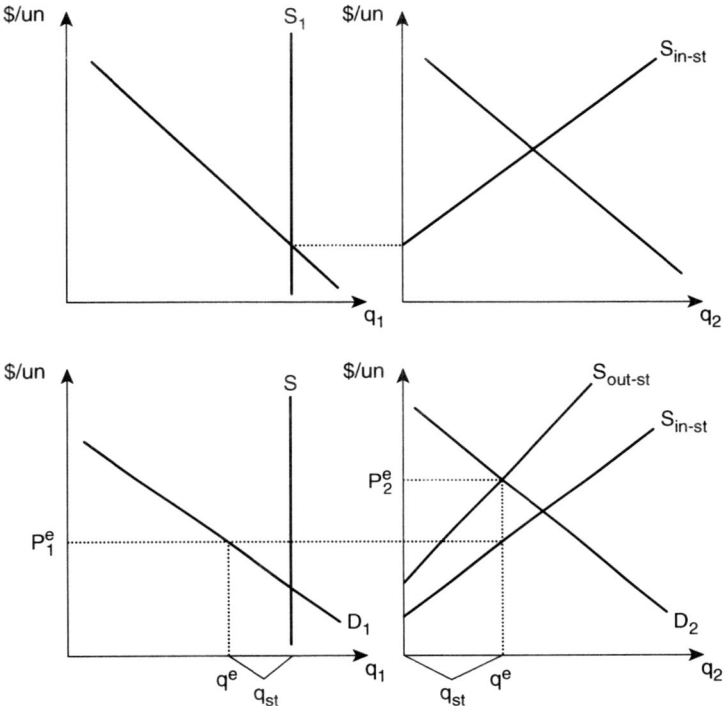

Figure 5.1 One-period production, two-period sales.

first-period supply is fixed. That translates into a vertical supply curve in the top-left panel of Figure 5.1. Figure 5.1 also depicts demand as being identical in each of the two periods. With no production in period 2, all the supply in the second period must come from storage. The available supply for storage is the surplus at any price above the "no storage" equilibrium price in period 1. This is very similar to the export supply function in a trade model. To find the available supply for storage, one simply subtracts the quantity demanded at a given price from the supply at that same price. This "surplus" at any price above the market clearing price is the amount that can be placed into storage for sale in a later time period. This is shown in the top-right panel of Figure 5.1.

However, we must use caution. The available supply for storage is not the same as the supply of product out of storage, available for sale in period 2. The difference is, again, marketing costs. In this case, the marketing costs are the storage cost (in the previous chapter, it was the export-import cost). Adding the storage cost to the supply of product into storage yields the supply for sale in period 2. This is displayed in the bottom-right panel of Figure 5.1, which shows how the storage cost leads to a supply curve in period 2 equal to the supply into storage shifted upward by the amount of storage costs.

Mathematical analysis of the two-period storage model

Having seen the two-period storage model graphically, it is now time to analyze this situation mathematically. In the mathematical example, we include a supply curve in period 2, so this is more general than the model displayed in Figure 5.1. However, it does not greatly complicate the math. To begin the analysis, write the supply and demand curves for each period as functions of price (that is, quantity on the left and price on the right); these are shown in Table 5.1.

To begin the analysis, first find the equilibrium price and quantity in each period with no storage. This is done simply by setting the two equations for q_i equal to find the equilibrium prices. For example, in period 1, $f(p_1) = h(p_1)$. After solving for the equilibrium price in each period, substituting those prices back into the supply and demand equations provides solutions for the equilibrium quantity in each period. Unlike in the two-region trade model, there is no need to find the direction in which storage moves; it can only go from period 1 to period 2, because time runs only in one direction. The supply-into-storage function can be found by subtracting the first-period demand, $h(p_1)$, from the first-period supply, $f(p_1)$:

$$\text{S-IS}(p_1) = q_{2,ST} = f(p_1) - h(p_1). \tag{5.4}$$

Next, find the supply-out-of-storage function by adding the storage cost. However, the supply-into-storage function in equation (5.4) has quantity on the left-hand side, so we need first to solve it for price before we can add the storage cost (since that is in money units (cost per unit stored)).

$$\text{IS-IS}(q_{ST}) = \text{S-IS}^{-1}(p_1). \tag{5.5}$$

$$\text{IS-OS}(q_{ST}) = \text{S-IS}^{-1}(p_1) + \text{SC} = \text{IS-IS}(q_{ST}) + a + cp_1. \tag{5.6}$$

$$\text{S-OS}(p_1) = \text{IS-OS}^{-1}(q_{ST}). \tag{5.7}$$

In the above equations, the inverse notation (superscripted "-1") with functions denotes the inverse, meaning in this case, interchanging the left-hand and right-hand variables. So IS-IS is the inverse supply-into-storage function with price on the left, IS-OS is the inverse, supply-out-of-storage function with price on the

Table 5.1 Initial equations for the two-period storage model

	Period 1	Period 2	Storage cost function
Supply:	$q_1 = f(p_1)$	$q_2 = g(p_2)$	$\text{SC} = a + cp_1$
Demand:	$q_1 = h(p_1)$	$q_2 = k(p_2)$	

left, and S-OS is the supply-out-of-storage function with quantity stored back on the left.

With the supply-out-of-storage function in hand, we can add that supply to any supply from production in period 2, $q_2 = g(p_2)$ from Table 5.1. However, the addition of quantities supplied from our two sources (storage and second-period supply) must be done at equal prices (that is, you need to add the supply curves horizontally). Because the supply-out-of-storage is determined by p_1 and the supply in period 2 is a function of p_2, keeping the prices equal is accomplished through the price-linkage equation. In a storage equilibrium, the price-linkage relationship that must hold is

$$p_2 = p_1 + SC = p_1 + a + cp_1. \tag{5.8}$$

Simplifying this, we get

$$p_2 = a + (1+c)p_1. \tag{5.9}$$

The final step to getting the total supply in period 2 is to add the supply produced in period 2, $g(p_2)$, to that coming out of storage, using the price-linkage equation to keep the prices in their proper relationship. Thus, we get

$$q_{2,TOT} = g(a + (1+c)p_1) + \text{S-OS}(p_1). \tag{5.10}$$

In solving systems of mathematical equations like this, it is always best to count the number of unknowns and the number of equations to make sure you can solve the complete system (remember, the number of equations must be at least equal to the number of unknowns). In the two-period storage problem, the unknowns are q_1, q_2, q_{ST}, p_1, and p_2—that is five unknowns. Between the two supply curves, two demand curves, and the price-linkage equation, there are five equations, so the numbers match, and a solution is possible.

Setting the supply in period 2 equal to the period 2 demand, $k(p_2) = k(a + (1+c)p_1)$, one can solve for the first-period price, p_1. Given the first-period price, next solve for the supply in period 1, $f(p_1)$, and the demand in period 1, $h(p_1)$. The quantity stored will be the difference between the first-period supply and demand, $q_{ST} = f(p_1) - h(p_1)$. Next, use the price-linkage equation to solve for p_2. Finally, using the second-period price, solve for the quantities produced and demanded in period 2 using the original supply and demand curves for that period, $g(p_2)$ and $k(p_2)$. That completes the solution; all the unknowns have been solved for. The application box 5.1 contains a numerical example of how all this works.

Multiple-period storage problems

Solving multiple-period storage problems (those with more than two time periods) is not particularly more difficult than the two-period problem. Each additional time period during which the seller could sell the product out of storage adds

Box 5.1 Numerical example

To make the conceptual math of the above section clearer, here is a specific numerical example using the supply, demand, and storage cost functions given below.

	Two-period storage	
Supply:	$q_1 = 100$	$q_2 = 0$
Demand:	$q_1 = 100 - p_1$	$q_2 = 100 - p_2$
Storage cost:	$SC = 1 + 0.05 p_1$	

1. Note that with no storage the equilibrium price in period 1 would be 0, so clearly some storage is going to be optimal. Solving the problem begins with finding the physical feasibility condition: consumption in the two periods cannot exceed supply in the two periods. To begin, assume total production equals total consumption.

    a. $100 + 0 = 100 - p_1 + 100 - p_2 \Rightarrow p_1 = 100 - p_2$

2. Now construct the price linkage equation, resulting in a second equation in the two prices:

    a. $p_2 = p_1 + SC = p_1 + 1 + 0.05 p_1 \Rightarrow p_2 = 1 + 1.05 p_1$

3. Substitute the physical feasibility constraint into the price linkage equation to solve for prices.

    a. $p_2 = 1 + 1.05(100 - p_2) \Rightarrow p_2 = 106 - 1.05 p_2 \Rightarrow 2.05 p_2 = 106 \Rightarrow p_2 = 51.71$

    a. $p1 = 100 - p_2 = 100 - 51.71 \Rightarrow p_1 = 48.29$

4. Plug the prices into the two demand equations to find consumption in each period.

    a. $q_1 = 100 - p_1 = 100 - 48.29 \Rightarrow q_1 = 51.71$
    a. $q_2 = 100 - p_2 = 100 - 51.71 \Rightarrow q_2 = 48.29$

5. Find the optimal amount to store by subtracting the second-period supply from the consumption in that period. In this case, period 2 supply is zero, so

    a. $q_{ST} = 48.29$

6. Check that all prices and quantities are positive and that total consumption equals total supply.

three more unknowns: the quantity produced in that period, the quantity sold in that period, and the change in the quantity stored in that period. These three additional unknowns can be solved for because we also add three new equations: a supply curve for that period, a demand curve for that period, and a price linkage equation. The general solution approach is very similar to that followed in our numerical example. Because all the prices for periods during which any storage is occurring are linked sequentially by a series of price linkage equations, all the prices for such periods can be reduced to functions of the price in the first linked period. That is, in a four-period problem with storage that exists between all four periods, if we used the same storage cost function as above, we would get

$$p_2 = a + (1+c)p_1$$
$$p_3 = a + (1+c)p_2 = a + (1+c)\left[a + (1+c)p_1\right]$$
$$= a(2+c) + (1+c)^2 p_1$$
$$p_4 = a + (1+c)p_3 = a + (1+c)\left[a(2+c) + (1+c)^2 p_1\right] \tag{5.11}$$
$$= a(3 + 3c + c^2) + (1+c)^3 p_1.$$

With these equations, we can replace all the prices with the first-period price and then begin solving the problem by finding the p_1 that gives us the total demand over the four periods equal to the total supply over the four periods. This physical feasibility constraint (I cannot sell more than I produce over the total period studied) is very handy for solving multiple-period problems such as this.

This approach involves one danger: an erroneous assumption. For the price linkage equations and the sequential substitutions shown in equation (5.11) to hold, the seller must be storing product between each pair of periods. If at any point before the end of the problem, the quantity stored hits zero, the price linkage will cease to hold. Because the math is much easier when the price linkage holds throughout the problem, the best way to solve these problems is to assume that the price linkage equations all hold (that is, assume that storage is positive between all periods), and then check the resulting answer for feasibility. If the assumption of positive storage was incorrect, you will get an answer that contradicts some constraint: a negative price, a negative quantity stored or sold in some period, or a total quantity sold that exceeds the total quantity produced. When you get an answer that violates one of these conditions and you cannot find a math error, the reason is generally that the storage equilibrium does not hold because at some point, the optimal storage was zero. Such problems can then be broken up into subsections of single periods or sets of periods that are linked and then solved in those smaller groups.

Finally, remember that the price linkage equation here involved an expected price (although it has not been displayed as such everywhere in the chapter; only at the start). Thus, as the seller moves through the time periods, unexpected changes in supply or shifts in demand may lead to prices that are not expected, and the price linkage equation may not hold once the later period's price is actually known. In multiple-period problems, the seller generally resolves the problem for each period, now treating what was period 2 as period 1 and with a total number of periods that is one less than what it was before.

In situ storage

A special class of storage problems involves products that have no direct storage costs because they can be stored at no expense. Economists refer to such a situation as *in situ* storage, because *in situ* is Latin for "in place" or "in position." Examples of *in situ* storage would include oil and gas wells; coal, metal ore, and gem mines; gravel and stone quarries; and certain agricultural products such as hay. All of these have this in common: if you choose not to sell now, you can pretty much just leave the product where it is until you choose to sell it later. Such storage problems reduce the storage cost to just the opportunity cost, so the price linkage equation becomes

$$p_{t+1} = (1+r)p_t \qquad (5.12)$$

where r is the interest rate that reflects the opportunity cost of the later sale.

Such *in situ* storage problems typically involve multiple periods because, especially in the non-agricultural examples, the common situation is a stock of some natural resource that is being slowly extracted and sold over time. However, if we know the total amount of product (hay, gold, oil, etc.) at the start of the problem and the total number of time periods over which the seller wishes to completely exhaust the resource, then these problems are easy to solve.

If you know the total quantity to be sold and the total number of periods, an *in situ* storage problem reduces to a single equation in one unknown, the initial price. Because in this type of problem, storage is assured in all periods, we know the price linkage equation always holds and that we can assume

$$\begin{aligned} p_2 &= (1+r)p_1 \\ p_3 &= (1+r)p_2 = (1+r)^2 p_1 \\ \text{and, in general,} & \\ p_{t+s} &= (1+r)^s p_1 . \end{aligned} \qquad (5.13)$$

If you substitute each of these price linkage equations into each period's demand curve, all the demand curves can be expressed as functions of p_1 rather than the price in their respective time periods. The sum of these demand curves can then be set equal to the total quantity to be sold (the initial supply), and the resulting single equation is solved for p_1. Once you have the initial price, you can solve for all the other prices. Then the quantity sold in each period is found by plugging each price into the appropriate demand curve.

In practice, a great way to solve these problems is with a spreadsheet on your computer. Let each row represent a time period. Create a column containing each period's price as a function of the previous period's price following the price linkage equations. The next column should have a formula that finds the quantity demanded for that price in that period. Take the sum of the quantity-demanded column, and display that in your spreadsheet. Now simply guess a price for the first period, and see what total quantity sold over the total number of periods is. If it is too high (demand > supply), raise the initial price; if you did not sell all the supply by the end of the problem, lower your initial price. In a few guesses, you will find the correct initial price to whatever precision is desired. You can probably solve the problem in this manner far faster than actually working out the math with paper and pencil.

Monopoly storage

In some cases, a single company manages to control the entire supply of a product, either in all periods or at least the supply out of storage. Such cases will be referred to as monopoly storage. Similar to the normal case of a monopoly firm, instead of being a price taker the monopoly storage firm selects prices and quantities together in order to maximize profit.

In the two-period case, a monopolist wishes to solve the following optimization problem:

$$\max \pi = p_1 q_1 + (p_2 q_2)/(1+r) - (q_{ST})(SC) \qquad (5.14)$$

where r is the discount rate that reflects the time value of money and SC is the per-unit storage cost as used in the price linkage equations earlier in the chapter. To solve this type of problem, begin by substituting inverse demand functions into the optimization problem so that it is reformulated only in quantities. Then q_{ST} can be rewritten as $q_2 - S_2$, where S_2 is the actual or expected production in period 2, and q_2 is the quantity sold; clearly, the difference is the amount that must have come out of storage.

Taking derivatives of this modified profit function with respect to both q_1 and q_2 and then setting each equal to zero yields the two first-order conditions. The first-order conditions will both recognize the marginal revenue from selling an additional unit in each period and the marginal cost of storage, as well as adjusting the second-period revenue by the discount factor to reflect the opportunity cost of waiting for that revenue. When these first-order conditions are combined with the physical feasibility constraint (that you cannot sell more than you produce), there are three equations in the three unknown quantities (q_1, q_2, and q_{ST}). Once the optimal quantities are solved for, the prices in each period can be found.

An intriguing feature of monopoly storage is that the price linkage equation does not hold. In fact, the price gap, $p_2 - p_1$, will always be smaller than the per-unit storage cost. This is because monopolists set marginal revenues equal to marginal cost instead of setting price equal to marginal cost as in perfect competition.

This feature of the monopoly storage optimum ensures that the monopolist can maintain its monopoly position. No other company would want to buy the product in period 1, store the product, and then sell in period 2 because the expected increase in prices is too small to cover the cost of storage. The price rise is enough for the monopolist because the monopolist realizes an extra benefit from the storage in the form of a higher price in period 1 on all units sold in that period. Thus, the optimal price pattern provides the monopolist with a built-in assurance that nobody will try to undercut its monopolist status by competing in the storage of its product.

Summary

This chapter has examined the economics behind storage of a product and applied the price linkage equation concept to find the equilibrium between markets for the same product in different time periods. This storage equilibrium is very similar to the equilibrium in a two-region trade model. Supply still must equal demand across all the markets. What were exports and imports now become product placed into storage and then that same product coming out of storage for sale. Storage will occur whenever the seller thinks that more profit can be made by paying for storage and then selling the product later (at an assumed higher price).

If the product is not stored between two periods, then the price linkage breaks down, and the markets in the two periods are not connected. Because time runs only in one direction, storage problems vary from trade problems in that we know at the start of the problem which direction the product needs to be moving if we are to find a new equilibrium that involves storing the product for later sale.

Monopoly storage problems involve solving a multiple-period, multivariable optimization problem in order to maximize the present value of discounted profit over the time periods. The solution of these problems require calculus. The solution for optimal sales over time by the monopolist yields prices over the periods that rise by less than the storage costs between periods because monopolists equate marginal revenue to marginal costs. This fact serves to preserve the monopolist's position in the storage market, since no competitor would choose to enter this storage market given that prices are not expected to rise by enough to pay for the cost of storage.

Multiple-period storage problems were found to be only slightly harder to solve than two-period problems, and *in situ* storage problems feature a simplified price linkage equation and can be solved quite quickly in a spreadsheet.

Chapter highlights

- Storage between two periods is another form of product transformation that allows producers and sellers to increase profit and better allocate their goods across different time periods.
- The different time periods are very similar to different locations in the trade models of the last chapter, so the graphical and mathematical versions of the problems look alike.

- The price linkage equation in storage problems shows how arbitrage in free markets will bring prices in two time periods into an equilibrium with an expected price difference equal to the cost of storing the product until the later sale date.
- One difference is that the price linkage equation holds in anticipation at the time the seller chooses to store the product; it may or may not turn out to hold when the later period price is actually determined. This cannot be avoided; the best one can do is update the solution when conditions change unexpectedly.
- Monopoly storage is characterized by prices that rise by less than storage costs. This is because monopolists focus on marginal revenue, not prices. The smaller price increases also serve to protect the monopolist's position as competitors have no incentive to enter the storage market (since they would lose money).

Practice problems

1. Solve a two-period storage problem in which production is 250 in period 1 and 150 in period 2. The demand in each period is $q_1 = 200 - p_1$ and $q_2 = 220 - p_2$, respectively. Assume storage costs of $5 + 0.10p_1$ for each unit stored. Make sure that you find both prices, quantities sold in each period, and the quantity stored.
2. Storage of Vidalia onions requires specialized storage facilities to control the atmosphere and limit quality loss. Assume all onions are stored in 100 lb bags. It costs $1.00/bag to put the onions into storage and take them back out. The facility's depreciation runs $0.10/month per bag. Insurance cost $0.03/month per bag. The quality loss can be approximated by a 2 percent drop in price each month of storage, and the onion company assumes its value of money is 1 percent per month.
   a. Construct the onion company's storage cost function for one month of storage.
   b. Now repeat, assuming the onions will be stored for two months.
   c. Why do the storage costs not simply double?
3. Resolve problem 1, but this time assume it is a monopoly storage problem. Confirm for yourself that $p_2 - p_1 < SC$. Compare the prices, quantities, and the total present value of the discounted profit over the two periods to your solution to problem 1 to see if being a monopolist increases profits.

6 Plant location and size decisions

This chapter will focus on the important business decisions involved in the starting and expanding of a business, rather than the daily operation and management of a business, which is what the rest of the book generally deals with. Rather than involving equilibrium concepts that are the focus of so much of economics, plant location and size decisions are discrete, lumpy decisions that revolve around comparison between alternatives. That means this chapter is more about the factors that determine these decisions and the process of making them, and less about math and specific numbers. Rather, in this chapter we will explore the important aspects of these infrequent decisions and their long-term implications. We will also have one of the few discussions in the book about actual on-farm decisions as we examine how plant locations and buying prices for ingredients influence farm planting decisions, profitability, and even land prices.

Optimal plant size

In deciding on the optimal plant size, a company must examine its average production level (per week, month, or year), the variance of its production, and its average cost versus the speed of running a plant. In chapter 2, we learned how to find the optimal speed for running an assembly line operation. This information tells a company how to produce its goods most efficiently in order to minimize its average variable cost. For a company that wants to have one plant, the optimal plant size would then be determined by finding the number of assembly lines needed to produce the total quantity while operating each line at minimum cost.

If the plant's production varies weekly owing to seasonal demand or seasonal supply of an agricultural product, then the plant size needs to be decided taking this variability into consideration. If demand is higher at certain times, the company needs to ensure either sufficient capacity to meet the peak demand or sufficient storage combined with the capacity to produce extra during the periods of lower demand, and store that production for the peak demand periods.

Because an investment in a plant is something done infrequently, a company may also wish either to install capacity for future production expansion or, more commonly, to construct a building with space for some expansion. The extra space is kept empty, delaying the expense of the assembly line equipment until it is needed. Because building shells are not particularly expensive, this is usually a cost-efficient way of allowing for an increase in plant size if the business grows, without incurring large expenses before they are needed.

Optimal number and location of plants

As a company expands in size, it needs to consider the possibility of multiple plants. Factors that enter these decisions beyond those mentioned above include transportation costs of raw materials to the plants and of the finished product to its markets, ease of management for different plant sizes, and the issue of risk in concentrating too much of the company's production or storage at a single location.

Different locations involve different costs for operating a production plant, for a variety of reasons. First, land costs vary by location, with the difference potentially being very large. The cost of industrial land can vary from a low of near $10,000 per acre to over $1,000,000 per acre for a location in a large city. Utility costs, labor costs, and construction costs all vary by location. The cost of bringing raw materials to the plant and then shipping the final product out to markets must also be included in the decision process. Another factor companies consider is local and state taxes (along with potential tax breaks for building a new plant). Computing an estimated cost for building and operating a proposed plant at a set of different locations is important and involves factoring in all these different component costs.

Given a starting list of potential locations (often with 10–20 possible sites on it), one simply adds up the different costs for building the plant (land, building, equipment) and for operating it (labor, utilities, transportation, taxes), and then compares them across the different locations. The business owner will locate the plant in the place that minimizes a combination of the initial investment and the ongoing operating costs (where some assumption about the number of years the plant will operate and the discount rate for computing a present value need to be made). It is also important before a final decision is made to ensure that the necessary raw materials and labor force can be obtained in the chosen location.

Transportation of ingredients (raw materials) and finished products is an especially important factor in many plant location decisions. First, it is often a fairly sizeable cost. Second, the costs are often very different between the cost of assembling ingredients and the cost of shipping out the final product. For example, oranges weigh much more than frozen concentrated orange juice, so a company could save a considerable amount on transportation by locating an orange juice concentrate plant near the orange groves and shipping the concentrate a longer distance to markets. Similarly, if either the ingredients or finished products need refrigeration or other special shipping, that may sway the location decision in order to minimize the distance involving expensive transportation.

Figure 6.1 shows an example of how the transportation cost of raw materials to the plant and then finished product to market can be combined to find the optimal location when other costs are roughly equal across locations. In cases where transportation costs are approximately linear in distance, the transportation cost

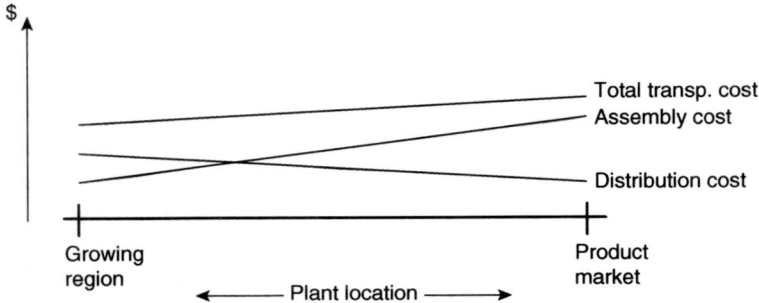

Figure 6.1 Components of transportation costs.

is likely to favor a location either very near the main ingredients or very near the product market.

Transportation costs (both assembly and distribution) also play a major factor in the decision about how many plants to operate. When ingredients or other raw materials come from multiple locations, placing food processing plants in a variety of sites near those suppliers can reduce assembly costs. When plants are located near various cities and concentrations of consumers of the company's products, then the distribution costs can be greatly decreased compared to a single plant with long shipping distances to multiple outlets. Additional advantages of multiple production plants are that operations can become difficult to manage beyond a certain size, infrastructure networks and local labor markets may be insufficient to handle plants that are large enough to produce a company's entire output, and geographical distribution of production provides risk reduction benefits against local disruptions such as fires, severe weather, and equipment breakdowns.

Because production plants generally reach a size where they approximate constant returns to scale (and thus a constant average cost) at a reasonably small output level, the plant operating costs are commonly fairly uniform across different plant numbers and location configurations. Plant investment costs can vary across these different possible numbers and locations of plants because of variations in land and construction costs and differences in incentives offered by local and state governments (usually in the form of direct subsidies or tax breaks). As discussed above, one expects transportation costs to decrease as the number of plants is increased and as they are dispersed geographically.

To determine the optimal number of plants, a company repeats exactly the same exercise that one would to determine the site of a single plant, but with options for multiple plants now in the mix. Figure 6.2 shows an example of the possibilities that might be considered by a company in such a decision-making process. Beginning with five possible locations and the possibility of operating with one to five plants, the company would have 31 different possible plant

		Number of plants		
One	Two	Three	Four	Five
A	AB	ABC	ABCD	ABCDE
B	AC	ABD	ABCE	
C	AD	ABE	ABDE	
D	AE	ACD	ACDE	
E	BC	ACE	BCDE	
	BD	ADE		
	BE	BCD		
	CD	BCE		
	CE	BDE		
	DE	CDE		

Figure 6.2 Possible combinations of plant numbers and locations.

number and location configurations to consider in its decision set. Just as with a single-location decision, the multiple-location decision begins by computing the total cost of plant investments, operating costs, taxes, and transportation costs for each of the 31 possibilities. Given a time horizon for the plant decision and a discount rate, a comparison can be made of the net present value of each of the 31 configurations, and then a decision can be made. Difficult-to-quantify items such as the risk reduction value of the geographic distribution of plants can be used to choose between different configurations that are close in economic costs if a company prefers that to attempting to turn them into dollar values. While this is fairly straightforward, it is tedious and involves collecting a lot of data, some of which is not easily accessible. Many large companies hire a site selection consultant to help find possible locations and to organize the information needed to make the final location decisions.

Net value surfaces

When a processing plant is considering how much to pay for an ingredient or what price to charge for a product, it needs to factor in any transportation cost that the firm must pay either to bring in the ingredient (assembly cost) or to deliver the product (delivery cost). In chapter 3, when we studied pricing rules, transportation costs were not included. However, companies sometimes must pay the cost of assembling ingredients and usually pay to deliver their products.

If the food processing company pays for the assembly of its ingredients (such as with chickens, where the processor picks up the chickens from the grow house), then the value to the company of nearby ingredients is higher. This concept can be represented mathematically by a net value surface that displays the value to the company of an ingredient as a function of the assembly cost of that ingredient. The net value of the ingredient is the buying price given by the formulas from chapter 3 minus the transportation cost of bringing the ingredient to the processing plant. If the transportation costs are linear in the distance from the farm to the plant, then the net value of an ingredient to the plant is given by

$$\mathrm{NV}(d) = r - s - td \tag{6.1}$$

where r is the value of the ingredient to the company at the plant, s is a fixed transportation cost that reflects loading and unloading costs, t is a per-mile transportation cost for the ingredient, and d is the distance in miles from the farm to the plant. If we imagined a series of farms located along a line with the plant in the middle of the line, then the net value surface will be a hill-shaped line with a peak at the location of the plant and two slopes declining as one moves away from that central point. An example of such a net value surface is shown in Figure 6.3. In a three-dimensional world, the net value surface would look like an inverted cone with the point at the center (where the plant is) and sides sloping away in all directions. Interestingly, the net value surface is the same regardless of which party is paying for the transportation cost because the money ends up with the transport company either way.

If transportation costs are a non-linear function of distance, either due to efficiencies or geographical factors such as topography or road conditions, then the net value surface would become irregular. The net value would always be decreasing with distance (that is, it will always decrease as distance increases), but the rate of that decrease would vary over the net value surface, so that instead of being a regular inverted cone, the net value surface would have ripples, wiggles, and other irregularities in it. However, it would still reflect the true value of an ingredient based on its location relative to the plant interested in purchasing it.

Different commodities may have different transportation costs owing to density (the space they take up relative to their weight), need for refrigeration, or other special handling needs. This would make the net value surfaces of different commodities slope downward at different angles. Also, because different commodities have different buying prices, the net value surfaces for different ingredients will start at different heights, reflecting the different values to the processing plant. An example of such a situation for two hypothetical ingredients is shown in Figure 6.4.

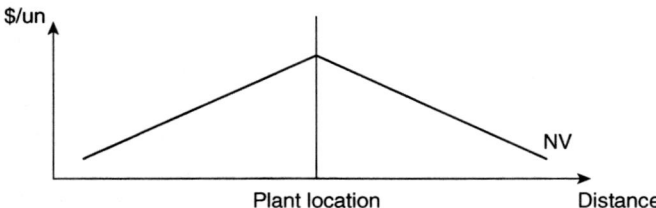

Figure 6.3 An example of a net value surface.

Plant location and size decisions 63

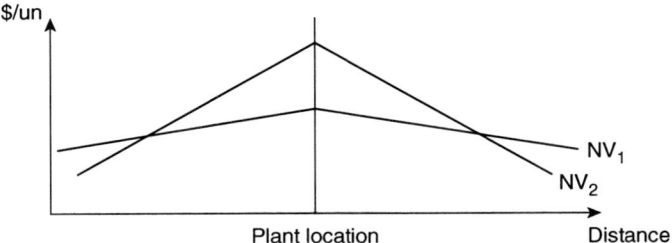

Figure 6.4 Net value surfaces for two ingredients shipping to one plant.

Boundary problems

Net value surfaces can be used to solve two types of boundary problems. They can be used to determine to which plant a farmer should sell a commodity and to decide what crops should be grown where.

Let us begin with the decision of which plant to sell a commodity to: this requires a modification of Figure 6.3, so that the line contains two plants, with farmers distributed along the line past and between the plants. This is shown in Figure 6.5. A farmer will sell to the plant whose net value surface for his commodity is higher at his farm; similarly, the plant with the higher net value surface will be willing to outbid the other plant for that farmer's commodity. Where the net value surfaces intersect, the net values of selling to each plant are equal, and a farm is indifferent as to which plant buys the commodity (and the prices offered by the two plants will be equal). This is the boundary between the two plants' buying areas. Mathematically, one can find the boundary between two plants' buying areas by setting the two net value equations as shown in equation (6.1) equal to each other for the unknown boundary point and then solving for the location of the boundary. For example, given a line that stretches from 0 to 100

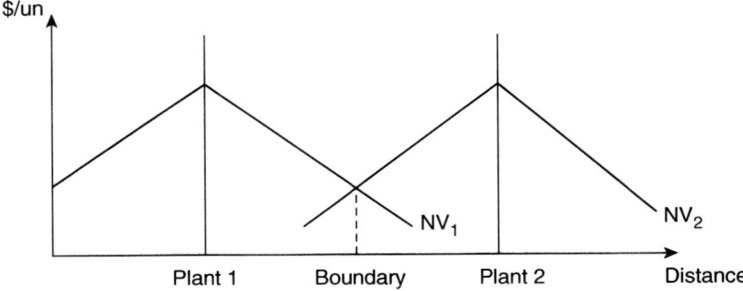

Figure 6.5 Net value surfaces for two competing plants.

64 Plant location and size decisions

with plants at 30 and 70, the boundary would be found by solving an equation of the form (where the subscripts refer to the plant offering to buy the commodity):

$$r_1 - s_1 - t_1(B-30) = r_2 - s_2 - t_2(70-B). \tag{6.2}$$

In equation (6.2), note that the two distances from the farm on the boundary to the respective plants are expressed by either subtracting the plant location from the boundary or vice versa, depending on which order makes the distance positive. When solving an actual boundary problem, all the variables in (6.2) would be known except B, so it would be a simple single equation in one unknown variable that can be solved by basic algebra.

If a plant cannot secure the supply of an ingredient it requires at the price it is offering, it must raise its price in order to increase the supply it can capture. An increase in the offer price, r, will raise the net value surface at all distances from the plant. If other plants do not raise their prices, this rise in the net value surface will result in the plant's boundary expanding (being farther from the plant), which will allow the plant to secure a larger supply. In this manner, if the plant knows the available supply of its ingredient and the suppliers' locations relative to the plant and its competitors, it can solve for the offer price that will produce a supply of each ingredient in any amount needed by the firm. Choosing an offer price is equivalent to selecting a boundary for the region within which the plant captures all supply, which is why adjusting the buying prices allows the adjustment in the amount of each ingredient purchased. For the math that links the quantity of an ingredient within a boundary and the offer price, see the appendix to this chapter.

Choice of crop by location relative to processing plants

For a farmer located within the boundaries of a plant or several plants willing to buy different ingredients that the farmer could grow, the net value equation can be modified to allow the farmer to make planting decisions. First, take equation (6.1) for the net value equation, and replace the buying price r by the formula from chapter 3 for the buying price:

$$NV_i(d) = \left[(1-gm)p - c(q)/q - u/q - \sum_{j \neq i} r_j n_j\right]/n_1 - s - t_i d. \tag{6.3}$$

where d represents the distance to the plant for the product whose values for product price, processing cost, and other ingredient prices are reflected in the equation. To make this net value (for one unit of ingredient i for use in a particular processed product) useful in making planting decisions, the units need to be converted from per unit of ingredient to per acre, and production costs must be factored into the equation. Then the equation would be transformed into one that showed a farmer the net value per acre of different commodities. Denoting the new net value as NVA to clarify that it is now net value per acre, the equation would be

$$NVA_i(d) = \left\{\left[(1-gm)p - c(q)/q - u/q - \sum_{j \neq i} r_j n_j\right]/n_1 - s - t_i d\right\} Y_i - PC_i \tag{6.4}$$

where Y is the yield in units per acre (e.g., bushels/acre) of the commodity, and PC is the per-acre production cost.

By evaluating the above equation for different commodities and plants in the geographical region of a farm, the farmer can determine the relative profitability of growing those commodities for sale to the nearby plants. Note that the farmer does not need to know every variable in equation (6.4) since the complicated part of the formula that serves to compute the ingredient buying price can just be replaced by r:

$$NVA_i(d) = (r_i - s - t_i d) Y_i - PC_i. \tag{6.5}$$

In this format, a farmer only needs to know the buying prices currently being offered, distance to the plant, his expected yield, and production cost. In fact, the form in equation (6.4) is likely only useful to the plant managers, who could use it to evaluate how they might need to change things in order to secure additional supply or are interested in seeing what an improvement in average processing cost might do to the attractiveness of growing commodities for their plant's purchase.

Site rent and plant locations

Site rent is an old, economic term for the profit earned by a company on account of its location. If a restaurant can charge extra for a wonderful beachfront view, that part of its profit is site rent. Similarly, if a farm can earn extra profit because it is located near a processing plant (thus saving on transportation costs), that extra profit is also site rent. Site rent reflects the reality that two different farms with identical average and marginal cost curves could actually have different profits from growing the same crop simply because one farm's location is more advantageous in the sense of lower transportation cost to the plant purchasing the crop.

If a new processing plant begins operating, farms located nearby capable of producing commodities used as ingredients in the plant will suddenly enjoy an increase in site rent and profitability. While such an increase in profits is obviously a wonderful benefit to the farmer, what happens when the farm is sold?

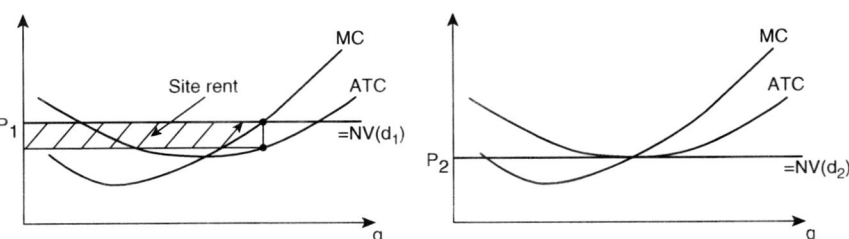

Figure 6.6 Site rent for farms two distances from the same plant.

Does the buyer of the farm enjoy the benefit of the site rent or is the future site rent captured by the seller in the form of a higher price for the farmland? The answer is that we cannot know for sure.

The seller of farmland that is earning site rent will surely try to sell for a high price per acre that reflects the presence of the nearby plant and its associated higher net value for the ingredients it buys. In fact, the seller is likely to ask for the present value of the flow of future expected profits from selling to the nearby plant. If the seller received that price, the buyer would have no site rent and would, in fact, face a zero-profit situation where the price received for the commodity would be equal to the average total cost (which would have shifted up from the position when the seller owned the farmland because the new buyer paid a high price for the land). The buyer will try to offer a lower price per acre in hopes of still enjoying some amount of site rent after purchasing the farmland. After all, why buy the farmland if the expected profit is zero? The buyer is also likely to point out that future site rents should be discounted to reflect the probability that the plant might close in the future. The purchase price will be somewhere between the fair price for the farmland before the new plant opened and the higher price that would eliminate all the site rent. Exactly where in that range the sale price will fall depends on the negotiating skill of the seller and buyer and the number of potential buyers for the farmland. The general idea is, however, that the site rent will be highest for owners of land at the point in time when the new plant opens for business. Each successive owner of the land will have less and less site rent as the price of the farmland rises to reflect its beneficial location.

There has been some research on how site rent gets capitalized into the price of land when it is sold. This research does not involve the nearby location of a processing plant, but the eligibility of the land for federal government farm program payments. Studies on a variety of crops and federal government subsidy programs have estimated that land prices can be inflated by between 15 percent and 20 percent owing to federal subsidy payments, with that amount often representing around 50 percent of the subsidy level. Less than the full amount is capitalized into the land price because there is no guarantee that the subsidy programs will continue indefinitely without change.[1] Similarly, a processing plant can close or move, so one should expect the site rent to raise land prices for future purchasers, but not by as much if the site rent was sure to last forever.

Summary

This chapter covered the process companies use to make decisions about where to locate their plants and how many plants to build. Companies must consider the investment cost of the plant and equipment, land costs, labor cost and availability, local and state taxes and tax breaks, and transportation costs in making location decisions. Choosing the optimal number of plants involves studying how having multiple plants impacts these costs, especially transportation costs, where multiple plants generally produce significant savings. Companies will scale their plants so that they can operate at the lowest possible average cost.

Plant location and size decisions 67

Net value surfaces display how the distance from a plant to a farm impacts the value of commodities produced on the farm. These net values provide a useful construct for understanding how farmers decide which plant to sell to, which commodities to produce, and why production of commodities is often concentrated geographically around processing plants. Net value surfaces from two competing plants produce a boundary where they intersect with farmers on each side of the boundary, all selling to the plant with the highest net value. A plant that needs to secure a larger supply of a commodity offers a higher price, raising the net value surface and thereby expanding the boundary of the region containing their suppliers. Net value surfaces can also be transformed to allow farmers to choose which commodities to produce in order to maximize their per-acre profits.

The last concept covered in the chapter was site rent. Site rent is the profit a farm or other business earns owing to its location. Site rent is created for a farm when a new processing plant opens near the farm that wants to buy a commodity the farm can produce. As farmland is sold, the site rent is capitalized into higher land prices so that over time the site rent disappears.

Chapter highlights

- Business location decisions are made by comparing the present value of investment, operating, and transportation costs for various possible locations.
- The same process can be used to find the optimal number of plants and where those plants should be located.
- Multiple plants help a plant reduce risk by providing alternative locations that protect against production disruptions at any single site.
- Net value surfaces show how the value of a commodity is affected by its distance from the plant purchasing it.
- Boundaries between two competing plants purchasing the same ingredient are located where the two net value surfaces intersect (where the net values are equal).
- To shift a boundary and capture more supply, a firm must raise the price it pays for the ingredient.
- Net value surfaces can be used by farmers to decide which commodities to produce.
- Site rent is profit earned by a farm owing to a favorable location near a processing plant.

Practice problems

1. Two tomato processing plants are located along a line 100 miles long. Plant 1 is at mile 30 and offers $2.00/lb minus transportation cost (which both plants pay). Plant 2 is at mile 70 and pays $1.75/lb minus transportation cost. Transportation costs for both firms are the same and are equal to $0.05/lb + ($0.02/lb-mi) D, where D is the distance from the farm to the plant.

a. Find the boundary between the two plants' supply regions.
b. Where does the boundary shift to if plant 2 matches plant 1's price?

2. Using information from problem 1(a) above, if a farm is located at mile 40 with a total cost curve per acre of TC = $1000 + 0.10q + 0.0001q^2$, where q is pounds per acre produced, find the optimal production in pounds per acre, the profit per acre, and the site rent of this farm relative to the farm located on the boundary.
3. How does the returns to scale of a processing plant impact the number of plants a company is likely to operate?
4. Farmland in an area is selling for $1000 per acre when a new processing plant opens that can add $100 per acre per year to farm profits. Assuming the plant has guaranteed to stay in operation for 20 years (to get some local tax breaks) and also assuming a discount rate of 5 percent per year, compute the range of possible farmland prices that might be reached in a negotiation to purchase land in this area.
5. For a circular almond supply region with transportation costs equal to $0.02 per mile per pound, production costs of $1.00 per pound, and yield of 1000 pounds per acre (which is 640,000 pounds per square mile), what price must a plant offer in order to secure a supply of 2,000,000,000 pounds (or 1,000,000 tons)?

Appendix: the boundary and captive supply

Captive supply is a term economists use to refer to supply that is essentially guaranteed to a buyer. In the context of food processing plants, farmers who are much closer to a particular plant than any other potential buyers of a commodity their farm produces represent captive supply. In terms of our net value surfaces, any farm inside the boundary of a particular plant and commodity is part of that plant's captive supply of that commodity. This appendix details the math needed for a plant to compute the amount of its captive supply as a function of its offer price to buy each ingredient it needs.

First, imagine all farms are on a line 100 miles long with a single plant located right in the center at mile 50. Assume the plant buys only one ingredient, and that is the only crop the farms can grow. To begin, assume that farmers produce 10 units of the crop per mile at a production cost of $1/unit. If the plant offers to pay $2/unit minus a transportation cost of $0.05 + ($0.02/mile)d, what is the captive supply for this plant?

The net value surface from the plant's perspective will be given by $2 − $0.05 − $0.02d = 1.95 − 0.02d$. However, farmers will subtract the $1/unit production cost to see a net value surface of $0.95 − 0.02d$. With no other plants, the boundary here will be the point where the farmer's net value equals zero, representing the point at which profit and site rent equal zero:

$$0.95 - 0.02d = 0 \Rightarrow d = 0.95 / 0.02 = 47.5. \tag{6.6}$$

Thus, the boundaries will be at B = 2.5 and B = 97.5. With an assumed production of 10 units per mile and a captive supply region 95 miles long (97.5 – 2.5), the plant can purchase 950 units of the crop at its offer price of $2/unit.

If a line has two plants, one would find the boundary by setting the two net value surfaces equal and solving for the boundary between the two plants. Then the net value surfaces can be used to confirm the outside boundary for each plant (in case some farmers are too far away from any plant to profitably produce and sell the crop). With all the boundaries known, the solution of the captive supply is the same as above: the product of the distance inside the plant's boundary and the density of production.

Also, note from the math above that raising the plant's offer price will move the boundary distance out by 0.5 miles for each one cent price increase (0.01/0.02 = 0.5). This is equivalent to 1 mile of total new supply region, which would produce an additional 10 units of captive supply. With this knowledge, the plant can raise or lower its offer price in order to appropriately adjust its supply of the ingredient and maximize its profit.

Now, what happens if farms are in two-dimensional space, spread across the countryside? Staying with a single plant, now at (x, y) coordinates of (0, 0), the same offer price, transportation cost, and production costs as above, but now a production density of 100 units per square mile, what is the firm's captive supply? The boundary distance is still d = 47.5 miles, but will now inscribe a circle around the plant with a radius of 47.5 miles. The total supply within that circular supply region is given by the product of the area of the circle and the production density:

$$S = \pi(47.5^2)(100 \text{ units} / \text{mi}^2) = 708,822 \text{ units}. \tag{6.7}$$

With a circular supply region, moving the boundary out by a mile has a more complicated effect on total supply, which can be found by taking the derivative of the area of the supply region with respect to its radius and multiplying by the production density.

$$dS / dr = 2\pi r (\text{production density}). \tag{6.8}$$

In the example above, that means that at the current boundary distance of 47.5 miles, moving the boundary out by 1 mile (which is equivalent to increasing the offer price by 2 cents) would increase the captive supply by $(2\pi)(47.5)(100) = 29,845$. Unlike the example along the line, in cases with circular supply regions, this marginal effect changes as the boundary distance changes, so the plant manager must factor that in and not assume a constant change in supply in response to buying price changes.

7 Risk management

This chapter covers a variety of practices that food industry companies can—and do—use to manage their risk. Food industry companies face an array of different risks. The prices of inputs can rise. The prices of their products can fall. Production equipment can break down. Deliveries can be delayed by transportation bottlenecks or road closures. Ingredients could become unavailable owing to market shortages caused by either weather conditions in growing regions or imbalances between supply and demand.

Using forward contracting to manage price risk

One of the simplest approaches to managing price risk is through forward contracting. A food processing company can contract with input suppliers (whether farmers or wholesale suppliers) for set quantities of ingredients the food processing company needs to be delivered at fixed dates in the future. For example, a tomato processing company might contract with a farmer for 10 tons of processing tomatoes each week to be delivered to one of its plants. In fact, such deliveries are generally scheduled for a specific date and time as the processing plant must ensure that it has a continual supply of tomatoes as any disruption in the plant's production is very costly.

Simply having forward contracts for inputs manages the risks involved in obtaining them, but does not address the price risk of the input cost. To do that, the food processing company must include price terms in the contract, which they commonly do. Prices in forward contracting can be specified in many ways, but two are the most common. The first method is a fixed price: so many dollars per pound for a specified quantity. In such contracts, the quality is also specified, and bonuses and deductions from price for higher or lower quality are sometimes included. This type of contract completely removes the price risk on the input cost side for a food processing company. The second method of specifying prices in forward contracts is to tie the price to be paid to some public price index. For example, a beef processing company could agree to pay $0.10/lb more than the futures market price for cattle on the date of delivery. Again, such contracts usually contain a schedule of bonus payments for higher-than-standard quality and penalties for lower quality. These types of index-linked prices do not remove the price risk by themselves, but they allow it to be done easily when combined with the next risk management tool to be discussed.

It is important to realize that the discussion above in which the food processor agrees to pay some premium above the futures market price in a forward contract (or a premium to a spot price or some average price over a specified period) is not an arbitrary assumption. Such forward contracts typically contain a price that is set at some amount above the price used as a base in the forward contract (what might be called the formula price). The processor usually rewards the commodity seller with some bonus above the formula price to compensate the seller for giving up other potential sales opportunities. That means that in order to reduce the ingredient supply risk, the processor is potentially paying more than it would expect to without the forward contract. Risk management techniques are designed to reduce some risk and therefore come at a cost (like paying your car insurance premium). Forward contracting and other risk management tools discussed below are meant to reduce the variability of costs, revenues, and profit; by intention, they will tend to produce a lower average profit over time. A company practicing risk management is willing to sacrifice a little expected profit in order to have more consistent and predictable profits.

Using futures markets to manage price risk

Futures markets are the most widely used risk management tool across the food industry. They are used by farmers, food processors, wholesalers, retailers, restaurants—pretty much all the participants in the food industry. Futures markets allow people and businesses to buy and sell futures contracts. Each futures contract specifies a commodity (corn, soybeans, cattle, etc.), a quality, an amount, and rules for delivery at the expiration date of the contract. At the expiration date, futures contract prices are expected to converge to the spot market price (and they generally do). Most commodities with futures contracts have multiple contracts trading simultaneously with one expiring either once a month or every other month.

Food processing companies can use futures markets to manage price risk on the input side and potentially on the output side, depending on what they are processing. When a company buys a futures contract, which is called taking a long position, it will make money if the price of the traded commodity rises and will lose money if the price falls. This procedure is called *hedging*. For a food processing company that needs to buy one or more agricultural commodities as inputs, buying futures contracts in those commodities allows it to lock in the cost of those inputs. If the price of the commodity rises, the food processor will pay more for the input but will earn a profit on the futures contract that offsets that cost increase. By buying the number of contracts that equates to the amount of the commodity it plans to purchase (with an expiration date close to or after the time of the planned purchase), a company can eliminate all uncertainty about the cost of that input (as long as the futures contract converges). A food processing company can also partially hedge its input cost risk by purchasing fewer contracts than needed to fully cover their input requirements.

For inputs that do not have futures contracts, a company can sometimes manage its input price risk by using the futures contract of a related commodity, a practice called cross-hedging. If a company needs to purchase corn meal, it can use the futures contract for corn as a cross-hedge; a restaurant chain that purchases steaks can use the futures contract for live cattle. To use a cross-hedge, the company must know the correlation between the commodity whose price risk it wants to control and the commodity whose futures contracts it will use to hedge. If the commodity to be purchased has a less variable price than the one with the traded futures contract, then fewer contracts would need to be purchased than the amount needed to provide an equivalent amount of the substitute commodity.

Some companies produce products that can also be hedged, either directly or by using cross-hedging. For example, there are futures contracts for frozen concentrated orange juice, pork bellies (basically bacon), soybean meal, and soybean oil. So a soybean crushing mill can actually hedge input and output price risk, although it may not bother to do so given that the prices tend to move in concert anyway, owing to market forces. However, an orange juice processor could definitely use the orange juice futures to remove the risk in the price it receives selling its product. It would do this by selling futures contracts equal to the amount of its sales. By selling futures contracts (taking a short position), if prices fall, the orange juice company would make a profit to offset the lower revenue when it sold the orange juice. If prices rise, it would make more selling its juice, but would lose money on its futures position by an offsetting amount.

Box 7.1 How many contracts are needed?

When a food processor wants to use futures contracts to hedge its input price risk, it has to calculate how many contracts are needed to accomplish its goals. For this example, the food processor is a bakery that uses a lot of corn to make its famous corn muffins. Corn futures contracts expire in the months of March, May, July, September, and December (on the last business day before the 15th of each month), and each contract is for 5,000 bushels, which is equal to 280,000 pounds of corn.

If the bakery uses 1,000,000 pounds of corn per month, that means it would need to buy roughly four contracts per month to offset all of its input price risk relative to corn purchases. The contracts are traded for a little more than a year before they expire, so when the bakery sees an attractive price, it can lock in that price by buying up to four contracts per month until the expiration date.

For example, in February if the bakery already owned four March contracts, it is fully protected against input price risk through mid-March. If the futures price on the May contract was below what the bakery had budgeted for corn costs, it would purchase eight May contracts to cover the price risk until then. If the price for the July contracts was also attractive, the bakery could buy another eight July contracts.

After purchasing all these contracts, the bakery would sell the appropriate contracts as it purchased the actual corn in order to close out its positions and not end up speculating on the price of corn. For example, if the bakery purchased 1,000,000 pounds of corn on April 5, it would then sell four of its May contracts to reduce its hedging position so as to stay in balance with the amount of corn still to be purchased.

Food processing companies cannot completely remove all price risk through futures markets because not all commodities have contracts and because contracts only expire at preset times (usually every two months, but for some commodities once a month). A food processor can still buy futures contracts for a listed commodity that it needs to buy as an ingredient and then sell the contracts (close out its position) as it buys the actual commodity. However, because futures prices need not converge to spot prices before expiration, when this process takes place between expiration dates there is still some small amount of price risk remaining.

In many situations, food processors and wholesalers do not use futures markets or forward contracting to manage their input or output price risk. There are a number of potential explanations for such behavior. The company might not be risk averse and instead be willing to accept the higher cost and/or revenue variability in exchange for higher average profits over longer time periods. The manager of some unit within the company may not want to hedge input cost risk in hopes of securing input supplies at lower prices leading to higher than expected profits and, potentially, a bonus for exceeding his budget target. Similarly, if the input price rises above the cost level projected in the company's internal cost and profit budgets, a manager may resist using futures markets to hedge the input price risk at that point since to do so would lock in a profit below the target level needed to earn a bonus. This can lead a manager to continue without hedging even as the situation continues to deteriorate simply because the manager still thinks there is a small chance that input prices will drop enough to allow the profit target to be reached (and a bonus to be earned). Finally, managers are sometimes reluctant to fix prices with futures contracts or forward contracting when prices are well above "normal" prices because of a fear of locking in a very high input cost only to see spot market and/or futures prices drop. Nobody wants to fix their acquisition costs right at the market peak, and the desire to avoid such a situation can lead a manager to continue without any hedging or forward contracting as the prices of the needed inputs continue to rise.

The reader should note that this section provides just a basic description of how futures markets could be used to manage price risk for food processors. To learn more, you can easily find whole books dedicated just to futures markets.

Using vertical integration to manage price risk

An alternative way for a food processor or retailer to manage price risk is through vertical integration. Rather than using forward contracting or futures markets to avoid price risk in the purchasing of inputs or (for food processors) the sale of outputs, a firm can instead use vertical integration. Vertical integration is the ownership of firms at different stages of production. So a food processor could purchase farms that grow commodities that it needs as ingredients, a bakery could purchase a flour mill, and a chain of steakhouses could purchase a beef packing facility. All the preceding examples have been framed as a way to reduce the risk of changes in input prices, but the direction of purchase can be reversed (e.g., the flour mill can buy a bakery) as a way to reduce the risk of changes in output prices.

Vertical integration allows prices at the intermediate stages (such as between the flour mill and the bakery) to be ignored. Since the transaction is between two arms of the same company, the price set is arbitrary and really only useful for figuring out the profitability of component units within the larger business. Thus, as long as production costs at the lower stage of production (lower means closer to the beginning, or farm,) are controlled to be fairly constant, the input cost risk is essentially eliminated for all ingredients that are part of the vertically integrated enterprise.

Clearly, vertical integration does not change the opportunity cost of using an ingredient. If the market price of a particular ingredient rises, a vertically integrated food processor's actual production costs do not rise, but the opportunity cost does because the ingredient could have been sold on the open market to some other processor. However, the vertically integrated company is likely to continue the use of the commodity as an ingredient in its own processing operations because of the importance of fulfilling contracts it has for finished products and maintaining its position in the marketplace. It should be clear that the profit of the vertically integrated is unaffected by the market price or opportunity cost of any commodity whose production is part of the company since the firm would have exactly offsetting revenue and expense if it tried to account for the internal transaction of "selling" the commodity to itself for use as an ingredient.

Note that vertical integration will be most successful in reducing price risk when the firm integrates vertically in such a way that the levels not owned have more stable prices than those that are integrated. For example, while commodity prices can be quite variable (both raw agricultural commodities and somewhat processed ones such as flour or high fructose corn syrup), retail food prices in the grocery store are much more stable. So if a company were to vertically integrate up to the final wholesale level, the remaining output price risk involved in selling to grocery store chains would be quite small. The price risk involved in selling to retailers also tends to be easy to manage through forward contracting as retailers generally want to control the cost of their purchases.

Spatial approaches to risk management

While forward contracting, futures markets, and vertical integration can all be successfully employed to manage price risk, they cannot address the issue of production risk. Production risk encompasses crop failure, yield or quality loss, production breakdowns within a food processing factory, labor shortages or strikes, supply chain interruptions, and any other issues that disrupt the planned operation of a food business. Production risk can never be eliminated (the real world does not go as planned). There are always at least minor mistakes and losses of production efficiency. However, production risk can, and must, be managed in order both to maximize profits and to minimize the long-term problems that will arise if your company cannot be relied upon to deliver promised products on time.

Dispersing the company's production geographically is an easy way to minimize most forms of production risk. The preceding chapter discussed the economics involved in a company deciding on the number and location of its production facilities, with the reduction of production risks mentioned as one factor that can play into those decisions. Here, that idea can be discussed in more depth. Multiple facilities mean that production breakdowns, labor shortages, and many forms of supply chain interruptions will only impact a fraction of the company's total production capacity, thereby significantly lowering the risk from these events. The risk from crop failures and supply chain interruptions can be further reduced by utilizing multiple input suppliers, preferably with some geographic dispersion between the suppliers for any input susceptible to weather-related or other place-dependent production risk. For example, most US orange juice companies now grow oranges in Florida and in Brazil, reducing production risk and allowing production to be spread out more evenly across the year owing to Brazil's different harvest season. Similarly, pecan processors are now procuring supplies from the United States and from Australia. On a smaller scale, Georgia peach growers own orchards in different counties in order to reduce their risk from localized weather events such as freezes or hail as well as problems such as pests.

Another method many large companies use to minimize supply chain interruptions is requiring input suppliers to locate within a prescribed distance of their production facility. With agricultural commodity inputs, this is not always possible, but processors can work to attract growers to be as close as possible. The best example of this can be found in chicken processing, where the processors recruit growers to build chicken houses near their processing facilities. In other cases, the location decision works in the reverse direction, with the processor building a production facility near existing growers of a key agricultural commodity input. For example, Vidalia sweet onions are grown only in a small region of east central Georgia. If you want to have a company that produces a Vidalia onion relish or simply pack Vidalia onions for sale to supermarkets, a logical move would be to locate the production facility within the sweet onion production region. Doing so minimizes the chance of transportation disruptions and quality loss during transit. Such coordinated location decisions lower the assembly cost of bringing inputs to the production facility, can improve the product quality because commodity inputs are delivered fresher, and reduce several of the production risks inherent in food processing. Overall, when possible, decisions to locate input production near a processing facility or to locate it near a concentrated production region can have many beneficial outcomes.

Summary

Firms face a multitude of risks and have a number of options for managing that risk. Production risk can be reduced by operating multiple facilities in different, spatially dispersed locations. Supply chain disruption risk can be minimized by using multiple suppliers and by either co-locating facilities or at least being located near suppliers and purchasers.

The risk from price changes in inputs or outputs can cause undesirable variability in firm profits. To make profit more predictable and smoother over time, a company can use forward contracting or futures markets in order to reduce or remove the risk from input or output price changes. Forward contracting can set the prices to specific amounts, removing all price risk. Futures markets can be used to hedge price risk by ensuring that the firm makes an offsetting profit or loss in the futures markets to any profit change resulting from changes in input or output prices. Forward contracting and futures markets can be used in tandem by first fixing input prices by a formula to some futures price and then taking a hedge position in that futures contract to remove the input price risk.

Companies also sometimes manage risks by vertical integration. Vertical integration involves a single company owning more than one stage of production between the farm and the kitchen. Chicken processors, for example, commonly own the chickens at every stage from the time the chicks hatch until they are sent to the retailer for sale. Vertical integration eliminates price risk at the intermediate market levels because the transaction itself is eliminated.

Chapter highlights

- Firms face production risk, input supply risk, delivery interruption risk, input price risk, and output price risk. They have a variety of options for managing and minimizing these risks.
- Production risk, input supply risk, and the risk of delivery interruptions can all be reduced by geographical dispersion. Having multiple production locations, multiple input suppliers, and multiple distribution facilities means that a problem in one location will not halt all production or deliveries.
- Forward contracting is a tool that can both ensure sufficient input supplies and also help to control input cost risk. A forward contract involves the promise of delivery of a specific quantity and a specific future date for some set price or formula to determine the price.
- Futures markets are an additional tool used by many farmers and food processors. By buying or selling a suitable number of futures contracts, a company can eliminate the risk from changes in input or output prices, respectively. As the input or outputs are actually bought and sold, an equivalent number of the futures contract positions would be closed out to keep the hedge at the right level.

Practice problems

1. Find the details of the soybean futures contract (easy to do on the Internet) and

   a. Determine how many contracts a processor should use to fully hedge the price risk of an expected purchase of 2.7 million pounds of soybeans next month.
   b. What if the company was going to purchase 2.5 million pounds?

2. What is an advantage of forward contracting compared to using the futures market to manage input price risk?
3. Discuss the risk management benefits of having your production facilities dispersed geographically. What about the location of suppliers relative to your factories?
4. Define cross-hedging, and give an example of an ingredient a food processor might use that would need to be cross-hedged to manage its price risk.
5. The poultry industry is completely vertically integrated from the hatching of chicks until the sale of processed products to grocery stores. The beef industry has very little vertical integration. Suggest some factors that might explain this difference.

8 The economics of the marketing sector

This chapter will detail the economics of the marketing sector. It deals with all the other costs that contribute to the price of the final product beyond raw materials and processing costs. Costs such as advertising, packaging, transportation, selling, and administrative costs have to be accounted for in proper pricing, or companies will fall short of their profit targets. This chapter also focuses on the multiple levels of the food industry on both the supply and demand sides of the market; thus, this chapter covers how to analyze markets with farmers, processors, wholesalers, regulators, and retailers all interacting with a product as it moves through the food industry on its journey from farm to consumer.

Transfer and marketing costs

In the broadest sense, the marketing sector is everything between the first level of production and the final consumption of a product. In this book, that is generally all the steps between when an agricultural commodity leaves the farm and when a consumer finally eats a food product containing that original, unprocessed ingredient. When a product goes through transformations (in form, time, and space) and is bought and sold as it moves through the supply chain from farm to table, each transaction involves a new marketing level with its own supply and demand equilibrium. Basic economics courses may not commonly deal with this important detail, but a farmer selling a cow is not interacting in the market with a consumer who wants a hamburger. Instead, the markets involved might be supply and demand curves for cows, processed beef, ground beef, and supermarket, tray-packaged beef. There might even be a wholesaler or two involved along the way. Realistically, there are somewhere from three to six levels to this market.

The marketing costs that must be accounted for as the agricultural commodity is transformed into the final consumer good include the obvious (processing costs, packaging, transportation, advertising) and the easy to forget (selling and administrative costs, depreciation, labeling, regulatory compliance, research and development, insurance, shrinkage/quality loss, debt payments, taxes). In addition to all these costs, each firm involved is trying to earn a profit, so the profit margins at each level should be allowed for (although the profit margin at each level is an open question and can be positive, negative, or zero).

Some of the marketing costs listed above are fixed (depreciation, debt payments, research and development), some are variable (processing costs, packaging, transportation, labeling, shrinkage/quality loss), and some could be either depending on the circumstances (selling and administrative costs, regulatory compliance, insurance). Taxes depend on prices, quantities, and costs, so they do not fit into either the variable or fixed category easily. They are definitely not fixed, but are very unlikely to be a linear or even monotonic function of quantity. In fact, taxes can change when the quantity does not, so taxes are a cost best left to their own category. A few other costs are tricky, such as insurance and selling and administrative costs, and may be not just functions of quantity sold but also of the total value of goods sold (or produced). Shrinkage/quality loss is a function of the value of the goods and the amount of time they are held in inventory. Costs will also vary in terms of their returns to scale. Some costs will display increasing returns (that is, average cost will decline as quantity increases), while others may show decreasing returns. Selling and administrative costs, for example, often show very strong increasing returns to scale, so that growing your business can lead to sharp drops in the average cost for that category. Cost components also vary by market level, and we studied the processor's costs in chapter 2. Retailers will be covered in chapter 12, but their costs tend to be more concentrated in fixed costs (rent, utilities, advertising) and labor costs, which vary with hours of operation more than quantity sold.

Because marketing costs are more likely to display increasing returns to scale than decreasing, a common form for an average marketing cost function would be something similar to

$$m(q_t) = a - bq_t \tag{8.1}$$

where $m(q_t)$ is the average marketing cost function, q_t is the quantity sold by the company, and a and b are positive constants. If the marketing cost function were decreasing returns to scale, the term in quantity would be added rather than subtracted from the function's intercept. Note that the total marketing cost function would still be increasing in q_t; it is only the average cost that decreases as quantity increases.

Marketing margins

A closely related concept to the average marketing cost function is the marketing margin. The term *marketing margin* is one that economists (unfortunately) use in several different ways, although it always refers to the difference in prices between two levels of a market. For example, the farm-to-wholesale marketing margin would refer to the difference in the price paid to farmers for an agricultural commodity and the price later paid to the food processor when it sells the processed product. This is not too complicated when the marketing margin is being computed for something like chicken and we are comparing the farm price for a whole, live chicken to the wholesale price for a processed, still whole broiler ready to be cooked. It gets much more complicated (and frankly impossible to compute without some arbitrary assumptions) when tracking something like the farm price for wheat versus the wholesale price of whole wheat bread.

Economists typically compute marketing margins as either the difference in prices or the ratio of prices. That is, sometimes the marketing margin is

$$M_{F,W} = P_W - P_F \tag{8.2}$$

and other times it may be defined as

$$M_{F,W} = (P_W - P_F)/P_F, \tag{8.3}$$

where $M_{F,W}$ is the farm-to-wholesale marketing margin, P_W is the wholesale price, and P_F is the farm price. The reader should carefully note that the above equations hide a rather large problem with the units involved that we shall discuss just below. In this book, we will generally stick to marketing margins in the difference form as in equation (8.2). Similar margins can be defined for the price difference between the retail and wholesale levels or between the retail and farm levels. A key distinction between the difference form of the marketing margin and the average marketing cost is that because the marketing margin is the actual price difference, it will be equal to the average marketing cost plus the average profit per unit. That is, $M_{F,W} = m(q) + \pi$, where π is the average profit per unit. If the profit is positive, the marketing margin will exceed the average marketing cost; if the profit is negative, the situation is reversed, and the marketing margin will be smaller than the marketing cost.

The fact that some economists use the ratio form of the marketing margin while others use the difference form is a little inconvenient because it means that whenever you see a marketing margin, you must check carefully to determine in which manner it is presented. A bigger difficulty is with the actual computation, and the problem here is in the units. As mentioned above, computing a marketing margin for a chicken is one thing, but what do you do when wheat is turned into bread or tomatoes, mushrooms, and spices are turned into spaghetti sauce? For processed products that are close to the same product as the unprocessed agricultural commodity, economists generally ignore the units problem. One cow becomes one processed cow worth of beef products, and one chicken becomes one chicken. It is only slightly more complicated to compute the farm price of the number of oranges needed to make one container of orange juice and then compare that to the price of one container of juice. In these cases, computing the marketing margin is reasonably straightforward.

In a more complex case, such as whole wheat bread, spaghetti sauce, or chicken noodle soup, assumptions need to be made to compute the marketing margin. The difference between the farm and wholesale price (or farm-to-retail or wholesale-to-retail) has to come from three sources: input costs, marketing costs, and profit. The problem in computing the marketing margin for complex, multiple-ingredient products is how to apportion the marketing costs and profit among the various ingredients. The simplest way is to use the share of the input cost. For example, if all the ingredients in spaghetti sauce cost $1.00 per jar (including jar, label, everything), marketing costs are $0.50 per jar, and the processor's profit is $0.30 per jar; the wholesale price of the spaghetti sauce will be $1.80 per jar. To find the farm-to-wholesale margin on the tomatoes, we need to know how many tomatoes are in the jar of sauce and what the farm price was. If 2 lb of tomatoes is used and the farm price is $0.25 per pound, then tomatoes represent exactly 50 percent of the total ingredient cost ($2 \times 0.25/1.00$). Thus, if we use 50 percent of the wholesale price, the farm-to-wholesale margin would be $0.90 − $0.50 = $0.40 per jar, or $0.20 per pound of tomatoes (since there are 2 lb per jar). Note that such an approach has allocated 50 percent of the total marketing margin to the tomatoes since they are 50 percent of the ingredient cost. In the ratio form, the marketing margin would be $(0.9 − 0.5)/0.5 = 0.8$. In either form, we see that the marketing margin when compared to the farm price of tomatoes suggests that a lot happens between the tomato leaving the farm and the sale of spaghetti sauce by the wholesaler.

What do high or low marketing margins mean? Advocates for farmers often complain that large marketing margins (either farm-to-wholesale or farm-to-retail) are evidence of unfair pricing behavior by processors. They claim an imbalance in market power (a small number of large-scale buyers negotiating with a large number of small-scale farmers) allows the processors to unfairly depress farm prices and capture an excessive share of the profit from the commodities that they grow. However, these claims should not be taken as valid unless evidence beyond a marketing margin is presented. After all, a large marketing margin can result from high processing costs, a large advertising expense, or other factors; processor (or retailer) profits are only one component of the marketing margin. In fact, while farm groups routinely point to expanding marketing margins over time as evidence of unfair practices by processors (usually referring to the farm-to-retail margin), this seems more likely to be a result of increases in the amount of processing being done to food between the farm and the retail outlet. When a supermarket sells boneless, skinless, pre-marinated chicken breasts, the farm-to-retail marketing margin is sure to be higher than when it sells a whole chicken. Over the last 50 years, retailers have shifted much of what they sell toward more highly processed products and the convenience they offer, so an expansion in the marketing margin should be expected. Thus, the reader is encouraged to remember that marketing margins and changes in them should be interpreted carefully and with a clear understanding of the products involved and assumptions made in computing the margins.

Derived supply and demand schedules

Having developed some understanding of the different levels of a market in the preceding chapters and the first part of this one, this knowledge can now be applied to integrating all these market levels into a unified treatment of their supply and demand schedules and the joint market equilibrium. To begin this discussion, we need to define original and derived supply and demand curves. Original supply curves are the supply curves for farm commodities (the original product); this is also called the farm-level supply. Original demand curves are the consumer (retail) demand for a final product that will not be sold again; this is also called the retail-level demand.

The other supply curves are derived supply curves because they are based on and derived from the original supply curve. The first problem with derived demand and supply curves is the same units problem that was encountered above in deriving marketing margins. Drawing demand and supply curves for farm peaches and supermarket peaches seems straightforward, but what units go on the quantity axis when the farm supply curve is for wheat and the retail demand is for bread? For now, let's assume that the units problem can be solved by standardizing all the products at the different levels by the number of units of the original product that are in that processed product. In such a system, a jar of spaghetti sauce that used 2 lb tomatoes as one of its ingredients would be graphed on a quantity axis labeled in tomatoes with each jar sold counting as a quantity of 2 (pounds of tomatoes). By this method, if all levels of a market are in equilibrium, then the equilibrium points will all line up vertically at the same quantity.

With the units problem "solved," we can proceed to determining the relationships between the different levels of supply and demand, beginning with supply. For simplicity, the following discussion will assume that we have a market with three levels: farm, wholesale, and retail. This is the most common case, although it is not that unusual to have two levels of processing (and thus two wholesale levels). Markets sometimes also have a distributor level (or "middleman") that lies between the wholesale and retail level. For example, many restaurants get their food from large suppliers such as Sysco, who do not process product but aggregate supplies from many processors and simplify the ordering and delivery processes for their customers. That would be an example of a distributor, which would add another level to the market. For now, we will try to stick to three levels.

Since the farm-level supply schedule shows the quantity the farmer is willing and able to supply at different prices, the wholesale-level supply schedule (after processing) should reflect the original price of the tomatoes plus the cost of other ingredients, all the marketing costs, and any profit margin. Thus, the marketing margin developed above that allocated marketing costs among inputs based on their cost share will not work here because it would show the processor willing to sell the processed product in the wholesale market for a price below what it really is willing and able to sell the product for. For analyzing the multiple levels of a market for an agricultural commodity that is one of many ingredients in a processed product, the marketing margin for a single commodity must be modified to include all the costs (including the cost of other ingredients) and any profits that are part of the markup from farm-to-wholesale price. For example, in the tomato to spaghetti sauce process described above, the marketing margin would be redefined to $M_{F,W} = \$1.80 - \$0.50 = \$1.30$ per jar or \$0.65 per pound of tomatoes.

If the marketing margin is constant returns to scale (not a function of quantity), then the wholesale-level supply curve can be derived from the farm-level supply curve by adding the farm-to-wholesale marketing margin to the farm-level supply curve. Continuing the spaghetti sauce example and keeping the quantity units in terms of pounds of tomatoes, the wholesale-level supply curve for spaghetti sauce would be $0.65 above the farm-level supply curve; that is, on a graph, the wholesale supply is shifted vertically upward from the position of the farm-level supply by $0.65. Assuming that the processor sells the spaghetti sauce directly to the retailer, the retail-level supply curve would then be derived from the wholesale-supply curve by shifting upward again by the amount of the wholesale-to-retail marketing margin. This process is illustrated in Figure 8.1. It is important to note that to use the marketing margins to find the derived supply curves, you must use the difference form of the marketing margin. The ratio form will not work, since we are adding, not multiplying.

Derived demand schedules are found by a similar process, but in reverse. Because the original demand is the consumer, or retail demand for the final product, we start there and subtract marketing margins to arrive at the derived demand schedules. So the wholesale demand curve will be the retail demand minus the wholesale-to-retail marketing margin; the farm-level demand will be the wholesale-level demand minus the farm-to-wholesale marketing margin. The marketing margins being subtracted are the exact same ones that were added in on the supply side to move up through the different levels of the market.

Thus, on the supply side, the original supply curve is at the bottom (the farm), and one works up to the derived supply curves by adding in the marketing margins; on the demand side, the original curve is at the top (the consumer), and one works down by subtracting the marketing margins. At any given quantity, when the marketing margin is constant, the vertical distance between the supply and demand curves on two different levels will be the same because the same marketing margin separates both curves. With a marketing margin that is a function of quantity, the curves will either get closer together or farther apart as the marketing margin changes. The equilibrium at any level of the market is

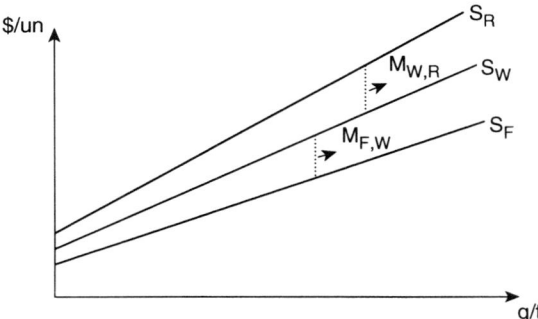

Figure 8.1 Farm, wholesale, and retail supply curves

84 The economics of the marketing sector

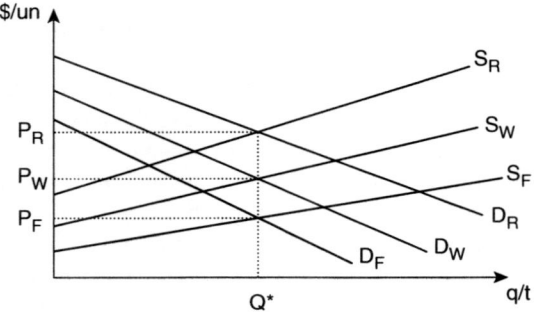

Figure 8.2 Market equilibrium at all levels

determined by the intersection of the supply and demand curves for that level (farm, wholesale, or retail). The intersection of curves at different levels means nothing; only intersections of curves for the same market level have economic meaning. In a complete market diagram, all the supply and demand curves for all levels can be seen (as in Figure 8.2), and all the equilibrium points should occur at the same quantity.

Algebraic approximations for marketing margin

To use the conceptual approach presented above to analyze a multiple-level market for some specific commodity, it is necessary to have some functional forms to approximate the marketing margins involved. Such a simplification will allow mathematical analysis to be employed so that applied policy analysis can be performed on a market and the impacts of various policies can be predicted.

Marketing margins typically are best approximated by either an increasing returns to scale function, a constant returns to scale function, a decreasing returns to scale function, or a constant percentage markup. Increasing or constant returns to scale are often the best approximations for the marketing margin of a food processor. Small food processors are often best represented as displaying increasing returns to scale because as they grow they are able to capture efficiencies by spreading their overhead (in particular, plant equipment and administrative costs) over the larger quantity of output. Larger food processors are generally very well approximated by constant returns to scale as their costs tend to be quite linear in output. However, even large food processors may capture some cost advantages as they grow and display at least slightly increasing returns to scale. Constant returns to scale marketing margins can be represented mathematically as

$$M = a, \qquad (8.4)$$

where *a* is a positive constant in dollars per unit. An increasing returns to scale marketing margin function would be decreasing in quantity and can be approximated by

$$M = a - bq, \qquad (8.5)$$

where q is the quantity sold and *a* and *b* are positive constants. The larger the value of *b*, the faster the average cost (or profit per unit) falls as quantity increases. A decreasing returns to scale marketing margin would look exactly like equation (8.5) with the "+" sign replacing the "−" sign.

Distributors (middlemen) and retailers are commonly assumed to have marketing margins well approximated by constant percentage markup functions; that is, the product is marked up (has its price increased) by some percentage of its cost to that distributor or retailer. While it is not plausible that such companies actually have costs that increase with the price of a product, in actual practice most clothes retailers use a constant-percentage markup almost exclusively. So-called *keystone* pricing refers to a 100 percent markup in which the retail price is simply double the wholesale price. Many retailers use percentage markups, but use different markup percentages for different goods. For example, jewelry stores use the highest markups on the least expensive pieces, while markups as low as 10 percent or less may be applied to very expensive jewelry with prices of over \$10,000. Mathematically, percentage markup can be represented as

$$M_{W,R} = cP_w, \qquad (8.6)$$

where $M_{W,R}$ is the wholesale-to-retail marketing margin, P_w is the wholesale price, and *c* is the markup percentage (in decimal form). A *c* value of 0.50 would be a 50 percent markup, and *c* = 1.00 would be the keystone, or 100 percent, markup. The wholesale-to-retail margin is employed here to demonstrate the percentage mark-up marketing margin because it is most common at that stage. Many retailers use percentage markup marketing margins in setting their prices. Note that the price to which the markup is applied is that for the lower level (farther away from retail) since the margin must be determined first before the price at the higher level (retail in this case) can be known.

Numerical solutions

The general technique for solving these multiple-level market problems is to find the matching supply and demand curves for at least one level, solve for the equilibrium quantity at that level, and then use that quantity and either supply or demand curves at each level to find the equilibrium price at each level. For example, starting with the farm supply, retail demand, and two marketing margins (farm-to-wholesale and wholesale-to-retail), one can use the marketing margins to derive the wholesale supply and then retail supply functions. This is accomplished by making sure that price is on the left of all equations (inverse supply functions) so that marketing margins can be properly added, since they are also in dollars per unit. Once the inverse retail supply function has been derived, it can be set equal to the inverse retail demand to find the equilibrium quantity. Substituting that quantity into the three inverse supply curves will yield the equilibrium farm, wholesale, and retail prices. An example of this with actual numbers is given in the application box 8.1.

Box 8.1 Numerical example—solving for equilibrium prices and quantity in a multiple-level market

In this example, imagine a market with three levels: farm, wholesale, and retail, and the ability to express all three levels in the same units so that we can treat all quantities as just Q. The information you are given to start with is the farm supply curve, retail demand curve, and the two marketing margins:

$S_F: Q = -50 + 10P_F \quad D_R: Q = 100 - P \quad M_{F,W} = 7 - 0.05Q \quad M_{W,R} = 0.4P_W$

Note that the farm-to-wholesale marketing margin shows increasing returns to scale and the wholesale-to-retail marketing margin is a constant-percentage markup. With a constant-percentage markup margin, it is always best to work from lower levels to higher levels, so the preferred way to solve this problem would be to start with the farm supply, derive the wholesale supply first, and then the retail supply. So, step-by-step, the solution would proceed as follows:

1. Solve for the inverse farm supply curve:

   $Q = -50 + 10P_F \quad \Rightarrow \quad 10P_F = 50 + Q \Rightarrow P_F = 5 + 0.1Q$

2. Derive the inverse wholesale supply curve by adding in the farm-to-wholesale marketing margin:

   $P_W = P_F + M_{F,W} \quad \Rightarrow \quad P_W = 5 + 0.1Q + 7 - 0.05Q \quad \Rightarrow$
   $P_W = 12 + 0.05Q$

3. Derive the inverse retail supply curve by adding in the wholesale-to-retail marketing margin:

   $P_R = P_W + M_{W,R} \quad \Rightarrow \quad P_R = P_W + 0.4P_W \Rightarrow$
   $P_R = 1.4(12 + 0.05Q) \quad \Rightarrow \quad P_R = 16.8 + 0.07Q$

4. Set the retail supply equal to the retail demand:

   $Q = 100 - P_R = 100 - (16.8 + 0.07Q) = 83.2 - 0.07Q \Rightarrow$
   $1.07Q = 83.2 \Rightarrow Q = 77.75$

5. Use the solution for the equilibrium quantity to solve for the three equilibrium prices:

$P_F = 5 + 0.1Q = 5 + 0.1(77.75)$ => $P_F = 12.78$
$P_W = 12 + 0.05Q = 12 + 0.05(77.75)$ => $P_W = 15.89$
$P_R = 16.8 + 0.07Q = 16.8 + 0.07(77.75)$ => $P_R = 22.25$

Note that the problem was completely solved without having to derive the wholesale demand or farm demand curves. These can be found by subtracting the marketing margins from the inverse retail demand curve. To check that the above answers are correct, they can be inserted into the demand curves to check that the same answers are obtained.

Policy analysis of multiple-level markets

Multiple-level market models such as those outlined in this chapter are very useful for estimating the outcome of various policies, regulations, and supply and demand shifts on various market participants. To analyze any such scenario, the first step is to determine the initial impact being analyzed. The initial impact has to be on one of the two original curves (farm-level supply or retail-level demand) or on a marketing margin. Then the model can be used to trace the indirect impact of those changes throughout the model.

For example, imagine that the government decided to provide a subsidy to peach farmers in order to encourage healthy eating. Using a model market with three levels (farmers, peach packers who wholesale the peaches, and retailers), a multiple-level market can be used to estimate how the subsidy will affect the retail price of peaches and the amount of peaches that consumers actually eat. A subsidy to peach farmers would be best represented as a shift down or outward in the farm-level supply. Because the wholesale supply and retail supply curves are derived by adding in the two marketing margins, which are unaffected by the new government policy, the wholesale supply and retail supply curves must both also shift down by the same amount as the farm-level supply curve does. These shifts keep the relationship between the supply curves the same (which they need to be since the relationships between them (the marketing margins) are unchanged. None of the three demand curves shifts, since retail demand and the two marketing margins are unaffected. Examination of Figure 8.2 allows one to see that the shifts on the supply side lead to a larger equilibrium quantity and lower equilibrium prices at all three levels. So the government policy works and consumers eat more peaches. However, one can also see from the figure that as long as the demand curves are not completely inelastic, the change in price is less than the value of the per-unit subsidy. Some of the subsidy is kept by the farmer rather than passed on to consumers, some is captured by the processor, and some by the retailer. The share that falls to each group is determined by the shape of the curves (their elasticities).

When a policy or change in either a farm supply or retail demand shifter causes one of the two original curves to shift, that will cause all the derived curves on the same side (that is, either supply side or demand side) to move in the same direction. In such cases, the price changes in the same direction at all levels of the market. However, when a policy or other change alters one of the marketing margins, the price moves in opposite directions above and below that marketing margin. For example, if the farm-to-wholesale marketing margin expands (say, owing to a rise in energy costs paid by a food processor), the equilibrium farm price will fall, while the equilibrium wholesale and retail prices will increase. An expanding marketing margin pushes prices away in both directions; a shrinking marketing margin pulls prices towards it from both directions.

If one has estimates of the actual supply and demand curves and the two marketing margins, the model can be analyzed numerically and an estimate of the change in retail price arrived at. In fact, you can try this sort of analysis for yourself in several of the exercises at the end of the chapter.

Summary

This chapter covered how to analyze markets for related products with different levels of transactions occurring as the product moves through the supply chain from farm, to processor, wholesaler, distributor, and finally retailer. The costs incurred as the product is transformed, transported, and stored as it moves through the supply chain are collectively called marketing costs. When these marketing costs are expressed as the average cost per unit and combined with the average profit per unit, they are referred to as marketing margins.

The farm-to-wholesale marketing margin represents the difference between the farm price and the wholesale price; the wholesale-to-retail marketing margin is the difference between the retail and wholesale prices. These marketing margins allow the derivation of wholesale and retail supply curves from the farm supply curve and of the wholesale and farm level demands from the retail demand curve. The farm-to-wholesale marketing margin is often approximately constant returns to scale or displays increasing returns to scale. Retail marketing margins should be increasing returns to scale based on the cost structure of most retailers, but often constant-percent markup pricing rules apply simply because that is the way the retailers operate.

Given estimates of the original supply and demand curves and the marketing margins involved in a market, the derived demand and supply curves can be found, and then the equilibrium prices and quantity can be solved for. Models such as these are very useful for analyzing market impacts, allowing economists to trace the impact of a policy change on all levels of a market. Even just using algebraic or graphical representations of multiple-level markets allows qualitative analysis of many policies so that economists can provide guidance to policymakers on the efficacy of various proposed policies.

Chapter highlights

- Marketing costs refer to the costs involved in transforming a product bought by one company as an input into a different product for sale. Sometimes the transformation is minimal (a peach from a farm into a peach at the supermarket), and sometimes it is significant (a tomato from the farm turned into spaghetti sauce).
- The marketing sector accomplishes transformations in form, location, time, or a combination of these.
- The marketing margin is a per-unit dollar value composed of the average marketing cost plus the average profit.
- Because marketing margins combine costs and profits, they should not be used in discussions about market power and fair pricing of farm products.
- Marketing margins can usually be approximated by a constant (meaning constant returns to scale), a linear function of quantity that displays some degree of increasing returns to scale (meaning it is decreasing in quantity), or by a percentage markup function. The first two are more common for processors, while the percentage markup form is common for distributors and retailers.
- Farm-level supply and retail demand curves are original, whereas all others are derived from those by adding or subtracting marketing margins.
- Policies that impact some level of a multiple-level market can be analyzed using a model of the supply and demand curves at the different levels, linked by the marketing margins. Policies must either affect an original curve (farm-level supply or retail demand) or a marketing margin. The effects of the policy can then be traced through all the levels to estimate price and quantity changes throughout the various market levels.
- When a policy changes a marketing margin, price changes at levels above and below the margin impacted will always be in opposite directions. When a policy causes a shift in farm supply or retail demand, price changes will all be in the same direction.

Practice problems

1. Find the equilibrium prices and quantities in the market for whole, roasting chickens given the information below for farm supply, retail demand, farm-to-wholesale marketing margin, and wholesale-to-retail marketing margin:

$$S_F: Q = 1000 + 1000P_F \quad D_R: Q = 2000 - 5P$$
$$M_{F,W} = 0.30 - 0.00001Q \quad M_{W,R} = 0.30P_W$$

2. Find the equilibrium prices and quantities in the market for milk given the information below for farm supply, retail demand, farm-to-wholesale marketing margin, and wholesale-to-retail marketing margin:

$S_F: Q = -100 + 20P_F \quad D_R: Q = 200 - 5P$
$M_{F,W} = 5 - 0.005Q \quad M_{W,R} = 4$

3. You are working for a senator who asks you to analyze the effects of some possible new policies on the poultry industry, which is a very important sector of your home state's economy. The poultry industry can be represented as a three-level market consisting of farm-level (supply of live chickens), wholesale-level (processing of chickens), and retail-level (further processing by flavoring, separating by parts, and packaging). For each scenario below, specify the expected direction of equilibrium price changes at all three levels and the expected change in equilibrium quantity:

   a. The government imposes new HAACP regulations on chicken processors to improve food safety.
   b. The price of soybeans used in feeding chickens increases.
   c. The beef industry decides to run a large television advertising campaign to encourage people to eat more beef.
   d. The minimum wage is increased by Congress, affecting wages paid at all three levels of the poultry market.
   e. Supermarkets create new convenient products for chicken, saving consumers time in meal preparation.

4. Explain why the average marketing margin in the US food industry has increased tremendously over the past 50 years. Include a discussion of the societal changes that helped spur this trend.

9 Price discrimination

Price discrimination is the practice of a seller segmenting its customers into two or more groups and selling to those groups at distinct prices. In its purest form, the good or service being sold to the separate customer groups should be identical; in practice, the products sold are often slightly different. Price discrimination is a more general form of the type of profit maximization pursued by a firm that uses storage. The ability to store a product allows sellers to divide their customers into customers *now* and customers *later*. The firm will not undertake storage without expecting to charge the later customers a higher price, so price discrimination is part of the plan in an optimal storage strategy.

Common definitions of the term *price discrimination* include first-degree, second-degree, and third-degree price discrimination. First-degree, or perfect, price discrimination is when a seller manages to charge every customer the exact maximum amount that each customer is willing and able to pay. That is, the customers get no consumer surplus at all; the producers capture the entire available surplus. The closest the real world generally gets to perfect price discrimination is when goods are auctioned. Second-degree price discrimination is when price varies by quantity, which typically means that a volume discount is offered to buyers of large quantities. Third-degree price discrimination constitutes the bulk of this chapter and involves separating customers into groups and charging each group of customers different prices. We will also discuss some forms of "near" price discrimination, referred to here as *quasi*-price discrimination, where a seller offers slightly differentiated products at different prices in order to capture the same sort of profit gains as in regular, third-degree price discrimination.

The why and how of price discrimination

Firms practice price discrimination in order to maximize profit. When a business can separate its customers into groups with different demands (particularly, as we shall see, with different price elasticities of demand), it can increase profits by price-discriminating and charging the different groups different prices. Note that implicit in the discussion of price discrimination is that the seller must have sufficient market power to face a downward-sloping demand curve and enough of a differentiated product that the seller can set prices for its product.

Price discrimination

Facing a linear, downward-sloping demand curve, a firm maximizes its revenue by setting a price where the price elasticity is equal to -1 (unitary elasticity; for proof of this, see the application box). Thus, if the company is currently selling at a price with an inelastic elasticity (an elasticity between 0 and -1), it should raise the price to increase revenue. Revenue increases, because with inelastic demand, price increases more than the quantity demanded decreases. Profit is certain to increase because costs definitely decrease since a smaller quantity can now be produced. More profit for less work is definitely a winning formula. If the current prices are in the elastic range, the price should be reduced in order to get a bigger percentage increase in quantity sold. Profit is not certain to increase in this case because more quantity must be produced. However, the beauty of price discrimination is that you never only decrease prices; instead, you do both of the above.

Elasticities and revenue maximization

For any given demand curve, the revenue to the sellers is maximized if the price is at the point on the demand curve where the price elasticity of demand equals -1 (assuming the demand curve has a point with that elasticity value). The justification for this is simple. In an elastic section of a demand curve, a fall in price causes the quantity sold to increase by a larger percentage than the price drops. This produces an increase in revenue since more revenue is gained in new sales volume than is lost to the lower price. In the inelastic portion of a demand curve, revenue can be increased by raising price. This works because the quantity sold decreases by a smaller percentage than price increases, so that the higher revenue on the remaining sales volume more than offsets the lower sales.

Mathematically, the fact that revenue is maximized at the point of unit elasticity is easy to demonstrate for a linear demand curve. Linear demand curves all have a price elasticity of demand that varies along the curve, being inelastic at the bottom right, elastic at the top left, and with a point of unit elasticity somewhere in the middle. This is because as one moves from top left toward the bottom right of a linear demand curve, if one took steps that kept the change in quantity equal, the percentage change in quantity decreases as you go (because it is the same change compared to a large base amount), and the percentage change in price increases (because the change in price is divided by a smaller and smaller base price). Using a little calculus, and remembering that the marginal revenue is the derivative of the total revenue with respect to quantity, the fact is proved as follows:

Inverse Demand: $p = a - bq$
Total Revenue: $TR = pq = (a - bq)q = aq - bq^2$
Marginal Revenue $= dTR/dq = a - 2bq$

Now, the total revenue is maximized at the point where marginal revenue equals zero, so set the marginal revenue above equal to zero and solve for q:

$$a - 2bq = 0 \Rightarrow q = a/2b.$$

At this quantity, the price is given by $p = a - b(a/2b) = a/2$. Elasticity of demand at a point on the demand curve is given by $\varepsilon = (dq/dp)(p/q) = (-1/b)(p/q)$. Substituting in the values of p and q that have been solved for yields:

$$\varepsilon = (-1/b)(a/2)/(a/2b) = (-1/b)(a/2)(2b/a) = -1.$$

This proves that for a linear demand curve, the total revenue is maximized at the point where the elasticity of demand equals -1.

To price-discriminate, there must be two (or more) groups of customers so that different prices can be charged. The secret to successful price discrimination is for a business to separate its customers into one group with inelastic demand and another with more elastic demand. Then the seller can raise the price for the inelastic-demand customers and reduce prices for the elastic-demand customers. This chapter will develop the math to show that this works a little later; first, it makes sense to discuss how to segment the customers, and then we will see how to keep them separated.

Discrimination by buyer characteristic

The most common form of price discrimination is where customers are separated by some personal characteristic. Price discrimination in this category includes such practices as student discounts (near and dear to many readers of this textbook), senior citizen discounts, and ladies nights at bars and clubs (a favorite of at least some of this book's readers). The key is that for pure price discrimination, the good being sold should be the same for both groups of customers. So, for example, student and senior citizen discounts are pure price discrimination as everyone is watching the same movie, in the same theater, at the same time, but not all for the same price. A kids menu in a restaurant is not price discrimination because the dishes on the kids menu are not the same as those on the regular menu, usually being smaller portions made with less expensive ingredients.

Discrimination by location

In addition to buyer characteristics, customer groups can be separated by location. A business selling shrimp might charge a lower price for sales at their dock and a higher price in cities where it faces a more inelastic or higher demand curve (or both). To be price discrimination the higher price in the cities must exceed the lower price at the dock by more than the transportation cost from dock to city; otherwise it would just be a normal marketing margin.

Customers are also segmented by location where the dividing characteristic is the level of competition in each location. In small airports with only one airline, prices are much higher than prices from airports with multiple airlines, even when the same airline operates in both airports. The airline can charge more at the small airport without competition because customers at such airports have more inelastic demand curves due to the lack of substitute goods (other airlines flying to their desired destination).

Discrimination by time or flexibility

In many cases, customers are separated into inelastic and elastic customers based on their ability to be flexible about exactly when or where they consume the firm's products. Restaurants offer early-bird specials with lower prices for customers who can come and eat dinner early (usually before 6 pm). Vacation resorts and cruise ships usually have high season rates for people who want to vacation at the time when weather or other amenities are at their peak and lower rates for people willing to visit at times when demand is lower. Those customers who are more flexible about when they vacation (meaning their demand curves are more elastic) choose to vacation at the off-peak time to get the lower price; customers who have more inelastic demands agree to pay the high, peak season prices to vacation when they want.

Another example of customers who are commonly separated by their ability to be flexible about timing is the case of airline customers. Business travelers have little to no flexibility about when they travel or their destinations; also, the money they are spending is usually not theirs, so price is less of a concern. Leisure travelers can usually shift their vacation dates to some extent and sometimes are willing to go to any of a set of possible destinations based on which is available at the most attractive price. Business travelers therefore have inelastic demands, and leisure travelers have more elastic demands. The trick for airlines was to figure out how to separate these customers since the business travelers are unlikely to volunteer their status and meekly accept the higher price. With more sophisticated information gathering that the Internet has made available airlines have changed their pricing practices somewhat, but when they began to price-discriminate, their customer separation mechanism was fairly simple. Airlines charged high prices for flights booked on short notice on the theory that those customers must be inflexible business travelers, while offering discounted prices for customers who booked far in advance (which was usually two or three weeks in advance). Airlines also tried to charge higher prices to business travelers by charging higher prices for return trips that did not include a Saturday night stay, reasoning that business travelers wanted to get home to their families.

Today, airlines practice a far more sophisticated form of price discrimination. Prices for flights change by day of the week, time of day, the number of unsold seats on a plane, how far in advance the purchase is, the airline's forecast of demand still to come, competition from other airlines (and the prices they are charging), and anything else the airlines can think of and model. Internet pricing and data gathering allow the airlines to change prices almost instantaneously as the airline monitors all these factors. For an example of how extreme airline price discrimination can get, see the application box on an infamous flight from San Francisco to Seattle.

A flight, a reporter, a story

A number of years ago, a reporter scooped a great story when he decided to take a flight and ask the other passengers what they paid for their ticket. Unfortunately, I was not able to track down a copy of the story as I wrote this book, but I remember it was a flight from San Francisco to Seattle.

The reporter bought a ticket like an ordinary passenger and brought a cameraman along. The flight had about 200 passengers. Once the seatbelt light went off, the reporter began going up and down the aisles asking other passengers how much they paid for their tickets. It turned out there was a huge range from highest to the lowest prices. Virtually everybody seemed to have paid a different price, with about 100 different prices among the 200 passengers.

As the passengers heard the different answers to the reporter's questions, those who had paid the higher prices became upset. By the time the flight was descending toward the airport in Seattle, there was a near riot onboard with passengers who suddenly felt overcharged demanding refunds.

The pilots, after being informed by a flight attendant what was going on, radioed ahead to the airline offices. The airline had customer service representatives at the gate when the plane landed to appease the angry passengers. The customer service representatives offered coupons for a future flight to upset passengers and worked hard to calm people down and regain the loyalty of their customers.

Similar uproars have occurred at other times when customers suddenly realize that different people are paying different prices (even if it seems they should have known that fact). Amazon was caught recently offering different prices on the same books to different customers (in an attempt to estimate elasticities of demand). Amazon was forced to apologize and said it would stop the practice. You can easily find stories about this controversy online.[1]

[1] For example, see Hargittai, Eszter, "Amazon's price discrimination," December 22, 2008. Available online at http://crookedtimber.org/2008/12/22/amazons-price-discrimination/

Discrimination by income

When it is possible, sellers may try to separate customers by income, with the higher-income customer assumed to be the inelastic customer (or at least possessing a higher demand for the product). Home repair and renovation firms are renowned for this type of price discrimination, with the practice of charging more for the same work in neighborhoods of more expensive homes being quite common. Note that this case involves firms using home value as a proxy for the true variable of interest—income—in order to separate their customers. Apparel stores that operate high-priced stores and outlet stores practice the same approach, charging more in the mainline store and then placing the remaining product in their outlets later at a lower price. This is price discrimination with the customers self-separating based on willingness to wait for the newest styles and to risk not getting the chance to buy them. The separation will be somewhat along income lines, but not entirely since preference for fashion helps determine the outcome as well.

Discrimination by effort: the case of coupons

An interesting way that some businesses separate customers is with coupons. Store coupons make customers separate themselves. If you are willing to expend the efforts to find, clip, bring, and use coupons for the company's product, then you get a lower price. Customers who are willing to put in this effort in order to receive a lower price are self-identifying that they have more elastic demands, because they are clearly willing to buy more of a product when offered a lower price. More inelastic customers will not bother to use the coupon, judging that the time and effort expended to do so is an additional, non-monetary expense that offsets the lower cash price the coupon offers.

Coupons have two advantages from the seller's point of view. First, the only cost of the price discrimination strategy is the printing and distribution costs of the coupons. No cost or effort needs to be expended on identifying customers by type, separating them into groups, or keeping them separated; the customers themselves do all the work. Second, the coupons double as advertising. Even people who do not use the coupons may see them in the newspaper, mailed advertisement, or the store. Seeing the coupon reminds previous customers to continue buying the product and also encourages people who usually buy a competing product to switch brands and try the product with the coupon. Making new customers with a "sale" price (the normal price minus the coupon amount) without having to offer it to all its existing customers can be quite attractive to many companies. Obviously some existing customers will use the coupons and get the lower price, but if the company puts the product on sale directly (with no coupon), all the customers get the sale price.

Implementation and policing of price discrimination

The first step for a company to implement a strategy of price discrimination is to study their customers to find out how to separate them. The company can try lowering and raising prices in order to collect information on both its average elasticity of demand and on how the elasticity of demand varies across its customers. If the company can spot customer types that have more inelastic demand and other types of customers with more elastic demand, then the price discrimination can begin.

The second step is to determine how to separate the customers into two groups that get charged different prices. When the customer groups are separated by a personal characteristic that is easily identifiable or verifiable, such as students or senior citizens, the company can simply post two prices for their product: a regular price and a student price, for example. When the customer groups are separated by more hidden characteristics, such as the leisure versus business travelers or gourmet food lovers versus "regular" food buyers, separating the customers can be much more difficult. Two strategies that are commonly employed are premium products and discount clubs. Premium products allow the company to charge a higher price for the inelastic customers who are willing and able to pay for higher quality, better service, or more desirable timing. Examples of premium products include first-class airline tickets; specially designated "estate" wines; top-grade meat, fish, and produce; and premium ice creams. Even in products such as canned or dry goods, there are premium brands in products such as soup, pasta, and even cake mixes. A premium brand is not an example of price discrimination unless the same company sells a lower-priced product that is nearly equivalent (at least in production cost). However, there are many examples in the supermarket of companies that sell high- and low-priced products in the same category under different brand names. For example, all the laundry detergents in the supermarket aisle are made by only three companies. Discount clubs and similar programs such as loyalty programs and even coupons are a way to post a higher price for the inelastic customers while offering ways for customers with more elastic demand curves to secure lower prices for either the same or very similar products. Airlines create e-mail lists of customers who want to be informed of last-minute sales or other special offers. Ice cream shops and restaurants offer loyalty cards that offer a free product after every so many purchased. These are all ways of selling the same product at different prices and avoiding the problem that must be dealt with next: preventing arbitrage.

With the customers separated, companies must keep them apart and prevent reselling of the low-priced product to customers who would have been the buyers of the high-priced product. Airlines, for example, go to great lengths to keep customers from gaming their systems in order to receive lower prices for flights that would normally be higher priced. When Saturday night stays were necessary to get the lowest airfares, a business traveler who knew she had to fly from Atlanta to New York every other week could book overlapping tickets instead. One ticket could be for Atlanta to New York this Tuesday and back on a Thursday two weeks later. The other ticket would be for New York to Atlanta this Thursday and back on Tuesday two weeks later. With these two tickets, the business traveler could make two round trips without staying over a Saturday night while getting the low price of leisure travelers who are staying over a Saturday night.

Airlines fought against such tricks, and if they caught somebody doing such things, they routinely cancelled the rest of the trips (without refunding any money). Bars offering ladies free drinks must try to ensure that the ladies do not order drinks and then let their boyfriends drink them. For some products, keeping separation is easy; movie tickets are generally purchased right before entry to the movie theater, identification cards are easy to check for these traits, so discounted tickets for students or seniors are easy to enforce and hard to resell to people not in such a group. Separations based on premium and lower-priced brands or products are also easy to police as people cannot buy the lower-priced product and attempt to resell it for a profit to people who having been buying the premium product; if such buyers want to switch from the premium to the lower-priced product, they can just go buy it themselves. Thus, on the whole, the policing of a price discrimination strategy is easier than the work involved in identifying and separating the customer groups in the first place.

Price discrimination among closely related products

Many examples of what we shall call *quasi*-price discrimination exist both inside and outside the food industry. These are cases where companies charge different prices for goods that are similar, but not identical, and the price difference greatly exceeds the difference in production cost. Outside of the food industry, some common examples include haircuts (women are charged more for theirs) and dry cleaning (again, women pay more). Women have claimed discrimination in the face of clearly higher prices, but the proprietors of the businesses selling haircuts and dry cleaning claim that the services provided to women involve more skill, and thus the higher price is a deserved reward, not price discrimination. Some cities have not believed such claims; Washington, DC, for example, has a local ordinance requiring hair salons to charge men and women the same price.

Within the food industry, there are further examples of quasi-price discrimination, where there are or seem to be some differences between products. Early-bird specials at restaurants are usually (although not always) discounts of normal menu items, so if you consider dinner at 5:00 pm the same as dinner at 7:00 pm, then this is an example of price discrimination. If the time makes it a different product, then it is only quasi-price discrimination. A clearer case of quasi-price discrimination is found in fresh versus canned or frozen fruits and vegetables. Fresh fruits and vegetables have lower production and marketing costs than their more processed "cousins," canned and frozen fruits and vegetables. Yet, the fresh products generally cost more than the frozen and canned ones. This is quasi-price discrimination, with the fresh product being the premium brand, and the canned or frozen being the lower-priced brand. Also, note that no policing of this type of price discrimination is necessary as nobody can buy the canned or frozen product and turn it back into fresh. Truly, there are many cases of this type of quasi-price discrimination in the realm of processed products, where a company transforms raw ingredients into multiple processed products (e.g., tomatoes into tomato paste, tomato sauce, canned diced tomatoes, canned whole tomatoes, pizza sauce, and spaghetti sauce, to name a few). When a company charges prices that differ by significantly more than the costs of producing these related products, it is essentially price-discriminating. Sometimes, customers can beat this type of price discrimination as one product may be easily turned into another. For example, you can save money by buying tomato sauce or canned diced tomatoes and then adding seasoning and maybe some vegetables to make your own spaghetti sauce.

When it looks like price discrimination, but it's not

In some cases, a company practices what looks like price discrimination, but the pricing policy may actually be based on cost considerations more than differences in demand. Restaurants must have staff in place before most customers arrive in order to prepare soups, sauces, perform other preliminary cooking tasks, set tables, and take reservations, so running an early-bird special is not just a way to price discriminate, but also a way to collect some revenue when the marginal labor cost is close to zero.

In a similar manner, diverting fresh produce into the lower-cost canned or frozen market might seem counterintuitive, but it has some characteristics in common with monopoly storage. When the company controls a sizeable share of the fresh market (such as Dole with pineapple), it faces a downward-sloping demand in that fresh market. By diverting some of the fresh fruit to the canned or frozen market, it can raise the price in the fresh market. If it had been in the inelastic part of the demand curve for fresh fruit, the company might increase its revenue and profit in the fresh market by selling less as fresh and moving more product into the frozen or canned markets (which serve as a storage market for later sale). This is not strictly speaking price discrimination since the seller does not have to expend any effort to separate customers and the products are different, but some of the spirit is there, along with the extra benefits found from utilizing storage to increase profits.

The math of price discrimination

An example is the best and easiest way to see how price discrimination can raise profits. To that end, the application box presents an example with some numbers and two customer groups with different elasticities of demand. The example demonstrates that profits can be raised by practicing price discrimination. It does not reflect any additional costs for researching the demand curve features and designing the price discrimination strategy. However, these costs are probably not significantly different from what a company would expend to price its products without price discrimination.

To analyze the potential for price discrimination to yield profits, a company needs to know its cost function and the demand curves of the two (or more) potential customer groups. Most companies should have a reasonably accurate estimate of their cost functions; not nearly as many have good estimates of the demand curve they face, and even fewer would have estimates of what the

Numerical example

Your company sells a differentiated product to two distinct types of customers. Group A and group B customers have collective demand curves for each group given by

$$Q_A = 100 - 0.5P_A \qquad Q_B = 140 - P_B.$$

The total demand from the customers of your company when the price charged to both groups (no price discrimination) is the same is then given by

$$Q = Q_A + Q_B = 100 - 0.5P_A + 140 - P_B = 240 - 1.5P.$$

Your company's total cost function is given by TC = Q^2, meaning that the marginal cost (dTC/dQ) is MC = 2Q.

If your company does not price-discriminate, it would maximize profits by setting the marginal revenue equal to the marginal cost. To find the marginal revenue, solve for the inverse demand curve, multiply it by the quantity, and then take the derivative with respect to the quantity:

$$Q = 240 - 1.5P \Rightarrow P = 160 - 0.67Q$$

$$TR = PQ = 160Q - 0.67Q^2 \qquad MR = dTR/dQ = 160 - 1.33Q.$$

Setting MR = MC gives

$$160 - 1.33Q = 2Q \Rightarrow 160 = 3.33Q \Rightarrow Q = 48 \Rightarrow P = 128.$$

Using the total revenue and total cost functions given above, the profit would be 3840.

If your company now practices price discrimination, separates the customers into their two groups, and sets two separate prices, it would maximize profits by setting the marginal revenue for each customer group equal to the marginal cost.

$$\text{Profit} = \pi = (200 - 2Q_A)Q_A + (140 - Q_B)Q_B - (Q_A + Q_B)^2$$

$$d\pi/dQ_A = 200 - 4Q_A - 2Q_A - 2Q_B = 0 \Rightarrow 200 - 6Q_A = 2Q_B$$

$$d\pi/dQ_B = 140 - 2Q_B - 2Q_A - 2Q_B = 0 \Rightarrow 140 - 2Q_A = 4Q_B \Rightarrow 70 - Q_A = 2Q_B$$

Setting these two first-order equations equal eliminates Q_B, and the solution can be found for Q_A:

$$200 - 6Q_A = 70 - Q_A \Rightarrow 130 = 5Q_A \Rightarrow Q_A = 26 \Rightarrow P_A = 148.$$

Then the value of Q_A can be used to find Q_B, which yields the value of P_B using the demand curve

$$200 - 6(26) = 2Q_B \Rightarrow 44 = 2Q_B \Rightarrow Q_B = 22 \Rightarrow P_B = 118.$$

The total profit can now be computed: profit = (148)(26) + (118)(22) − (26 + 22)² = 4140.

Since 4140 is greater than 3840, your company can increase profits by price discrimination as long as any extra costs that are incurred to implement the price discrimination are less than 300.

demand curves of the separated customer groups would be if they began practicing price discrimination. In order to gain the information necessary to do the math as shown in the application box, a firm must find a way to approximate the demand curves of the planned customer groups if they do not already have such information.

The most straightforward way to gain the information is to find some way of identifying and tracking customers and then collect purchasing pattern data as the company varies prices experimentally. Companies use loyalty cards (the Kroger Plus card, for example); information collected online either in sign-ups for e-mail lists, Facebook pages, or similar efforts; and even credit card numbers to identify and track their customers. Online purchasing is ideal for tracking purchase histories as customers must identify themselves to receive their orders. Companies then see how purchases vary as prices are raised and lowered. The customers who do not change their purchasing much when prices change (especially when they rise) are potential members of the inelastic customer group. Customers who sharply reduce purchases in the face of higher prices and increase purchases when prices are lowered are likely candidates for the elastic customer group.

The seller uses the data collected in two different ways. First, the demographic data on the customers can be used to construct the customer groups to be separated. If it appears that a simple trait such as student or senior citizen status is highly correlated with group membership, then the business has an easy path to initiate price discrimination. The same goes for location and a number of other traits. If no particular variables seem to explain which customer group a person belongs to, meaning it is just individual tastes and preferences, then the company will be best off pursuing a discount club or loyalty program for the elastic customers and perhaps an elite program with some higher quality (in product or level of service) for the inelastic group that can be used to justify raising prices for those customers.

The second way to use the collected data is to estimate the demand curves of the separated customer groups. This usually involves statistical regression analysis techniques as learned in a linear regression class from a statistics department or an econometrics class in an economics or agricultural economics department. This book does not teach how to do this, but suffice it to say that given pairs of price and quantity purchased data, the company can estimate the demand elasticities of its two customer groups.

Legal aspects of price discrimination

Price discrimination in many forms is illegal in the United States under antitrust law and some specific court rulings. However, other forms are legal, and some illegal forms of price discrimination are still widely practiced. Under the Clayton Act (1914), Sherman Antitrust Act (1890), and the Robinson–Patman Act (1936), it is often illegal to practice price discrimination. Two key issues are that it is almost always illegal to price-discriminate in ways that are designed to reduce competition or to reward larger purchasers with lower prices. If a dairy company offered lower milk prices to supermarkets that also bought its brand of ice cream, that would be illegal because it would lessen competition and make it harder for businesses to survive that sold only milk or only ice cream. Offering lower prices for buying in larger volumes is generally considered illegal. For example, in 1962 the US Supreme Court ruled against two dairies in Chicago that offered chain grocery stores lower prices for the larger volume that the entire chain bought. The dairies claimed that the lower prices were justified by the lower cost of serving larger customers and submitted cost studies to support that contention. The court ruled that the Clayton Act prevented such behavior because the cost differences did not explain all the price discrimination and the separating of the dairies' customers into groups was not dependent only on the difference in cost of servicing the distant accounts.[1]

However, different prices can be charged to different customer groups as long as the seller is not trying to diminish competition in the market for the product for which it wants to price-discriminate or in a related product. It is legally okay to price-discriminate if the only goal is to charge different customers different prices and the strategy has nothing to do with any competitors. Also, drug distributors, operating at the wholesale level, are legally allowed to offer volume-based price discounts under the Prescription Drug Marketing Act of 1987. Even better, the law essentially prohibits the high volume purchasers from reselling the drugs at a profit, so the price discrimination strategy is enforced by the federal government.[2] Finally, gender-based price discrimination, such as ladies nights and different prices for haircuts and dry cleaning, are generally considered illegal discrimination against the gender getting the higher price unless the business can establish that there is sufficient difference in the service being provided to justify the price difference. California, Massachusetts, Washington, DC, and New York City all have specific laws banning differential prices for services based on the gender of the person receiving the service. Of course, price discrimination based on race, ethnicity, or religion is essentially always illegal under civil rights laws.

Overall, companies should be careful to check the legality of any price discrimination strategy before implementing it. However, as long as the customer groups are not separated by gender and the purpose is not to harm any competitors, price discrimination strategies can be legal.

Summary

This chapter covered price discrimination. Price discrimination is a conscious strategy practiced by companies in order to increase revenue and profits. In the most common forms of price discrimination (both third-degree and quasi-price discrimination), a company separates its customers into two (or more) groups of customers with different price elasticities of demand. The company sells its product at a higher price to the customers with more inelastic demand and at a lower price to the customers with a more elastic demand.

Customers can be separated by personal characteristic (senior citizens, students), gender, income, location, or anything else that is highly correlated with the customers' price elasticities of demand. Customers can also be separated by their demand elasticities directly if the company can devise a scheme for identifying the members of each group. Once separated, the company may have to devise a strategy to ensure that customers in the group buying for a lower price cannot resell to members of the group buying at a higher price in order to arbitrage away the company's profit from price discriminating.

Price discrimination is legal as long as it is designed only to extract more revenue from customers and is not based on gender. Price discrimination is illegal if a company tries to use price discrimination to diminish competition or to gain market share in another product. Additionally, the Robinson–Patman Act makes most price discrimination based on volume illegal.

Chapter highlights

- Price discrimination is the practice of charging customers in two groups different prices for the same good or service.
- The most common price discrimination strategies encountered are student and senior citizen discounts.
- When restaurants offer early-bird specials, it is usually a combination of price discrimination and the ability to supply meals at a lower cost during the early dinner hours when staff are not very busy.
- Loyalty clubs, discount clubs, coupons, and premium memberships are all ways to convince customers to separate themselves into the elastic or inelastic demand groups so that the seller can offer them the lower or higher price, respectively.
- Total revenue is maximized when only a single price is offered at the point where elasticity is equal to -1.
- Separating customers into groups boosts revenue and profits by allowing the firm to move both customer groups closer to unitary elasticity on their separated demand curves.

104 Price discrimination

- Under US law, some types of price discrimination are illegal. Companies cannot use price discrimination to hurt competitors or to gain market share in another product.
- Volume discounts are illegal some of the time, but not always.
- Gender-based discrimination is often illegal and is very clearly banned in a number of states and cities. Racial, ethnic, or religious discrimination is illegal.

Practice problems

1. For the inverse demand curve $P = 150 - 1.5Q$:
    a. Find the (price, quantity) pair at which total revenue is maximized.
    b. Show that the price elasticity of demand is equal to -1 at that point.
    c. Show that the demand curve is elastic above the point of unitary elasticity and inelastic below that point.
2. List four types of price discrimination you encounter regularly in your life. What characteristics are used to separate the customers into groups? What, if anything, is done to prevent arbitrage by reselling?
3. Your company has produced 500 cases of chicken pot pies to sell. You have customers in two cities: Atlanta and Birmingham. The demand curves in each city are given by (with prices in $/case and quantities in cases):

    Atlanta: $P_A = 120 - 0.1Q_A$ Birmingham: $P_B = 90 - 0.2Q_B$.

    Transportation from the factory to the cities is $15 per case to Atlanta and $20 per case to Birmingham.

    a. Find the price the company would charge and quantity to be sold in each city without price discrimination, but accounting for the different transportation costs.
    b. Find the price elasticity of demand in each city in the solution from part (a).
    c. To practice price discrimination, your company should raise the price in which city? Lower the price in which city?
    d. Now find the optimal solution for what price to charge and what quantity would be sold in each city with price discrimination (still accounting for transportation costs).
    e. Ignoring any production costs (since they are sunk) but accounting for transportation costs, compute the company profit with and without price discrimination, and see if your company benefited.
4. On the Internet, find a news story about price discrimination. Write a paragraph summarizing the story and any controversy about the price discrimination being practiced.

10 Imperfect competition and game theory

Game theory is a subdiscipline within economics that studies decision making in a competitive environment. In traditional economic analysis, a company takes as given its cost structure and the demand curve that it is facing and uses those to find strategies that maximize its profit or other objective function (such as market share or a discounted flow of profits over some multi-year planning horizon). Game theory suggests that most companies are smarter than this (or operate in a more complex economic environment than this) and realize that competitors will respond to whatever strategy they choose. When a company makes decisions in a game-theoretic framework, the company considers how to choose an optimal strategy given its cost structure, the demand curve it faces, and the anticipated reactions of its competitors. For example, if Coca-Cola is deciding on an optimal pricing and advertising strategy for the next year, it factors into those decisions the most likely responses of Pepsi instead of the traditional economic assumption that Pepsi would just continue with whatever it had been previously doing.

In this chapter, basic game theory concepts will be covered and then built upon to move through more sophisticated games and ways to model strategic behavior. Both static (single-period) and dynamic (multi-period) games will be discussed. Similar to the chapter on price discrimination, there will also be some discussion of the legal constraints on the practice of some of these strategies.

Basic game theory concepts and solutions

Game-theoretic ideas date back to at least the early 1700s when James Waldegrave used it to develop strategies for a card game. The first application of game theory directly to economics was by the French economist Antoine Cournot in 1838, who used the concepts to study a duopoly case where firms chose the quantity to produce.[1] Another French economist, Joseph Bertrand, in reviewing Cournot's paper, presented a duopoly case with prices being the chosen strategies instead of quantities.[2] The economic application of game theory did not really catch on until the 1960s. This was precipitated by John von Neumann and Oskar Morgenstern's 1944 book, *Theory of Games and Economic Behavior*, which fully developed the mathematical constructs behind game theory and proved many theorems about game solutions. This set the stage so that as economics became a mathematically based field in the 1950s and 1960s, game theory was ready for economists to adopt and modify to suit their purposes.

Modern game theory strives to formalize the theory and mathematics of decision making in a strategic environment. These models of decision making incorporate awareness of the consequences of those decisions. The consequences can be a response from competitors, such as matching a competitor's prices, or responses from consumers, such as lower future demand in response to quality issues with the company's product. Games can include competitors cooperating with each other (even to the point of illegal collusion), cheating on agreements that were made to cooperate, and strategies implemented in order to punish firms that break agreements. Some simple examples and basic definitions will begin to make these concepts clearer.[3]

Definitions

Games involve two or more *players* who are the people or companies making decisions, often referred to as *strategies*. Once the decision, or strategy, of all players is known, each player receives a *payoff* based on the set of all decisions made by the players. The payoff may be a quantity sold, a profit made, a market share, or a loss incurred, depending on the structure of the game. The payoffs can be a continuous function of the strategies chosen by the players or can be discrete, especially when the strategies chosen are discrete.

A game in which the sum of all payoffs is fixed is called a *constant game*; a *non-constant game* is one where the sum of payoffs varies depending on the strategies chosen. Non-constant games tend to encourage more cooperation and collusion among players since they can change the size of the pie being divided, so side deals (think "bribe") can be made in the hopes of benefiting everyone by dividing up a larger total payoff.

Duopoly games have two players, *oligopoly* games have a "few" players, which is generally taken to be somewhere between three and ten. Game theory becomes more complicated as the number of players becomes large, since it becomes less plausible that any other player really cares about the individual strategies of another single player among many. In games with many players, some formulation is needed detailing how each player expects other players (either individually or collectively) to respond to their strategy choices. Sometimes games are constructed with a few players operating strategically and the remainder of the industry represented as a *competitive fringe*, meaning that those firms act as in perfect competition and do not practice strategic behavior.

Repeated games are when the same players repeat the same game, either a set number of times (called *rounds*) or an infinite number of times. Repeated games add more strategy to *single-period* games (*non-repeated* games) because in repeated games, players can not only encourage cooperation, but threaten other players with punishments in later rounds. Punishments generally are carried out by a player choosing a strategy that leads to a unfavorable payoff for the players being punished. As will become clear below, punishments involve serious thinking because the player doling out the punishment usually must incur a poor payoff itself in order to deliver the punishment to its intended target.

Punishments lead us to an additional definition. A repeated-game strategy is *time-consistent* if it is optimal when announced at some point in time and is still optimal at future time periods during the repeated game. The alternative is a *time-inconsistent* strategy. In repeated games with the possibility of cooperation and cheating, it is often optimal to announce a strategy of planned cooperation with punishment to be administered should another player cheat. However, in many cases, once that point in time is reached, it becomes suboptimal to actually administer the punishment because the punishment usually lowers the payoff to the player administering it. In particular, the fewer periods left in a game, the more likely it is that the punishment will become suboptimal. Thus, the announced, initial strategy is time inconsistent because it is the right strategy when announced, but does not continue to be optimal through the later rounds of the game.

A simple example of a two-player game

To see these concepts in action, Figure 10.1 displays the basic features of a two-player, non-constant game in the manner the information is frequently summarized. Player 1's two possible strategies (A and B) are represented by columns of the box; player 2's strategies are in the two rows. The two-by-two box shows the four possible combinations of strategies that can arise depending on the pair of strategies the players choose. Within each quarter of the payoff box, the number shown in the top-right is the payoff to player 1, while the bottom-left is the payoff to player 2. For example, if player 1 chooses strategy A and player 2 chooses strategy B, the payoff is 4 to player 1 and 8 to player 2. The game is a non-constant game because the sums of the payoffs in each box-quarter change. From the diagram, one cannot tell if the game will be repeated or not. Strategy choices

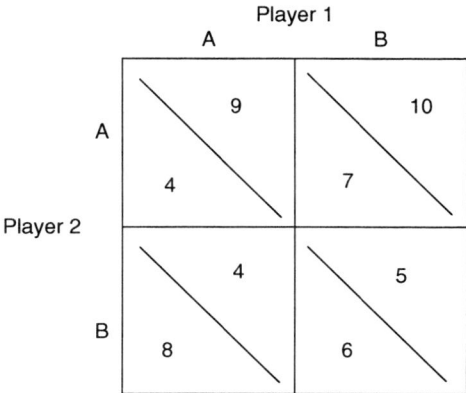

Figure 10.1 Basic 2 × 2 game.

are often denoted by pairs in parentheses, such as (B, B), where the first is player 1's choice and the second is player 2's.

To analyze a game and determine what strategies each player will choose requires assumptions about the objective function each player is trying to maximize. Two objective functions that fit discrete games like the one in Figure 10.1 are called the maxi-max and maxi-min solutions. A player with a maxi-max objective function will choose the strategy that gives that player the chance to end up with the highest possible payoff. This is a risk-lover's or optimist's objective function.[4] In Figure 10.1, if both players followed a maxi-max objective function, each player would choose strategy B (and neither would end up with the payoff they were hoping to get). A player with a maxi-min objective function will choose the strategy that maximizes the worst possible outcome. This is a risk-averse or pessimistic objective function. In Figure 10.1, if both players followed a maxi-min objective function, they would again choose strategy B because those strategies have the largest minimum possible payoff. Game players can also have more complex objective functions that strive to maximize profits, the present value of a flow of profits over time (for repeated games), or any other objective that can be employed in normal economic analysis.

Once all players have chosen strategies and payoffs have been determined, it is possible to analyze the outcome and determine if the solution reached is an equilibrium solution. An equilibrium in a game is a solution that is stable. A particularly famous type of game equilibrium is the Nash equilibrium. A Nash equilibrium is a very stable solution to a game because the definition of a Nash equilibrium is a solution from which, if given the chance to revise its strategy after seeing the strategies chosen by all competing players, no player would want to change their already-announced choice. Again referring to the game in Figure 10.1, with the maxi-min objective functions, the strategies chosen were (B, B). This is not a Nash equilibrium, as can be shown by an examination of the player's strategies. Player 1, seeing that player 2 has chosen B, would not want to switch to strategy A to earn 4 instead of 5. Player 2, seeing that player 1 has chosen B, would want to switch to strategy A to earn 7 instead of 6. If even one player wants to switch after knowing the other player's choice, the solution is not a Nash equilibrium. It does not matter that players are likely not allowed to switch strategies in this manner; that is just how a Nash equilibrium is defined. The reason a Nash equilibrium is so stable is that no player has any reason to try to cheat or deviate from an announced strategy since any change would yield an inferior payoff.

The prisoner's dilemma

The most famous game in all of game theory is a simple two-player game. Sometimes it is a repeated game, and sometimes it is not. It is always a non-constant game. It is called the prisoner's dilemma. Figure 10.2 shows a version of the prisoner's dilemma game. While the exact payoffs can vary, what remains constant is that the total payoff is the highest if the two players both choose strategy A; think of (A, A) as the cooperative solution. However, each individual player

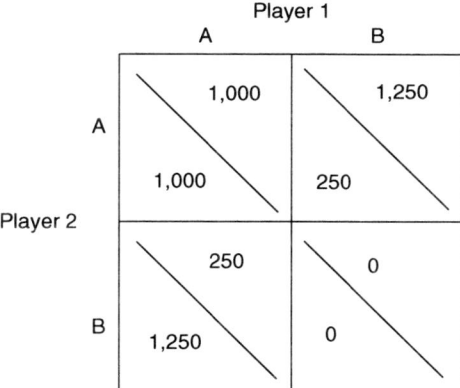

Figure 10.2 The prisoner's dilemma.

gets a higher payoff by choosing strategy B while the other player chooses A. Unfortunately for the players, if they both choose B, they get the worst of all possible outcomes.

The name of the game comes from the following story: two crooks rob a bank and abscond with $2,000. They agree to split the proceeds 50/50, give $250 to their wives immediately, hide $1,000 in a fantastic hiding spot to retrieve later, and each take $250 with them. However, the cops suspect them and bring them both in for questioning. The police offer each crook immunity from prosecution if he will testify against his partner and give up the $250 in cash they found on him. Each crook has two possible strategies: keep quiet (A), and testify against his partner (B). If they both remain quiet, they get away with the crime and each end up with $1,000; that is (A, A) in Figure 10.2. If one testifies while the other stays quiet, one prisoner goes to jail while the squealer goes free and collects the remaining money; this is either (A, B) and (B, A). If they both squeal, the cops actually prosecute them both, take their cash and find the rest of the money before they are released from jail; this is (B, B).

The prisoner's dilemma encourages a cooperative solution of (A, A), but each player has a strong incentive to cheat; that is, to promise to play strategy A but actually choose strategy B. This incentive to cheat makes it highly likely that the players will end up at (B, B), the worst possible outcome. If the prisoner's dilemma game is played repeatedly by the same two players, the incentive to cooperate and end up at (A, A) is much stronger, especially in the early rounds. As the end of a finite repeated game nears, the cooperative solution will tend to break down, and cheating (switching from strategy A to B) is likely to occur.

Competition in prices and quantities

When companies play games, their strategies can be a quantity to be produced, a price to be set, a level of advertising expenditures, a combination of these, and

110 *Imperfect competition and game theory*

many other factors within the company's control. Two types of games are actually named after what variables the strategies deal with: Cournot games are games where the strategies are based on the quantity companies choose to produce, whereas Bertrand games are games where the strategies are based on the prices that companies set. These games do not fit into a simple two-by-two box, because demand curves are continuous, and so the payoff functions are also continuous. However, by assuming an objective function for each firm playing the game, a solution can generally be found by solving standard optimization problems.

Cournot duopoly games

The most likely scenario for a Cournot duopoly is an industry with a fairly homogenous product so that the two competitors cannot set separate prices. Instead, they face a single downward-sloping demand curve where the price is determined by the sum of their two output decisions. A linear inverse demand curve of this form would look like $p = a - b(q_1 + q_2)$. If the two firms had cost functions denoted by $c_i(q_i)$, then we could represent the profit function for each player as

$$\pi_i = a - b(q_1 + q_2)q_i - c_i(q_i). \tag{10.1}$$

If the objective function of each player in this Cournot duopoly game is taken to be single-period profit maximization, then each player wants to choose the strategy (output level) that maximizes his profit subject to the other player's output level. If each player solves the problem of maximizing equation (10.1) by choosing q_i, what each one gets is called a *reaction function*. After taking the derivative of (10.1) with respect to the firm's output, setting the derivative equal to zero, and solving for the optimal output, the result will be a formula for the optimal output level as a function of the other firm's output; that is, the reaction functions are

$$q_1^* = f_1(q_2) \text{ and } q_2^* = f_2(q_1). \tag{10.2}$$

These reaction functions let each firm know how to respond to the other firm's strategy. If firm 1 knows what q_2 is, the reaction function will provide the value of q_1 that will maximize firm 1's profit. On their own, these reaction functions are very useful and provide a quick way for a company to respond optimally and quickly in a competitive situation. However, the reaction functions alone do not provide a solution to the Cournot duopoly game. There could be a continual back and forth as firm 1 responds to firm 2's strategy, necessitating firm 2 to respond to firm 1, with this cycle repeating endlessly. Luckily, we can search for an equilibrium to the game by looking for a point where the two reaction functions intersect. If the reaction functions intersect, then the point of intersection will be a (q_1^*, q_2^*) pair that satisfies both reaction functions. At this point, neither player would want to change strategies; it would be a Nash equilibrium.

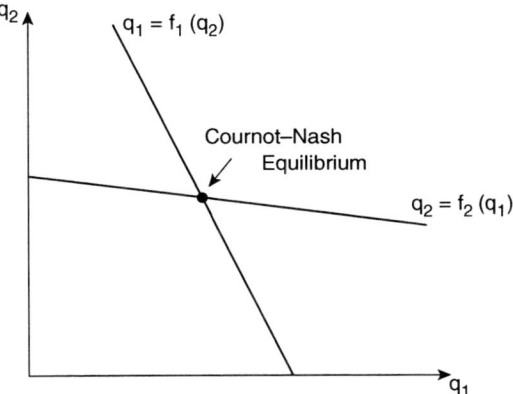

Figure 10.3 Cournot reaction functions and Nash equilibrium.

All that is needed to find such a Nash equilibrium is to substitute one reaction function into the other (since there are two equations in two unknowns, the solution is straightforward). The result will be to solve for one output at the Nash equilibrium that can then be placed in the other firm's reaction function to find the second half of the solution. The reaction functions for a typical Cournot duopoly and the resulting Nash equilibrium are pictured in Figure 10.3. All the steps for solving a Cournot duopoly game are shown in the application box.

Bertrand duopoly games

A Bertrand duopoly or oligopoly, where the concerned firms set prices, is very applicable to much of the food industry. Many processed food sectors have a small number of dominant firms that sell differentiated products which are well branded and can be sold for prespecified prices that do not need to be identical to their competitor's price. Soft drinks, canned soups, snack foods such as potato chips, ice cream, cheese, lunch meat, and pasta all fit into a Bertrand duopoly or oligopoly model reasonably well.

Bertrand duopoly (and oligopoly) games are solved in a manner very similar to that used for Cournot games. Because demand is now assumed to be differentiated, each firm has a separate demand curve; for example

$$q_1 = a - bp_1 + cp_2 \text{ and } q_2 = d + ep_1 - fp_2. \tag{10.3}$$

Note that these demand curves imply that the two firms' products are substitutes (since the implied cross-price elasticities are positive). If this were not the case, they would not be competing, and modeling their behavior with a Bertrand game would make no sense. Again, assuming that the firms want to maximize single-period profit, these demand curves and the firms' cost curves would be used to

Solving a Cournot duopoly game

The market demand is given by $p = 500 - 2(q_1 + q_2)$. The two companies' cost functions are $c_1(q_1) = 3q_1$ and $c_2(q_2) = 4q_2$. Assume that each firm maximizes the single-period profit.

Firm 1's problem

$\max \pi_1 = pq_1 - c_1(q_1) = [500 - 2(q_1 + q_2)]q_1 - 3q_1$

Firm 2's problem

$\max \pi_2 = [500 - 2(q_1 + q_2)]q_2 - 4q_2$

Now take the derivative of the profit with respect to the firm's quantity and set it equal to zero:

$d\pi_1/dq_1 = 500 - 4q_1 - 2q_2 - 3 = 0$

$d\pi_2/dq_2 = 500 - 2q_1 - 4q_2 - 4 = 0$

Solve the above first-order conditions for the firm's quantity to derive the reaction functions:

$497 - 2q_2 = 4q_1 \Rightarrow q_1 = 124.25 - 0.5q_2$

$496 - 2q_1 = 4q_2 \Rightarrow q_2 = 124 - 0.5q_1$

Next, find the intersection of the reaction functions to find the Cournot–Nash equilibrium. Do this by substituting one reaction function into the other:

$q_1 = 124.25 - 0.5q_2 = 124.25 - 0.5(124 - 0.5q_1) = 62.25 - 0.25q_1 \Rightarrow 0.75q_1 = 62.25 \Rightarrow q_1 = 83$.
$q_2 = 124 - 0.5(83) \Rightarrow q_2 = 82.5$.

The quantities can be used to find the market price and then the companies' profits:

$p = 500 - 2(q_1 + q_2) = 500 - 2(83 + 82.5) = 169$.
$\pi_1 = pq_1 - c_1(q_1) = (169)(83) - 3(83) = 13,778$.
$\pi_2 = pq_2 - c_2(q_2) = (169)(82.5) - 4(82.5) = 13,612.5$.

set up a profit function for each firm that is similar to that in equation (10.1). However, this time, the quantity is substituted out, and the profit is expressed in terms of prices since that will be the choice variable. For firm 1, the profit function would look like

$$\pi_1 = (a - bp_1 + cp_2)p_1 - c_1(a - bp_1 + cp_2). \tag{10.4}$$

Firm 1 would solve the implied maximization problem by taking the derivative of the profit function with respect to p_1, setting it equal to zero, and solving for p_1 as a function of p_2. That will yield a reaction function that is similar to the one in

Imperfect competition and game theory 113

the Cournot game except that here the reaction function tells the firm the optimal price to set in response to the price set by its competitor. To find the Nash equilibrium, find the point where the two reaction functions intersect.

Cournot duopolies tend to be very stable and virtually always have a Nash equilibrium. Bertrand duopolies are somewhat more finicky. Depending on the own and cross price elasticities and the marginal cost of each firm, the reaction functions may slope upward or downward, meaning it is possible for no Nash equilibrium to exist because the reaction functions may not intersect within the space of positive prices. Figure 10.4 shows some possible shapes for Bertrand reaction functions and the Nash equilibriums to go with them. Further, it is possible to have reaction functions that intersect, but an unstable equilibrium. In such a case, a Nash equilibrium exists, but there is no plausible way to get there except by collusion between the competitors. In these unstable equilibriums, once the firms are at some point other than the Nash equilibrium, their reaction functions cause them to adjust prices away from the Nash equilibrium so that each successive response takes the firms farther away from the Nash equilibrium until either prices go to infinity or one firm's price hits zero.

As stated above, Bertrand games are likely a good approximation for many segments of the food industry in which two or a few large firms dominate a category of branded, differentiated products, competing for customers partly with price. Alcoholic beverages, energy drinks, ground and instant coffee, margarine, yogurt, cake mixes, detergents, and paper products are other examples of product categories that could be modeled as Bertrand duopolies or oligopolies. One advantage of Bertrand games is that they are easy to generalize to games with a menu of strategies where firms are choosing strategies involving price, coupons, advertising budgets, and other promotional variables. All that is required is to specify demand functions similar to the one shown in equation (10.3) to include shifts for the other choice variables such as advertising expenses, both for the company's own promotions and its competitors. That demand curve goes into the

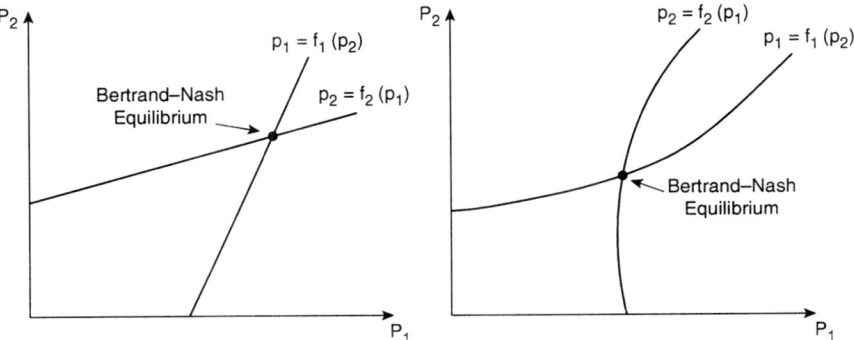

Figure 10.4 Bertrand duopoly, reaction functions in different shapes, and Nash equilibriums.

profit function, and derivatives are taken with respect to all the choice variables that are part of the firm's strategy. In such a game, reaction functions would be derived for each choice variable, and each reaction function would depend on all the other choice variables of that firm and its competitors. The Nash equilibrium is still at the point of intersection of the reaction functions and would be found simultaneously for all choice variables. There is a practice problem at the end of the chapter that involves such a game.

Moving from duopoly to oligopoly

To extend the duopoly games shown so far to oligopoly games is not difficult. For a Cournot oligopoly game, the first step is to modify the demand curve to allow for the larger number of firms. Thus, the inverse demand curve is now assumed to be of the form

$$p = g(q_1 + q_2 + \ldots q_k) \qquad (10.5)$$

where $g(\cdot)$ is the inverse demand function and q_1 through q_k are the output levels of the k firms that comprise the oligopoly. Other than this change to the inverse demand function to incorporate the presence of more than two firms, the profit function remains the same. The reaction functions will now tell each firm in the oligopoly the profit-maximizing output to produce in response to the total output of all the other firms in their industry.

In a Bertrand oligopoly game, the demand curves must be adjusted to include the prices and other relevant variables (like advertising expenditures) for all of each firm's competitors. That means that the demand curves can become rather complex; firms need to collect a good amount of data in order to be able to estimate the demand curves they have and be able to solve the required profit maximization problem. However, the basic process is the same as in the Bertrand duopoly, with the end result being a set of reaction functions that tell each firm the optimal price to set in response to the price (and other) strategies of its competitors. The Nash equilibrium is still found at the point of intersection of the reaction functions.

Even without going to continuous strategies, Bertrand concepts are useful in oligopoly settings. One can construct a game as simple as one with two possible strategies: match a price change or don't match a price change. In such games, it can often be shown that optimal strategies are to match price decreases, but not to match price increases. This leads to the famous "kinked" demand curve where a firm in an oligopoly perceives its demand curve as very elastic above the current price and very inelastic below the current price. See Figure 10.5 for what the kinked demand curve looks like. The figure also shows how the firm's marginal revenue curve has a gap in it at the current quantity (matching the point of the kink). This gap in the marginal revenue means that when a firm such as this experiences changes in its costs, it is unlikely to pass those cost changes on to consumers through price changes.

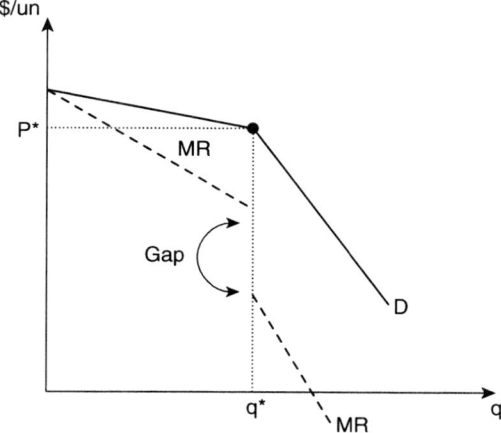

Figure 10.5 Kinked demand curve with marginal revenue curves.

Competition with leaders and followers

While the games presented so far in this chapter demonstrate how firms can incorporate strategic thinking into their decision making, the strategic thinking and strategies allowed can be developed even further. In the Cournot and Bertrand duopoly and oligopoly games above, each firm first assumes that its competitors' strategies will remain unchanged in order to derive the reaction functions; there has been no discussion of any explicit process of how the firms' continual adjustment to each other's changing strategies leads them to reach a point where the adjusting can stop and the strategies actually do remain unchanged. Using the reaction functions, and assuming that firms take turns adjusting their strategies, one can see how such successive optimal responses would bring the firms to the Nash equilibrium, but that still leaves the question of why firms would follow such a process.

An alternative approach to how firms might reach an equilibrium has been advanced and formalized into what is now called a Stackelberg duopoly game. In a Stackelberg game, one firm (called the *leader*) realizes that instead of using its reaction function to respond to its competitor's strategy, it can actually make a larger profit by finding the strategy that maximizes its own profit subject to its competitor's reaction function. That is, instead of taking its competitor's strategy as given, the leader is really choosing both its own strategy and the strategy of its competitor (called the *follower*). This generally allows the leader to earn higher profits.

To see how this works, refer to Figure 10.6, which shows the reaction functions for two firms in a Cournot duopoly game. Added to the diagram are isoprofit lines, which show all the pairs of (q_1, q_2) that produce the same profit for one of the firms. Profit increases for each firm as one moves toward the intercept of its

116 *Imperfect competition and game theory*

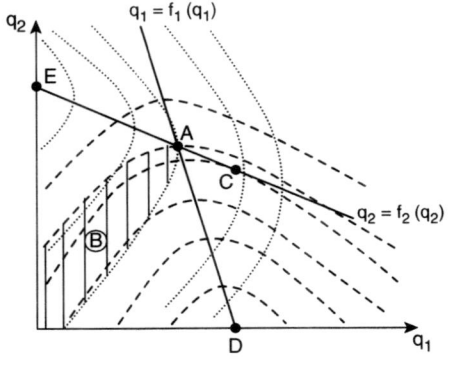

A=Cournot–Nash Equilibrium
B=Collusive Lens
C=Stackelberg Equilibrium with Firm 1 as Leader
Dashed lines are firm 1's isoprofit lines with maximum profit at point D
Dotted lines are firm 2's isoprofit lines with maximum profit at point E

Figure 10.6 Stackelberg Cournot with isoprofit and collusive lens.

reaction function on its own quantity axis. At that point, the other firm's quantity is zero, as a result of which the remaining firm earns maximum (monopoly) profits. In a Stackelberg game, the leader searches for the point on the follower's reaction function that is on the highest possible isoprofit line. This point is marked in Figure 10.6. You can see that the profit of the leader firm is definitely higher than at the Cournot–Nash equilibrium, while the follower receives a lower profit.

Interestingly, in Cournot duopolies, it is always preferable to be the leader in a Stackelberg game, but in a Bertrand duopoly, the follower in a Stackelberg game can often gain a larger profit than the leader and also a larger profit than it would have received at the Bertrand–Nash equilibrium. Thus, when strategies are based on prices, firms may not be eager to follow the Stackelberg behavioral model until another firm takes the lead.

There are numerous examples in the agribusiness industry of firms competing in a market that fits either the standard Bertrand game or a Bertrand Stackelberg game. The US almond industry has a clear, dominant processor/wholesaler. Blue Diamond Almond has about two-thirds of the market and takes the role of a Stackelberg leader. Blue Diamond performs market research, predicts the annual supply, and sets its price. The remaining firms follow along, basing their prices on the price set by Blue Diamond. Coca-Cola and Pepsi can certainly be characterized as playing a Bertrand duopoly (with a small fringe of other soft drink sellers), choosing strategies of prices and various promotional and advertising programs. Pepsi can also potentially be characterized as a Stackelberg leader in the snack food category, where it owns the Frito-Lay brand.

Antitrust laws, collusion, and non-competitive behavior

The United States (and most other countries) have laws against companies colluding (a legal term for cooperating) in order to raise prices (and profits) at the expense of consumers. In the United States, there are three main antitrust laws that govern such collusive behavior and strive to make sure markets stay competitive. These laws are the Sherman Antitrust Act, The Clayton Antitrust Act, and the Federal Trade Commission Act. The simplest summary of these laws is that they ban any practice by which companies collude to reduce competition. That means companies cannot agree to keep prices high, to split a market with agreed-upon market shares for each company, or to fix bids for contracts that are supposed to be competitively decided. The other purpose of these laws is to determine whether two companies can merge (where one company buys the other and combines operations). If a proposed merger is deemed anticompetitive, the government can block the deal in order to maintain a suitable level of competition in that industry. The approval of a merger depends on the market share of the proposed combined company and the estimated elasticity of demand that the new firm would face in any markets that are under review. The more inelastic the estimated demand will be, the more likely the merger request will be denied, since that implies less competition.

Models of collusive behavior

Referring back to Figure 10.6, which shows a pair of reaction functions and two sets of isoprofit lines for a Cournot duopoly, note that there is a lens-shaped area below and to the left of the Cournot–Nash equilibrium. This area represents higher profits for both firms than the Cournot–Nash equilibrium since both companies would be moving toward higher isoprofit lines. That area is the area where collusive behavior can lead to gains for both companies. Thus, if one company offered to collude with the other to reach some point within that area, its "competitor" would have an incentive to agree; any such collusive agreement would be a win-win for the two companies. Economics cannot guide us on where within the collusive region the two companies might agree to move; any agreement is based on the relative strength and negotiating skill of the two companies.

Such collusion could be accomplished by agreeing to each restrict output, by agreeing to maintain prices above some specified level, by agreeing to place artificially high bids for some contracts so that each company won a certain number of sales, a combination of the above, or any other form of anticompetitive agreement they can think of. An application box covers some examples of agribusiness companies that have been caught violating these laws, to give a feeling for the variety of methods and markets involved.

The most famous example of collusive behavior is a legal one. The Organization of Petroleum Exporting Countries (OPEC) is a cartel of some of the largest oil-producing countries including Saudi Arabia, Venezuela, Nigeria, Iraq, and Kuwait. They meet periodically, analyze the current level of demand in the

A sample of antitrust violators

- Ivy League universities were caught coordinating their financial aid offers to students so that students were faced with the same net price for all schools. They claimed this helped students choose the college they like best, but the US Department of Justice called it an antitrust violation.
- In 1961, and again in 1972, General Electric and Westinghouse were charged with fixing prices on electrical generators that they were selling to the Tennessee Valley Authority and other commercial customers.
- Between 1988 and 1991, the US Justice Department filed charges against 50 companies for fixing the price of milk sold to public schools in 16 states.
- Two makers of baby formula agreed to pay $5 million in 1992 to settle Florida charges that they had fixed prices of baby formula.
- Coca-Cola Bottling Co. of North Carolina agreed to pay a fine and give consumers discount coupons to settle charges of conspiring to fix soft drink prices from 1982 to 1985.
- Archer, Daniels, Midland, Co. paid a record $100 million fine in 1996 for fixing prices on the animal feed additive lysine. This is an amino acid added to animal feeds, not anything that you eat.

world oil market, and then set production levels. While they do not represent a majority share of world oil production, OPEC produces enough oil to matter and represents a larger share of the world trade in oil than its share of world production. OPEC sets both an overall production target for oil production and individual quotas for each member country. The output levels are set with the goal of maintaining some price or price range in the world oil market, and OPEC is often successful in doing so. However, OPEC also frequently suffers from cheating by its members who, as predicted by the theory on repeated games, have a strong incentive to agree to output restrictions that raise the world oil price and then produce more than their quotas in order to earn more money. The fewer countries that cheat, the more the cheaters can benefit, so every country pledges fidelity to the agreement before many secretly break their word. Because OPEC involves countries and not companies, it is above antitrust laws. While the higher oil prices OPEC is responsible for are no fun, they offer economists a chance to observe collusive behavior and confirm many of the predictions of game theory.

Summary

This chapter examined game theory, a subdiscipline within economics that studies decision making in a competitive environment. Game theory predicts how firms might make decisions when accounting for the likely responses of their competitors. In many agribusiness markets with a small number of branded, differentiated products that dominate the market, game theory has strong predictive ability of the behavior we are likely to observe.

Cournot games have companies choosing output levels as their strategies, whereas Bertrand games involve price setting as strategies (or choice variables). At the retail level and much of the wholesale level within the food industry, Bertrand games are more plausible. Many product categories such as soft drinks, breakfast cereals, margarine, cheese, yogurt, canned soup, and pasta can be reasonably modeled as Bertrand duopoly or oligopoly games. Cournot games might make sense with products such as flour and sugar that are not really differentiated products for most buyers.

Based on assumed objective functions for the players in a game (such as profit maximization), these continuous strategy games can be solved for each player's (or firm's) reaction function. A reaction function allows each player to easily find the optimal response to other players' strategies rather than needing to resolve the entire optimization problem every time another player changes strategy. The intersection of reaction functions is the Nash equilibrium as no player will want to change its strategy once the players get to that point.

Players in games can also abandon their reaction functions, either to become a Stackelberg leader in order to gain an advantage over its competitors or to collude with competitors in a manner such that all players do better than at the non-cooperative Nash equilibrium. Collusion is generally illegal for companies to practice, but companies nevertheless try it often enough that the list of those caught is not all that short.

Chapter highlights

- Game *players* choose *strategies*, and the set of strategies chosen determines the *payoff* to each player.
- *Repeated* games involve the same players having multiple rounds choosing strategies for the same possible payoffs. Repeated games open up the possibility of *cooperation, cheating*, and *punishment* for cheating.
- A Cournot game has output as the choice variable; Bertrand games have players choosing prices.
- *Reaction functions* allow a player to respond optimally to the other player's strategy.
- A Nash equilibrium is a set of strategies, or a solution to a game, at which no player has any incentive to change their strategy choice after seeing what all the other players have chosen. Thus, a Nash equilibrium is self-enforcing and needs no cooperation to be maintained. A Nash equilibrium is where reaction functions intersect.
- In a Stackelberg game, a *leader* finds the profit-maximizing strategy to play subject to allowing the other player (or *follower*) to be on its reaction function.

The Stackelberg leader does not use a reaction function, because it is leading, not reacting.
- Companies can also collude (or cooperate) in order to increase industry profits while making an agreement that covers how to split up the profits. Collusion is almost always illegal.

Practice problems

1. Consider an industry with two firms, each with marginal costs equal to 10 at all levels of output, meaning that their cost functions are $c(q) = 10q$. The market level (inverse) demand function is
   $p(Q) = p(q1 + q2) = 250 - 4Q = 250 - 4(q1 + q2)$.
   a. If there was perfect competition, what would be the equilibrium output level?
   b. What would be the profit levels of each firm?

2. Now assume that the firms play a Cournot duopoly game. Demand remains as in Problem 1 above, but the cost functions are now $c_1(q_1) = 5q_1$ and $c_2(q_2) = 10q_2$.
   a. Find both firms' reaction functions for q_i given q_j.
   b. Find the Cournot–Nash equilibrium levels of output.
   c. Find the equilibrium price and profits for each firm.

3. A town has two ice cream shops that sell only ice cream cones, and they play a Bertrand duopoly game as they compete for business. The ice cream shops each have a constant marginal cost of $1 per ice cream cone and face daily demand curves given below
   shop 1: $q_1 = 200 - 20p_1 + 10p_2$ shop 2: $q_2 = 200 + 5p_1 - 25p_2$
   a. Assuming each ice cream shop is trying to maximize its daily profit, find each firm's reaction function.
   b. Find the Bertrand–Nash equilibrium.
   c. Find each firm's daily profit.

4. Repeat all the parts of Problem 3 above with the new demand curves below that now include each ice cream shop's advertising expenditures (on ads in the local newspaper). You should end up with reaction functions for price and for advertising.
   shop 1 demand: $q_1 = 200 - 20p_1 + 10p_2 + Adv_1 - Adv_2$
   shop 2 demand: $q_2 = 200 + 5p_1 - 25p_2 - Adv_1 + Adv_2$

5. A company has a monopoly selling microwavable French fries. Its cost function is $c(q) = 5 + 0.5q^2$ and its inverse demand curve is $p = 100 - 0.5q$.
   a. Find the monopolist's profit-maximizing price and quantity and the profit it earns.
   b. Now a new entrant comes along and enters with a competing product. The new entrant's cost function is $c_2(q_2) = 10 + q^2$. If the two companies

play a Cournot game splitting the monopolist's old demand, what profit will each firm earn at the Cournot–Nash equilibrium?
c. How does the total industry profit now compare to the monopoly profit before?
d. The monopolist is interested in negotiating a collusive solution to this new game. State a possible offer the monopolist might make to the new entrant.

11 Spatial competition

Spatial competition is an important factor in the food industry. Food processors have to decide where to locate their processing facilities, and those location decisions are influenced not just by the location of farmers producing needed ingredients and retailers who want to buy the product but also by the location of other competing processors. Retailers also must choose locations, deciding where to place stores relative to the location of both their customers and competitors. There are benefits from locating away from your competitors and benefits from locating near competitors. As we will see, the particular features of an industry determine which benefits are larger and whether firms in a specific sector of the food industry tend to disperse spatially or cluster together. A second feature of spatial competition is price competition. Firms choose not only where to locate their business but also what price to set, and both of these decisions are done while considering your competitors and their likely responses to your choices. This chapter will explore some spatial competition models and how the results of these models translate into what we see in the food industry.

A basic Hotelling location model

Harold Hotelling was a mathematician who made enormous contributions to economics as both a researcher and teacher (he taught two people who went on to win the Nobel Prize in Economics: Milton Friedman and Kenneth Arrow). His spatial competition model is one of the simplest and allows us to start with a simple model and add complexity slowly.

To begin, consider two retailers each selling a single product to consumers located along a line. A common scenario that fits such a model is two ice cream stands located on a beach. Imagine that the consumers are spread evenly along the beach and that the ice cream vendors can locate wherever they wish to on the beach. If we designate locations on the beach by numbers from 0 (at one end) to 100 (at the other), where will the two vendors choose to set up their ice cream stands? It turns out that the answer to that question depends on exactly how the vendors react to each other, whether they can change prices along with the location, and even on how the buyers behave.

If all buyers are guaranteed to purchase one ice cream and vendors cannot compete on price (perhaps it is a public beach and the government regulates the price of snacks sold on it), then the vendors will end up in the middle of the beach (at 50) right next to each other. How does this happen? Imagine that the two vendors start at the opposite ends of the beach, at 0 and 100, respectively, and that the vendors assume that consumers will purchase an ice cream from whichever vendor is closer. Given these assumptions, each vendor will have an incentive to move toward the center of the beach in order to gain more customers since moving toward the center increases the share of customers closer to your ice cream stand if your competitor does not match your move.

This outcome of both vendors ending up in the center of the beach is the result of the set of assumptions listed above. It can be changed by many factors. For example, if customers are only willing to walk a certain distance to buy an ice cream (which is less than 50, or half the beach), then the vendors will move toward the center, but not all the way to the center of the beach. If the vendors can choose their prices and customers make a trade-off between price and the distance they have to walk, again we get the vendors moving toward the center but not all the way. In fact, for plausible assumptions about vendor and consumer behavior, the two vendors will end up somewhere near the locations of 25 and 75. Since the customers respond to price, if the vendors get too close to each other, price would become the determining factor, and competition would force the vendors to lower price until their profits were gone. By remaining some distance apart, the vendors will not have to compete on price so fiercely.[1] The business owners face a trade-off between the desire to move closer to center of the beach and steal some of the competitor's customers and the desire to be farther away from the competitor so as to have more pricing power. If moving closer to another business means having to lower price in order to compete, a business that moves closer to a competitor will gain revenue from the new customers that it captures but will lose revenue on all its preexisting customers owing to having to lower its price. To determine which of these impacts is larger, one needs to know how a firm and its competitor will compete with each other on price and how the consumers will react to price changes (in other words, the price elasticity of demand).

Conjectural variations

A firm solving a spatial competition problem by choosing a location and price combination must make an assumption about how it expects its competitors to react to its choice of price. This assumption about how other firms will adjust their prices in response to your firm's selection of price is called the conjectural variation by economists, because it is the firm's "conjecture" (a fancy word for guess) about how other firms will "vary" their prices. There are several famous assumptions about price responses that are worth knowing as they are often used in spatial competition models.

The first conjectural variation is that competitors will fully match any price change. When this price response is assumed, the model is referred to as

Löschian competition. A second common assumption is the complete opposite: competitors will not respond at all to price changes. When this price response (or lack thereof) is assumed, the model is referred to as Hotelling–Smithies competition. Note that Hotelling–Smithies competition is simply a Bertrand game in space, and the solution to a Hotelling–Smithies competition model is the same as a Bertrand–Nash equilibrium (as covered in Chapter 10). A third famous conjectural variation is that the price at the boundary of a firm's market area is fixed. This model is called Greenhut–Ohta competition and assumes either that the firm practices price discrimination or that the fixed price at the boundary refers to price plus the costs the consumer bears to shop for the product.

Conjectural variations are not restricted to the above examples and can be quite general. For example, a firm in a spatial oligopoly can assume that competitors will match price reductions but not price increases (creating the familiar "kinked" demand curve). All that is required is a reasonable assumption about what other firms' responses will be to your firm's price change; mathematically, one is making an assumption about $\partial p_j/\partial p_i$, where i denotes the firm being modeled and j denotes a competitor. With some type of conjectural variation in place, a firm can build a mathematical model of its spatial competition and solve for the strategy that maximizes its expected profit. If the model is in two-dimensional space (such as an actual city or region) and the firm wants to choose location (or locations) plus prices, these models can become very complex quite rapidly. In fact, they generally result in the need to solve a system of non-linear equations, which is beyond the scope of a course such as this. Instead, we shall move to a qualitative discussion of spatial competition in the food industry as observed in the real world before returning to a simple mathematical model of price competition in space.

To cluster or not to cluster, that is the question

As you go about your day, you see examples of retailers that cluster together and ones that work hard to stay separated. For example, car dealers and fast food restaurants often cluster together, whereas supermarkets tend to separate themselves. In the real world of spatial competition among retailers, there are a number of factors at work guiding these decisions. The above-mentioned opposite effects on revenue play a role: clustering might bring more customers if a business gains something from their surrounding competitors, but will cost the business revenue if clustering means it has to lower prices. Additionally, customers face search and transaction costs in purchasing items; for some purchases, these costs are large (either in absolute terms or relative to the purchase price of the items), and retailers that are clustered lower the search and transaction costs for customers. Finally, for some types of retailers, the location can have an enormous effect on their business. In such cases, clustering may be almost forced on a business because if they avoid that location (where other competitors are already located), any other location choice will be far inferior.

Within the food industry, fast food restaurants are an obvious example of clustering. If you find one fast food restaurant, there is a good chance that you have found four or five. This is a sector where location is very important, with restaurant owners wanting high visibility, high traffic counts on the street they are located on, and to be in a location that people pass on their way to somewhere else (such as at a highway interchange). Because all the fast food restaurants are looking for a site location with the same characteristics, they often end up next to each other. This co-location lowers the search cost of customers who might see a billboard for one brand, but upon arriving at that location find that they can actually choose from a number of fast food restaurants. Fast food restaurant owners do not worry much about clustering increasing the price competition among their restaurants since they already feature low prices and brand loyalty that leave their demand curves fairly inelastic in terms of their own price elasticity. The feeling among fast food restaurant owners is generally that if they can get a good enough location, a fair share of the consumers choosing one of the multiple restaurants in that location will choose to eat at their restaurant. They believe that the benefits of the location outweigh any negatives from sharing the location with competitors. A group of fast food restaurants clustered at an interstate highway off-ramp or in a mall's food court is visible testimony to these beliefs.

An example of the opposite solution to spatial competition can be seen in the supermarket sector. Supermarkets work very hard to never cluster together. In rare cases, you will find two supermarkets within a short distance of each other, but in most cases they try hard to separate themselves so that each has an area within which it is definitely the closest supermarket for a population of approximately the number of people needed to support a supermarket of that size. Supermarkets also often have some type of loyalty program that rewards customers who frequently shop in their brand of store. Both the spatial separation and the loyalty programs are designed to reduce the need for price competition among supermarkets. To further that goal, supermarket chains routinely sign leases with shopping centers that ensure they will be the only supermarket in that shopping center. In fact, supermarket chains that close a store have been known to pay rent on an empty store for years in order to block a competitor from moving into that location. This usually occurs when the chain that closed the store has other stores in that town and wants to encourage the people who used to shop at the closed store to drive to one of their other stores in town. All of these actions are designed to increase the cost of shoppers going to another (farther away) grocery store and allow supermarkets to compete less fiercely on price (although they still do compete on price). Because margins in the food retailing business are so low (an average supermarket earns only a 2 percent profit on its gross revenue), they have little room left for more price competition.

Another example of spatial competition in which firms try to spread out is food processing. Particularly with main ingredients that are expensive and difficult to transport (such as pears or grapes), food processors try to locate near farmers producing the needed commodity, but not next to each other. By using the spacing to create a local monopsony[2] for the closest farmers, the food processors can offer lower prices. If they located closer together, the food processors could be forced to compete on price for farmers in order to secure the necessary supply of their main ingredient, raising the price paid to farmers and the costs of the food processors. Because farmers generally have to sell their commodities quickly to avoid deterioration, a spatial monopsonist has even more pricing power than a monopolist since at some price consumers will not purchase a product.

A mathematical model of spatial competition[3]

To demonstrate a fairly simple mathematical model of spatial competition that has enough features to make it realistic, we return to the Hotelling model with a linear market, although this time we will fix the location of the two firms at opposite ends of the line.

The concept of a linear market actually can be quite representative of real-world situations in the food industry if one connects the simple features with characteristics we all face in real life. For example, think about competing products in a supermarket such as different brands of spaghetti sauce. When a consumer decides which of these competing products to buy, they compare them by product characteristics such as taste and nutritional content. The differences in the competing products separate them in a manner that is exactly analogous to identical products separated by distance on our imaginary linear market. As we build the model below, we will point out how each feature can translate into aspects of spatial competition in the food industry.

The model begins with two firms selling a single identical product at prices that each firm sets so that prices can differ between the two sellers. The two firms are located at opposite ends of a line. For simplicity, specify the line as 1 unit in length so that one firm is at 0 and the other is at 1. Both firms can manufacture the product at a constant marginal cost of $\$c$ per unit and sell their products for some price $p \geq c$ (that is, firms will not set a price at which they lose money). Consumers are located along the line with a uniform density of consumers at all points and face a transportation cost of $\$t$ per unit of distance to get to the store and purchase the product, so that the total price to buy the product is the price p plus td, where $0 < d < 1$ is the distance from the consumer's location to the store. Consumers have no preference between the two firms and their products (since they are identical) and simply purchase from the seller offering the lowest total cost as long as that total cost $(p+td)$ is less than a value R. That means that consumers will be separated into two markets, with a boundary somewhere between the two firms that divides the customers and those on each side buying only from the firm on their side of the boundary. The value of R, a reservation price, can best be thought of as the total cost at which the consumers would instead purchase a different (substitute) product in order to maximize their individual utility. For such a model to be interesting, then, $R > c$ is a necessary condition, otherwise no consumer will buy any of the product, and the two firms will just go out of business. In fact, if we had perfect competition, $(R - c)$ would be the consumer surplus.

At the opposite extreme from both firms going out of business, if $R < c + td/2$, then some consumers in the middle of the line are guaranteed not to purchase the product even at the firm's break-even price (equal to the average cost, c). Each firm will set the price to maximize profit accounting for the effect of the transportation cost on consumer demand. Note that this case of high relative transportation costs can also represent products that are differentiated rather than identical, with differentiation increasing instead of transportation costs[4]; the extreme is then when the products become so differentiated that they cease being substitutes and the firms become monopolies. Also, this case shows how it is relative transportation costs that matter, implying that spatial competition would extend farther for products that are more expensive. That is, people will travel a long way to save money on an expensive piece of farm equipment or machinery for a food processing facility, whereas people will only travel so far to save money on groceries or a fast food meal.

There are two in-between cases for this model. In the first case, when $(R - c) > 1.5t$, the firms will compete in a spatial duopoly. If one firm sets its price lower than the other, the firm with the lower price will capture extra market share, meaning that the boundary between consumers who shop at one store and those that shop at the other will shift away from the low-price firm, giving it the larger share of customers. However, in such a case, the competing firm will lower prices to respond in an attempt to recapture its customers. For this case, the Nash equilibrium (remember this concept from chapter 10) has both firms setting a price $p = c + t$, which will put the market boundary in the middle at $d = 0.5$. An implication of this is that as transportation costs rise, so does the product's price. Remembering that transportation cost plays a role in the model that is analogous to differentiation among products, this case of the model shows that as competing products become differentiated, the prices of the products will rise. This occurs because as products differentiate, consumer taste differences will cause the demand for each product to become more inelastic in terms of cross price elasticity.

The final case for this model occurs when $t < (R - c) < 1.5t$. In such a case, each seller perceives a kinked demand curve as in the classic oligopoly model. The conjectural variation assumed by each seller is that its competitor will match price decreases, but not price increases. Mathematically, this conjectural variation could be written as

$$\partial p_j / \partial p_i = 0 \quad \text{if} \quad \Delta p_i > 0$$
$$\partial p_j / \partial p_i = 1 \quad \text{if} \quad \Delta p_i < 0,$$
(11.1)

where Δp_i is the change in the firm's own price. That makes the demand curve very elastic above the current price and very inelastic below the current price; hence, a kink in the demand curve occurs. In this case of the model, the spatial competition manifests itself differently than in the case above. Now, as the transportation cost increases, the equilibrium prices decrease. This is because if the price did not drop as transportation costs rose, consumers in the middle of the line would stop purchasing the product. That suddenly makes the demand facing each firm more elastic, which results in a lowering of the equilibrium price. This case

128 *Spatial competition*

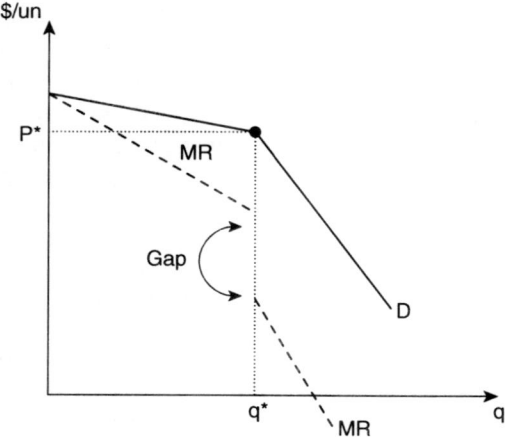

Figure 11.1 A kinked demand curve.

of the model also is characterized by multiple equilibria (as opposed to the single Nash equilibrium in the previous case), so the solution is more complicated, and it is unclear exactly what prices will result for any given set of parameters. This case would be representative of an industry with multiple firms selling differentiated but still closely similar products, such as many branded grocery products. Spaghetti sauce, bread, or salad dressings could fit the concepts represented by this case of the model.

Turning the model into a buying model

The same basic model can be "reversed" so that instead of two sellers the model has two buyers, one at each end of the line. The consumers located all along the line who each buy one unit are replaced by farmers who each have one unit of a commodity to sell if the buyers are processors, or even manufacturers each selling one unit of a manufactured product with the buyers being retailers. With buyers in the place of sellers, anything that led sellers to raise prices will now cause buyers to lower price. The model can provide insight into spatial competition when transportation cost is measured relative to the offered buying price, shining light on how behavior changes in markets as transportation costs vary relative to the net value of the product to the buyer. In the model of farmers selling to processors, transportation cost and distance are best interpreted simply as transportation cost and distance to the buyer. In the model of manufacturers selling to retailers, the distance could represent differences among retailers who perhaps attract customers with stronger or weaker preferences for a particular product.

Summary

This chapter covered spatial competition. Models were introduced in which firms competed by choosing the location and price of a product that they are selling. While there is an inclination to move closer to each other in order to gain customers in the region between the two sellers, moving closer also leads to stiffer price competition that results in a lower price. These two effects at least partially offset each other, and while the firms may move somewhat toward each other, generally they will not end up next to each other.

Some stores cluster with other retailers with which they compete; this tends to occur in industries with higher search and transaction costs relative to price (jewelry, fast food) and where location is very important to consumers. Other industries dislike clustering, and retailers (or processors) disperse themselves hoping to each have a local (spatial) monopoly for their product or monopsony for an important input they purchase.

A mathematical model of spatial competition, originally due to Hotelling and recently explored by Mérel and Sexton (2011), was presented. This added some rigor to the insights and intuition on the spatial competition models previously discussed. With the location of competing retailers fixed, the relative magnitude of transportation cost compared to the reservation price minus production cost (which under perfect competition would be the consumer surplus) determines the type of spatial competition and the price levels that result. If relative transportation costs are large enough, the two sellers become local monopolies. This case represents products where the cost of purchasing the good and transporting it to your home or business is expensive relative to the product's value, situations where sellers are widely separated geographically, or products that are relatively differentiated. An opposite case has low transportation costs, resulting in fierce competition between the two sellers and a Nash equilibrium where both firms set price equal to average cost plus the transportation cost for the distance between sellers. There is also an in-between case where sellers perceive a kinked demand curve as usually depicted in oligopolies, with competing sellers expected to match price cuts but not price increases. In this case, multiple solutions are possible, and the impact of an increase in transportation costs on price is counter-intuitive (the equilibrium price drops).

Chapter highlights

- A common model of two ice cream stands on a beach that are able to choose their location produces ice cream sellers that move toward the middle, but do not meet in the center of the beach unless there is no price competition and consumer demand is completely inelastic.
- Conjectural variation is the term for one firm's assumption about its competitor's reaction to its own price strategies. A few famous ones:
    - In Hotelling–Smithies competition, rivals are assumed to have no reaction to a price change.

130 *Spatial competition*

- In Löschian competition, rivals are expected to match any price changes.
- In Greenhut–Ohta competition, rivals are assumed to maintain a constant price at the firm's market boundary.

• Retailers and processors sometimes cluster together and at other times spread themselves out across the area of potential customers or suppliers. The choice of spatial pattern depends on the relative transportation costs, the amount products are differentiated, and even the frequency of the product's purchase.
• Supermarkets almost never cluster and food processors rarely do either, trying to reduce the need to compete on price with each other.
• Fast food restaurants commonly cluster; already having low prices, they benefit more from drawing in large numbers of potential customers, and all the restaurant owners want to be at the most favorable possible location.
• A mathematical version of the Hotelling spatial competition model with fixed sellers was analyzed to show how the relative transportation costs affected price competition between the sellers. The relative transportation cost can also be seen as a stand-in for product differentiation or increased spatial dispersion of the sellers.

Practice problems

1. The beach in Coastal City is 3000 feet long with two taco stands. One is located 300 ft from the north end of the beach and the second stand is 500 ft from the south end. Each taco stand sells fish tacos for $2.00. Beachgoers have no preference between the tacos sold at the two stands and are willing to buy tacos as long as the price plus the cost of walking back and forth to the taco stand is less than $4.00.

    a. If the cost of walking along the beach to a taco stand is $0.001/foot, what is the market area for each taco stand?
    b. If both stands charge the same price, what is the highest price that would cause the market areas to meet at a shared boundary?
    c. What happens to the market areas if the southern taco stand cuts its price to $1.50 per taco?
    d. If the southern half of the beach (from the 1500 foot mark and up) is smoother and the cost of walking on that half of the beach is only $0.0005/foot what are the market areas both when the southern taco stand charges $2.00 and when it charges $1.50?

2. Name two industries in the real world that you believe reasonably fit the mold of

    a. Hotelling–Smithies price competition
    b. Löschian price competition

c. Classic oligopoly-style price competition (matching price decreases but not price increases)

For example, airlines would be a good example for part (c).

3. In your town, what businesses cluster with their competitors and what businesses spread out? Try to name three examples of each.

12 The food service industry

A significant segment of the food industry is the food service sector: bars, restaurants, cafeterias, delivery pizzas, college dining halls, and caterers, all the places that prepare and serve ready-to-eat food for us to consume. While the basic economics of the food service industry is no different than that of any other food processor, there are some special features of food service that warrant a separate chapter. Labor issues are especially important. Customer service gets more attention because a small restaurant probably has many more different customers in a year than does Campbell's Soup. Pricing rules are not as precise, partly owing to less managerial ability at many food service establishments, but also owing to the impracticability of continually adjusting prices to keep up with ingredient costs (and sometimes even recipes) that are often changing on a daily basis and to the fact that customers complain fiercely when menu prices are increased. Finally, food service marketing plans must be designed to appeal to people directly, while large food processors market to people, wholesalers, and retailers. A restaurant does not need to deal with a supermarket chain over its shelf space, but it is producing a final good, so its products cannot hide from consumers. Consumer loyalty must be earned continually and with as few missteps as possible.

Costs in restaurants and food service locations

To begin a discussion of costs in restaurants and other food service locations, it helps to understand the relative size of different cost categories in the food service industry. The following figures come from the 2007 US Census Bureau's Business Expenditure Survey for the business category of food service establishments. Thus, sit-down restaurants, fast food restaurants, pizza delivery businesses, bars, and cafeterias are all lumped in together even though they would have some differences between them in the different categories. Still, the data is informative and sets a good stage for understanding where most of your food-away-from-home dollars go. Of the average dollar of expenses in the food service industry, 52 percent went to labor costs, 4 percent to materials and supplies, 5 percent to utilities, 3 percent to repairs and maintenance, 4 percent to advertising, 8 percent to lease and rental payments, 2 percent to taxes and fees, and 4 percent to depreciation. The Other category, which for food service is where the ingredient and food product costs are recorded, was 14.5 percent. On average, only about one-seventh of food service expenses go to purchases of food or beverages. Labor costs almost four times as much as the food! Food cost typically runs much more than 14 percent, but beverage costs are very low compared to the price of beverages, so when all restaurants (which sell beverages along with food) and bars (which sell mostly beverages) are combined, the percentage of expenses that food costs represent is quite low.

The above data gives us some quick insight into what are the important items to focus on in minimizing costs in the food service industry. Getting a favorable rent or purchase price for your building and equipment is nice, watching spending and waste in materials and supplies is worthwhile, but to really make a difference in the bottom line (that is, profit), there are only two places you can look: food costs and labor costs. This is borne out by actual observation in the restaurant and food service industry. Food is inventoried and tracked; if too much is being ordered and then thrown out due to spoilage, action is taken to correct it. It is not uncommon to spot-check kitchen staff to ensure that the portions being served are the correct size (so that food is not "wasted" by being given away for free in the form of larger servings). For example, ice cream stores will tally the day's sales in scoops, calculate how many gallons should have been used, and then check to see how close the staff came to hitting their target. If extra ice cream is disappearing, the manager will start to either check individual workers or try to determine who is over-scooping by comparing use rates to work schedules. Fast food restaurants monitor their food use versus items sold ratios very closely, checking reports weekly or even daily to ensure that, as far as possible, the amount of food purchased equals the amount of food sold. The book author has personally observed the bar staff in a restaurant undergoing a pouring test to see if they are mixing drinks with the right amount of alcohol. This restaurant prefers its bartenders to "free pour" drinks, meaning not use any sort of measuring device, because they think it looks more impressive. Using water in old liquor bottles with the same pour tops as used for the real drinks, the bartenders have to free-pour six drinks, with a mixture of singles and doubles. The manager then pours the drinks into measuring tubes marked with the target amounts. If the bartender misses twice (either high or low), she either doesn't tend bar that night or she has to use a measuring device (a jigger).

While food cost is controlled by portion control and through efforts to avoid spoilage and other waste in preparation, labor cost management is more straightforward. Labor costs are controlled by managing hourly wages and benefits and by carefully monitoring the number of hours worked, particularly relative to the number of customers served or meals prepared. Restaurants routinely schedule workers such as wait staff for a shift and then if the restaurant turns out not to be very busy, send some of them home. No restaurant wants to pay a worker to sit around without work to do. With few unionized workers in the industry (outside of large food service organizations such as large hotel restaurants), managers rarely have to worry about minimum hour rules. A worker can be sent home 30 minutes after starting work and only be paid for those 30 minutes.

A later section will detail some of the special rules for pay that apply to food service workers who get tips, but for now we will just note that these employment laws help to hold down labor costs. Restaurants and bars can pay workers below minimum wage as long as the tips earned bring the worker up to the minimum wage. This helps the business hold down labor costs, although as we will see later in this chapter it can lead to some complications.

It is also worth noting that while caterers will not really be mentioned in this chapter, they are part of the food service sector, and most of what is discussed relative to restaurants applies to the catering business as well. The main difference is that in catering, the meals are served to customers at a different location every time. Most caterers still have a permanent kitchen and food storage facility somewhere that is similar to a restaurant in terms of having fixed costs and needing inventory control. Most caterers will provide servers upon request, so labor issues are very similar. Caterers do have one large advantage compared to regular restaurants: it is easy for caterers to adjust prices daily if necessary to keep up with changes in food costs or labor costs. As is discussed in more depth later, restaurants try hard to avoid changing their menu prices because of customer complaints when the price of their regular meal changes.

Restaurant pricing strategies

Proper pricing is crucial to the success of a restaurant.[1] Setting prices too high will drive customers away; too low, and business will be good until the restaurant closes down owing to lack of profitability. Prices must provide a large enough gross margin per meal that when multiplied by the number of meals served, the restaurant can cover its fixed costs and hopefully even leave some profit for the restaurant owners.

To set menu prices, a restaurant manager must first understand the restaurant's costs. Restaurant costs fall into two categories: fixed costs and variable costs. Fixed costs will generally include rent or loan payments on the building and equipment, annual taxes and fees, insurance, advertising, and salaries for any employees not paid hourly (such as the manager and chef). Variable costs will include food, beverages, supplies, utilities, and hourly labor expenses. Given an understanding of the costs, a restaurant manager can begin with calculations such as a simple break-even analysis.

Imagine a barbeque restaurant that only sells barbeque sandwiches with a side of coleslaw and a side of beans. The variable cost of preparing this meal is $4. The restaurant has monthly fixed costs of $5,000 and a profit goal of $3,000 per month. With this information, the restaurant manager can choose a price and then determine how many sandwiches need to be sold to break even or reach the profit goal. For a given quantity sold, the manager could also find the price that would allow the restaurant to break even or reach the profit goal. The break-even and profit goal quantity formulas for a selected price are

$$Q_{BE} = FC / (P - AVC) \qquad (12.1)$$

$$Q_\pi = (FC + ProfitGoal)/(P - AVC) \tag{12.2}$$

where AVC is the average variable cost, FC is the total fixed costs in the selected time period (say, monthly), P is the price per meal, ProfitGoal is the desired profit, Q_{BE} is the number of meals that would need to be sold to break even, and Q_π is the quantity of meals sold that would achieve the desired profit goal. Given the above numbers for the barbeque restaurant, if the sandwich is sold for $6, equation (12.1) tells us the restaurant must sell 2,500 sandwiches per month to break even, and equation (12.2) shows that the restaurant needs to sell 4,000 sandwiches per month to reach its profit goal.

Equations (12.1) and (12.2) can be rearranged to find a desired price if the quantity of meals sold is assumed. In this case, the equations would be

$$P_{BE} = FC/Q + AVC \tag{12.3}$$

$$P_\pi = (FC + ProfitGoal)/Q + AVC \tag{12.4}$$

where P_{BE} is the price that would enable the restaurant to break even, while P_π is the price that would allow the restaurant to reach its profit goal. If the restaurant expected to sell 5,000 sandwiches per month, it would break even with a price of $5 per sandwich and would reach its profit goal with a price of $5.60.

Equations (12.1) through (12.4) can help a restaurant assess, with simple calculations, the feasibility of a business plan for a new restaurant or determine how much business would have to improve (or prices be raised) in order to reach certain economic goals. The above equations, however, cannot be used to select the full set of menu prices that a restaurant needs. After all, most restaurants have more than one item on the menu and more than one price. Selecting menu prices is a complicated process, and a restaurant owner or manager has several possible approaches from which to choose.

Subjective pricing strategies

One set of options for setting menu prices is referred to by the collective term *subjective pricing rules*. The term means what it implies, that these "rules" are not really rules but are guidelines or methods that are not based on exact mathematical formulas. Within this category fall such pricing "rules" as loss-leader pricing, highest price, and competitive pricing.

Competitive pricing is somewhat ad hoc in that no definitive rule is involved, but it at least has research behind it. A restaurant owner or manager would collect information from restaurants that are operating nearby in the same market niche and try to price comparable menu items at comparable prices; in fact, competitive pricing could just as easily be called comparative pricing. Competitive pricing has the advantage that it is based on what essentially is very inexpensive market research. If other similar restaurants are charging those prices and staying in business, that is an indication that customers are willing and able to pay those prices and that those other restaurants are able to serve the meals at a cost that is low enough to make a sufficient profit at those prices. Of course, the new restaurant may have higher (or lower) costs than its established competitors, so competitive pricing is no guarantee of financial success. Also, if customers do not judge the meals (and overall dining experience) to be of equal quality to those comparable restaurants, people may not be willing to pay equal prices for what they judge to be an inferior meal. The reverse is also possible; if a restaurant is better than its chosen competitors, then comparable pricing would cause a restaurant to leave money on the table by charging less than it could.

Highest-price menu pricing is similar to competitive pricing but with a twist. After researching what other restaurants charge for similar menu items, the restaurant owner or manager sets prices at the highest level they think the market will support. This might be the highest price observed in their market, or it might even be 5 percent or 10 percent higher. While such a pricing strategy carries risk (of ending up with very few customers), if diners can be convinced that the dining experience is worth those prices, the highest-price menu pricing is likely to lead to very healthy profits for a restaurant. A restaurant planning to use the highest-price menu pricing strategy should probably also be willing to incur higher costs than its competitors in either ingredients, dining room décor, service, or all three. This will help convince customers that the dining experience is worth the additional expense.

The opposite of highest-price menu pricing is loss-leader pricing. No restaurant can build an entire menu of loss leaders, since the point of a loss leader is that the restaurant loses money on that menu item in order to bring in customers, in the hope that some members of each group will order other items that are profitable. A daily special is sometimes a loss leader. A loss leader is more a form of advertising than a true price-setting strategy, so we will have nothing else to say about it here.

Objective pricing strategies

Objective pricing strategies are formula-based methods of setting menu prices. Three common objective strategies will be mentioned here: profit goal pricing, food cost markup pricing, and margin contribution pricing.

Profit goal pricing is a mathematical approach to menu price setting designed to select prices so that the restaurant reaches a pre-selected profit goal. It involves a number of steps and assumptions by the restaurant owner or manager. First, one must know the fixed costs (FC) and the profit goal (π). Then one needs to know the average non-food variable costs per meal (ANFVC). That is the cost of any disposable products used (like paper napkins or table cloths), washing and wear costs for reusable items such as glasses, dishes, linen napkins, and table cloths, and hourly labor costs involved in preparing and delivering the meal. The owner or manager also has to estimate the number of meals that will be served (N). Finally, the owner or manager must select the target for the food cost percentage (Food%). The food cost percentage (which will figure prominently in the food cost markup pricing rule) is pretty much exactly what it sounds like: the percentage of a menu price that represents the cost of the food ingredients in that meal. This number is typically somewhere between 28 percent and 36 percent. Given all these facts and assumptions, the restaurant owner or manager solves for prices in two steps. First, the total revenue target (TR) is computed with the equation

$$TR = (\pi + FC + N \times ANFVC)/(1 - Food\%). \qquad (12.5)$$

Then, dividing by the number of meals served will yield the price that should be set:

$$P = TR/N. \qquad (12.6)$$

For a restaurant with a large number of diverse menu items, the above process obviously needs to be generalized as salads, desserts, and main dishes will all have different prices. A possible approach is to apportion shares of the fixed costs, non-food variable costs, and profit goal to each menu category or subcategory, and then solve for an average target price for each category. Possible categories might be appetizers, salads, pastas, steaks, other main dishes, desserts, and beverages.

Food cost markup pricing is the most commonly used objective pricing strategy. It is simpler and more amenable to complicated and diverse menus. A restaurant chooses a food cost percentage. Prices for each dish are then set at the level that would make the food cost equal to the desired percentage. Mathematically,

$$P = \frac{Food\,Cost}{Food\%}. \qquad (12.7)$$

For example, if a restaurant wants a food cost percentage of 32 percent and a dish has a food cost of $3.52, the price would be P = $3.52/.32 = $11.00.

A restaurant using the food cost markup pricing strategy needs to establish the food cost in each dish. This is straightforward since the restaurant knows all its own recipes and certainly should be tracking the cost of all ingredients being purchased. Two factors complicate this seemingly simple strategy as restaurants actually practice it: changing ingredient costs and different food cost percentages for different types of dishes. Ingredient costs will change on a weekly basis for at least some of the ingredients that a restaurant uses. Because it is expensive to reprint menus and because regular customers do not like it when a restaurant's prices change frequently, most restaurants will not recompute the ideal price each time an ingredient's cost changes. Instead, the restaurant manager or owner is more likely to use an average ingredient cost over some recent period of time, say six months. Using these average ingredient costs and the desired food cost percentage, the menu prices for each dish can be solved for with equation (12.7).

The second complication to the food cost markup pricing strategy that is often employed is for a restaurant to use more than one food cost percentage, varying the desired target by menu category (appetizers, main dishes, desserts, beverages). For example, most restaurants use a lower food cost percentage for drinks than for food dishes. The food cost percentage for beverages is more commonly in the 15 percent to 25 percent range, making beverages the highest profit margin category in a restaurant. Restaurants also often use a lower food cost percentage on desserts. The high profit margins on drinks and desserts helps to explain why the wait staff in restaurants so commonly ask you whether you want something to drink or to order dessert. Using multiple food cost percentages does not make the math any harder in terms of implementing a food cost markup pricing strategy; it just means that the food cost percentage used in equation (12.7) changes depending on the menu item being priced.

The food cost markup pricing rule is the most commonly used menu pricing strategy in the food service industry for two reasons. First, it is easy to apply to multiple menu items. There is no need to apportion out fixed costs or profit across different menu items or categories. Instead, the rule works for each menu item individually without any modification or generalization. Second, the only information needed is the target food cost percentage and the cost of ingredients in a dish. This is a considerably smaller set of necessary information than needed for the profit goal pricing strategy. Food cost markup pricing is, for both these reasons, much easier to apply in real-world restaurants and bars.

The final objective pricing strategy is margin contribution pricing. This strategy is closely related to the break-even analysis studied earlier in the chapter. A restaurant owner or manager selects the average margin contribution desired from each item. The margin in question is usually gross profit plus non-food costs, where the non-food costs and the fixed costs plus the non-food variable costs. Once the average margin contribution (AvgContrib) is determined, it is added to each menu item's food cost to determine a menu price. Using the notation from earlier in the chapter, this approach can be expressed mathematically in two steps with the equations

$$\text{AvgContrib} = (\pi + \text{FC}) / N + \text{ANFVC} \qquad (12.8)$$

and

$$P = \text{FoodCost} + \text{AvgContrib}. \qquad (12.9)$$

This approach requires as much information as the profit goal pricing strategy, but is as flexible in regard to multiple menu items as the food cost markup pricing rule. Although as presented above the average margin contribution would be the same for all menu items, because food cost varies, each menu item would get a unique price. However, those prices would likely be rather close together, and if drinks are treated the same as main dishes, drinks would be very expensive in such a restaurant. Thus, it is more realistic for a restaurant to apportion the profit and fixed costs at least between beverages and food items and also to determine separately the average non-food variable costs for those two categories. Then one target average margin contribution can be computed for beverages and another for food items. This will produce more realistic pricing of beverages (assuming the apportioning is adjusted with that as the goal).

Such an approach will still produce a somewhat compressed set of menu prices compared to the range that will be observed if the food cost markup pricing approach is used. Food cost markup pricing implicitly is assigning a higher margin contribution to the menu items with higher food costs. So an expensive steak will add more to the margin than pasta primavera and much more than a cup of coffee. If you tend to order inexpensive items, you want to find a restaurant using food cost markup pricing; if you order filet mignon, you are better off under the margin contribution pricing strategy.

Changing menu prices

The reluctance of restaurants to change their menu prices is so renowned that in economics, "sticky" prices that change more slowly than economists think they should are referred to as *menu costs*. Menu costs refer to the actual cost of changing the prices (printing new menus). In the old days, restaurants did not change their prices often for two reasons: menus were actually quite expensive to print, and customers did not like prices to change. Today, many restaurants use paper menus printed in-house and could change prices easily using a personal computer and a little paper. In fact, restaurants that focus on seasonal food and fresh ingredients often print menus daily to emphasize their specialty. Clearly, the actual price of printing menus is less important today (in most cases) than it used to be. However, restaurants still do not like to change prices.

The reason that remains is that restaurant customers are very resistant to price increases. More than most consumer products, restaurants have repeat customers who buy the same product over and over and do not simultaneously buy other products that might help disguise price changes. We all buy certain items at the supermarket over and over, but we are generally buying an entire basket of goods, so if one or two items change prices, we just know groceries are getting more expensive, not necessarily which items are the cause. At a restaurant, many people stick to the same order and know what they are used to paying for it. To make matters worse, many restaurants offer takeout service and have distributed menus with their prices on them. Customers keep those menus and refer to them frequently. If the price charged does not match what they expect (even if the menu they looked at is several years old), the customer tends to complain. This is not necessarily rational, but it nonetheless really does happen—and happens frequently.

Obviously, restaurants do raise prices; they are not fixed forever. However, a restaurant will generally accept some noticeable loss in profit before raising prices and also expects many complaints and some (at least short-term) loss in business after it finally does increase its menu prices. Printing menus is much less expensive than it used to be, but restaurant prices are still "sticky" and slow to change.

Special pricing and marketing concepts

The above section has described a number of commonly used menu pricing methods. However, actual food service establishments use one or more of the above strategies as a starting point with modifications made for purposes of simplicity, based on competition, and for marketing purposes. For example, most restaurants would take the menu prices produced by whatever of the above menu pricing strategies they used and either round them to even dollar prices or to prices that end in a common amount such as $12.95, $14.95, etc. After that, more complicated marketing strategies can be applied to the menu.

One of the more common marketing strategies used in restaurants and bars is price discrimination. Early-bird specials are the most common form of price discrimination practiced by restaurants. An early-bird special offers diners a specified menu item (or choice from some subset of the full menu) at a reduced price if they eat early enough (usually from 5:00 to 6:00 pm or from 5:00 to 6:30 pm). The equivalent in bars is happy hour, where drink specials are used to entice customers to arrive at the bar early and start drinking. As mentioned in chapter 9, early-bird specials and happy hours make economic sense because staff must be on-site anyway to prepare for the peak business hours to come, so the labor costs are lower during those early hours (since much of the labor is essentially a sunk cost). The early-bird and happy hour special prices are also a form of advertising. Restaurants and bars hope to bring in new customers who will return later to pay full price; in fact, a bar can do both in one night as customers arrive for happy hour but stay long enough to buy full price drinks later in the same evening. Ladies nights are another form of price discrimination. Bars use ladies nights to bring in female customers by offering them lower prices with the hope that the women will bring in male customers who will have to pay full price for their drinks. Children's menus are a similar marketing mechanism for restaurants. These lower-priced (and usually low-profit) menu items encourage families to dine out, so the restaurant can benefit from the regularly priced menu items that the adults order.

Restaurants also use coupons and daily specials as common marketing devices. Coupons are a great way to bring in new customers who may be more willing to try a new restaurant if offered a lower price. The hope is that regular customers will not be looking for (or at least not notice) the coupon, and thus will still pay full price. Daily specials are sometimes a regular menu item offered at a special, lower price on one day per week, and other times are a new item that is not part of the standard menu. The first type of daily special is a marketing plan designed to attract customers to the restaurant who particularly like that menu item. The restaurant hopes that they either bring people with them who order higher-priced menu items or order other menu items themselves while there (like beverages and desserts). The other type of special is often one of the more expensive menu items. It has two purposes: to encourage customers to order more expensive items (either the expensive special or a regular menu item that is perhaps slightly less expensive) and to allow the chef to use a particular ingredient. When a chef sees a particularly attractive ingredient, she may want to buy it and create a special menu item so she can feature it. Alternatively, when a chef has too much of some ingredient and needs to use it before it spoils, the chef may create a special to help use up the ingredient more quickly.

The final marketing topic is menu design. A well-run restaurant carefully plans every aspect of its menu from layout, fonts, and the order that menu items are presented in. Generally, a restaurant menu starts with appetizers, salads, and soups, then lists main dishes, and finally covers desserts (unless the desserts are listed on a separate menu). Within a category such as main dishes, a menu designer has the opportunity to decide on the order the menu items are presented in. Usually, similar items are placed together (pastas, steaks, chicken dishes, fish, etc.); however, the ordering of those groups is done differently by different people. Some start with the inexpensive items and end with the most expensive, whereas others do the reverse; some do not order the dishes by price at all. A further price-related marketing ploy is the stand-out high- or low-price menu item. For example, with most main dishes ranging from $15 to $25, a menu might contain one main dish (perhaps steak or lobster) that is $30. The stand-out high price menu item is designed to make those $22–$25 dishes seem to be reasonably priced and get more people to order those rather than the more inexpensive dishes on the menu. Customers are not really expected to order the stand-out high price item very often. The stand-out low price menu item is different. It is usually a dish with a very low food cost (perhaps a simple pasta dish), so that while it may be the lowest-priced dish in its category, it is by no means the least profitable. The restaurant owner is quite happy to have customers order the stand-out low price menu item.

Labor and pay issues

Cafeteria, restaurant, and bar management has more than its share of labor issues. The industry has some special pay rules that allow a lower minimum wage to be paid to workers who receive tips. Food service businesses also tend to have higher labor turnover rates than most other businesses, and the costs of that turnover are not trivial.

Special minimum wage and tip rules

Employees who regularly receive tips are allowed to be paid below the minimum wage by their employer as long as the tips bring the total hourly wage up to the minimum wage (currently $7.25). Employers still must pay a direct wage of at least $2.13 per hour, regardless of how much an employee earns in tips. Employees who do not typically receive tips, such as dishwashers and kitchen staff, cannot be paid this lower wage. It is the employer's responsibility to keep track of each employee's tips sufficiently to ensure that all employees receive at least the full minimum wage.

The federal government also has a set of rules about tip pools, which are not uncommon in restaurants. A tip pool is some sort of system by which tips are shared among different members of a restaurant's service team, often moving some money from wait staff to bussers and/or bartenders. Tip pools can only include workers who receive tips. Restaurants must clearly explain any tip pool to all employees and cannot use the tip pool to distribute any of the tips to employees who do not typically receive tips, such as cooks, chefs, managers, or hosts. While the law is very clear on this point, restaurants seem to violate these rules constantly. A recent example involved celebrity chef Mario Batali who agreed in 2012 to settle claims that eight of his restaurants had been operating illegal tip pools since 2007; management was accused of keeping some of the money. The settlement will involve management paying $5.25 million, which will be distributed to over 1000 employees who participated in the tip pools that violated the law.[2]

Minimum wage impacts

Restaurants often have many workers earning at or near the minimum wage. Restaurant owners and managers need to be aware of the minimum wage even when they have no or few employees getting paid at that mark. Workers who earn at or near the minimum wage know what the minimum wage is and, if they are above the minimum wage, they know how far they are above minimum wage. When the minimum wage is increased, restaurant owners must pay any minimum wage employees more, and they also need to give raises to any workers who were above the old minimum wage but are below the new minimum wage. Beyond that, workers who are getting paid slightly above the new minimum wage will feel slighted if they do not receive a raise to put their earnings back to roughly the same amount above the new minimum wage as they were above the old one. Thus, an increase in the minimum wage has a cascade effect on the food service industry. Owners are forced to increase wages for a large number of employees because each time they raise the pay of one worker, other workers who made a little more than the first employee expect a similar raise.

The overhead costs of employees

The overhead costs of employees have three components. The first is the cost of any benefits offered to the workers that are paid by the employer. The second is the cost of taxes levied on employers based on employee wages. The third is the administrative, accounting, and training costs of the employees that are born by the employer. These will be covered in order below.

Most food service employees are offered few benefits that add to the owner's cost of the employees. Workers in larger food service organizations (big cafeterias, hotel kitchens, and dining rooms, university food service employees, etc.) are the most likely to get benefits such as health insurance or retirement plans, especially in locations where the workers are unionized. Some higher-end restaurants may also offer such benefits to their workers because they want to minimize employee turnover and they can charge high enough menu prices to pay the extra labor costs. If an employer offers paid sick or vacation days, these must also be accounted for as an employee benefit with a cost.

In addition to any benefit costs, employers are always required to pay employment taxes. In the United States, the federal government charges two employment taxes: one for social security and one for Medicare. The social security taxes, to pay for promised future retirement payments, are levied at a rate of 6.2 percent of wages and tips paid up to a wage ceiling in 2012 of $110,100, with the employees having to pay an equal amount that is withheld from their paychecks. Each year, the wage ceiling on which social security taxes are collected is raised to keep up with inflation and to try to collect enough money to fund the system. Medicare taxes, which go toward qualifying for health insurance after the age of 65, are an additional 1.45 percent of wages, with no limit this time. Employees again pay an equal 1.45 percent in Medicare taxes on their wages and tips. On top of these federal employment taxes, food service businesses will generally also pay an unemployment premium tax to their state government. This tax is designed to pay unemployment benefits to workers who have been laid off. The amount of unemployment taxes vary by state but generally is based on the total wages paid to eligible employees and the employer's past track record of layoffs. Together, these three taxes make up the employment tax cost of employees in the food service (or any other) industry.

The cost of employee benefits and taxes are obvious overhead costs associated with direct labor costs. However, it is important not to neglect indirect costs such as managerial oversight, accounting and payroll costs, and training expenses. Accounting and payroll costs are not trivial and should not be ignored. An employer has to pay to have a new employee's tax withholding information collected and entered into her accounting system, for the owner or her accountant to add the new employee to the payroll system, and for whatever advertisement, interviews, and background and reference checks are carried out as part of the hiring process. Training costs are also important. A food service business must divert another employee to train a new one, while paying both of them to likely do less work than one fully trained employee.

In total, these costs are not inconsequential. The hiring and training of a new employee costs a minimum of $300. Then the taxes, benefits, and administrative costs add somewhere between 10 percent and 30 percent to the hourly cost of an employee above their stated wage rate. These costs give food service businesses an incentive to minimize employee turnover. If workers do not stay with one employer long enough to cover these costs, the business will lose money. Thus, an important part of restaurant and bar management is to identify the better workers and to keep them happy so that they stay with the business longer. Common ways to keep these workers happy include raises, giving better workers their choice of shifts, and increasing benefits with longevity.

Franchises

One common feature of the restaurant industry is franchise restaurants. Many of the best-known names are franchises: McDonalds, Wendy's, Subway, and

Baskin-Robbins, to name just a few, are all chains comprising mostly franchise stores. In simple terms, a franchise restaurant is one where a franchiser who owns the restaurant concept sells franchisees the right to operate restaurants using the specific brand name, menus, and all-around look and feel of the restaurant. In other words, the franchisee, who owns the actual restaurant, pays for the privilege of copying a successful restaurant's format.

Operating a franchise restaurant has advantages for the franchisee (who operates the restaurant) and the franchiser (who owns the intellectual capital of the restaurant concept). The franchisee greatly lowers the risk involved in opening and operating a restaurant. Government statistics typically find that 95 percent of restaurants close in any five-year period. Franchise restaurants have a much higher success rate, because the concept is proven already and because franchise restaurants have the additional benefit of enormous advertising and familiarity. A single restaurant cannot possibly afford to advertise as much as a chain of restaurants can; so franchisees gain a benefit by pooling their advertising dollars and reaching a larger audience of potential customers. Familiarity is also very helpful. When people travel or move to new locations, franchise restaurants provide a known quantity, a restaurant that customers can go to with clear expectations of what meals will be available and, often, what menu items they like. The benefit of familiarity is why franchise restaurants are so prevalent along highways; the owners are counting on travelers to choose the familiar over taking a risk trying something new.

Franchisers get a different benefit: access to capital to fund the expansion of their chain. It is possible to build an enormous chain of restaurants without franchising, Chick-Fil-A has over 1,000 restaurants all owned by the corporation, but it takes longer and means investing profits into the expansion instead of the owners getting to enjoy spending those profits. Under a standard franchise model, the franchiser takes a share of the revenue from licensed restaurants, while not having to pay anything to open those restaurants. The franchisee invests the necessary capital to expand the chain. While the franchiser ends up sharing profits with the franchisees, the profits gained from more rapid expansion are deemed more valuable than the eventual larger profits from maintaining full ownership of all restaurants in the chain.

The basic franchise operation works as follows. Somebody starts a restaurant that proves to be successful. After a period of time, the owner opens more stores, confirming that the concept works and can be replicated. With a suitable history of successful operation behind it and a desire to expand more rapidly than the restaurant's profits would allow, the owner decides to enter the franchise business. To do this, a company is formed to be the franchiser. This corporation owns the brand trademarks (logos, menus, packaging), anything distinctive that identifies the restaurant chain to its customers. The franchiser then sells the right to operate restaurants using the brand to individuals who will open and operate restaurants under the umbrella brand of the franchiser. These restaurants will look the same, have the same food, and are designed to be more or less exact duplicates of all other restaurants in the chain. The franchiser and franchisee sign a franchise agreement that covers all the terms. This agreement spells out the initial franchise fee paid for the right to open the restaurant, the share of operating revenues that will be paid to the franchiser while the restaurant operates, any other fees that must be paid (a fee for joint advertising is common), and exactly how much control the franchiser has over the look, feel, and operation of the restaurant. For example, does the franchiser control menu prices and choice of input suppliers; can the franchiser force the franchisee to remodel, to offer new menu items, to be open certain hours? The agreement also usually has a term with an option for renewal perhaps requiring payment of another fee, and often gives the franchisee some protection that the franchiser will not allow another restaurant to open within some set distance of the restaurant or that would reduce the population closest to that restaurant to below some level.

Thus, the operator of a franchise restaurant gives up a fair bit of control over the operation of her restaurant. The gains include the above-mentioned lower risk, advertising muscle, a central research and product development team, and the advantage of not having to invent a new restaurant concept. Opening a new business involves a fair amount of creativity and perhaps coming up with something new that will attract customers. A franchise operator can concentrate on running the restaurant, rather than on strategy.

To give the reader some idea of the numbers involved in some common franchise restaurants, Table 12.1 shows the franchise fees, royalties paid, and several other features of some common national and regional franchise restaurant chains. You can see that there is some significant variety to these licensing arrangements, as well as to the total investment needed by the franchisee in order to open a restaurant.

In addition to the standard franchise models, there are a few hybrid systems to be found in the restaurant industry. McDonald's is the most famous, with the franchiser owning the actual land and building for the restaurant while the franchisee operates the store and pays rent to McDonald's. In some sense the McDonald's franchising company is more a real estate than a restaurant company. There are also some franchising companies that prefer their operators to own

Table 12.1 Franchise terms and details for some common chains

Restaurant	Number of restaurants	Franchise fee	Royalty fee (% of sales)	Advertising fee (% of sales)	Estimated cost to open ($)
Arby's	3,700+	$37,500	4%	4.2%	500,000–2,500,000
Burger King	7,000+	$50,000	4.5	4	1,200,000–2,200,000
Jamba Juice	700+	$25,000	6	2–4	350,000–640,000
McDonald's	33,000+	$45,000	4		1,000,000–1,850,000
Moe's	850+	$30,000	5		450,000–769,000
Subway	36,000+	$15,000	8	4.5	115,000–$260,000
Wendy's	6,300+	$25,000	4	4	1,600,000–2,700,000
Zaxby's	500+	$35,000			

multiple stores. For example, Jamba Juice wants franchisees to open at least three stores. Panera Bread sells rights to a market area within which the franchisee can open up to 15 stores.

Some small franchise chains are not big enough to have their own input suppliers or supply chain, and so franchisees order food and other supplies from large industry wholesalers such as Sysco in a manner essentially the same as an independent restaurant would do. As chains grow larger, they tend to increase control over input supplier choices and eventually move to a single, standardized set of suppliers (who often ship to distribution centers from where supplies are sent to restaurants in a single truck that contains all the items needed to keep the store operating). The centralization of the supply chain tends to lower costs and also provides for standardization of the restaurant product, so that customers see the same food, wrapping, and even drink cups no matter what restaurant they go to in that chain.

Franchise restaurants are a common feature of the restaurant industry. They operate similarly to an independent restaurant in the sense that both of them serve meals to customers. However, they are different in that franchise restaurant owners cannot revamp the menu unless the entire chain does, may not have full control over prices, and generally purchase food and supplies from either their franchiser or from a list of approved suppliers. While franchise restaurant owners have less control over these features, they can focus even more on efficient restaurant operation since that is fully within their control. The next section describes some ways to evaluate the efficiency of a restaurant's operation.

Evaluation metrics

To evaluate the performance of a food service business, managers and owners have a number of quantitative metrics they can use as tools to guide them in attempts to lead their business to higher profitability. Different metrics can be used to test the financial health of the business, the quality of inventory management, the skill of overall business operations management, and the performance of the business from an investment point of view.

Operating metrics

Beginning with some operational management metrics, a good place to start is with the inventory turnover ratio. The inventory turnover ratio is defined as

$$\text{Inventory turnover ratio} = \frac{\text{annual cost of goods used}}{\text{average monthly inventory}} \quad (12.10)$$

where higher numbers are good. If the inventory turnover ratio is low, that means the restaurant is carrying too large an inventory. This is particularly bad management in the food service industry because customers do not want to be eating food that has been in the restaurant for a long time. If a restaurant does a good job of managing inventory, it will not run out of food needed to fill orders, but will not tie of large sums of capital by carrying extra inventory either. Most bars and restaurants get deliveries daily for fresh ingredients and several times a week for items with longer shelf lives. Thus, for most items there is little need to carry excess inventory beyond what is needed for a few days.

Another operational management metric that applies mainly to sit-down restaurants is the seat turnover. This measures how good a job the restaurant is doing of utilizing its seating capacity. Seat turnover is defined as

$$\text{Seat turnover} = \frac{\text{guests served}}{\text{number of seats available}}. \quad (12.11)$$

To properly compute the seat turnover, the time frame for the numerator and denominator must be the same. So if the guests served number is for a week, then the number of seats available should be for the number of seats in the restaurant times the number of meal slots that the restaurant was open. For example, if a restaurant is evaluating just their dinner efficiency, and the restaurant is open for dinner six nights per week, the number of seats would be six times the actual number of seats in the restaurant and the number of guests served would be total dinner customers in a week. A restaurant can also compute the seat turnover for a whole day, combining the guests served for all meals that the restaurant serves.

Seat turnover is generally referred to in the industry as *turns*, where a seat turnover of 2.3, for example, would be called 2.3 turns. For dinner service, most restaurants need 2 turns or greater to make money; at lunch time, a somewhat lower figure is often okay, perhaps 1.5 turns. More turns are better because that means the restaurant is earning more revenue for the same investment in rent, kitchen, and dining room décor. More turns means spreading those fixed costs over a larger number of meals served, so that the average fixed cost per meal drops. A restaurant with a low seat turnover is wasting money on more space than it needs, which indicates poor management in terms of matching space needs to space rented or purchased.

Restaurant and bar managers are also specifically evaluated based on their performance separated as much as possible from other facets of the restaurant's operation. One simple metric is the labor cost ratio. The labor cost ratio is given by

$$\text{Labor cost ratio} = \frac{\text{labor cost}}{\text{total sales}} \quad (12.12)$$

where a manager should be trying to keep labor costs low relative to the total sales. A value somewhere around 30 percent would be considered good performance on managing labor costs. If the labor cost is too high, it would indicate that the manager is overstaffing the restaurant. A manager in such a situation would work hard to send workers home when business is slow in order to better manage staffing levels.

A sophisticated metric for evaluating a restaurant manager is the managerial operating efficiency ratio, which is given by

$$\text{Managerial operating efficiency ratio} = \frac{\text{operating income} + \text{depreciation} + \text{occupancy costs}}{\text{gross revenues}}. \quad (12.13)$$

Operating income is the restaurant profit before taxes, to which are added the depreciation expenses and occupancy costs in the form of rent or loan payments for the restaurant's space and major equipment. The reason for adding the depreciation and occupancy costs to the operating income is to remove the effect of those expenses on profit because the depreciation and occupancy costs are generally based on decisions made by the owner, not the manager. They are fixed costs while the goal is to evaluate managerial skill in the ongoing operation of the restaurant. Adding back in these two big fixed costs makes the ratio essentially a gross operating profit margin. A higher managerial operating efficiency ratio is better as it implies that the manager is doing a good job of producing lots of gross operating profit from each dollar of sales.

Financial metrics

Many of the metrics that can be used to evaluate the financial performance of a restaurant or bar are just standard metrics used to evaluate businesses in any industry; thus, they may be familiar to readers who have taken finance classes. A simple metric to assess the financial health of a food service business is the current ratio. The current ratio is given by

$$\text{current ratio} = \frac{\text{current assets}}{\text{current liabilities}} \quad (12.14)$$

where current assets are cash, accounts receivable (money owed to the business), the value of inventory, and any prepaid revenues (such as money from selling gift cards); and current liabilities are short-term debts such as accounts payable, accrued wages, and other short-term debts. Bars and restaurants should watch their current ratio for deterioration. Changes in this ratio are probably more informative than its actual level, so a restaurant or bar owner should compute and track this metric monthly.

A measure of the financial management in a bar or restaurant is the accounts receivable turnover ratio. This metric is defined as

$$\text{charge sales turnover ratio} = \frac{\text{charge sales}}{\text{average charge sales receivable}} \quad (12.15)$$

where charge sales are the total for a year, while the average is the average amount owed to the restaurant by the credit card companies at any point in time.

A high ratio is good as that means that the business is collecting its money quickly. In fact, if you divide 365 by the charge sales turnover ratio, the result is the average number of days the business is waiting to get its money.

Two important metrics for measuring the financial performance are the return on equity (ROE) and the return on assets (ROA). These two metrics are given by

$$\text{return on equity} = \frac{\text{annual net income}}{\text{average owner equity}} \quad (12.16)$$

and

$$\text{return on assets} = \frac{\text{annual net income}}{\text{average total assets}}. \quad (12.17)$$

The return on assets measures the business's net income relative to the total assets being employed to earn that income. Higher ROAs are better, and a value of approximately 5 percent would not be unusual. If assets are not earning a sufficient return, then the owner of those assets could earn more money by reinvesting them more profitability and will not want to stay in the restaurant business. The return on equity uses only equity in the denominator, not total assets (the difference being debt financing). ROE is always equal to or greater than ROA because equity cannot be larger than total assets. If a restaurant or bar has borrowed to finance assets (such as their building or kitchen equipment), that leverage allows for a higher return to be earned on the actual amount invested by the owner. While ROA is often around 5 percent, the ROE should generally be above 10 percent. Over any five-year period, somewhere around 50 percent–70 percent of restaurants go out of business.[3] Given the risk involved in investing in a food service business, the return on that investment should compensate for that risk.

A regulatory metric

A final metric that restaurants sometimes need to track is the food–beverage sales ratio. This measure is generally computed as

$$\text{food-beverage sales ratio} = \frac{\text{food sales}}{\text{total sales}}. \quad (12.18)$$

The reason that this metric can be important is that in many cities restaurants and bars are governed by different local ordinances controlling issues such as operating hours, allowable locations, and the cost of annual operating licenses. The way that most local governments decide whether a business is a bar or a restaurant is the food–beverage sales ratio. If the food sales do not constitute a large enough share of total sales, the business will be declared a bar and regulated accordingly.

150 *The food service industry*

Therefore, some restaurants that do a large amount of business in alcoholic beverage sales must watch this metric carefully to ensure that they stay on the correct side of the regulatory line.

Summary

This chapter covered one of the more visible sectors within the food industry: the food service sector. Bars, restaurants, cafeterias, and catering businesses all face some special situations along with all the regular precepts of economics that govern the behavior of any business. Labor issues and inventory control tend to be more important facets of management in the food service industry.

Labor issues are important in the food service industry because labor costs are a large share of total costs and because they are one of the easiest ones to control through effective management. Therefore, a large part of the management effort in the food service industry is directed toward hiring, training, scheduling, firing, and retaining workers. The food service industry also has some specialized laws and regulations concerning labor and pay, so care must be taken to obey all the rules, and some special education is necessary in this area even if one is used to dealing with payroll and labor issues in another industry.

Various methods for determining the pricing of menu items were discussed in this chapter, ranging from the extremely ad hoc methods to fairly "scientific" ones with clear rules and numerical formulas for implementing them. By far the most common in the industry is the food cost markup pricing rule, where menu items are priced as a multiple of the cost of the ingredients in each menu item. This method is flexible, in that it can handle all sorts of menu items and can be generalized easily to use different markups for different categories (such as drinks). Common rules set the food cost to somewhere between 28 percent and 36 percent of the menu price, while drink prices usually keep the beverage cost in the 15 percent to 25 percent range. The chapter also explained why restaurant prices tend to be "sticky," with owners reluctant to raise prices even when costs are increasing.

The chapter also discussed a variety of ways to evaluate the performance of a food service business. Some of the metrics covered apply to the daily operation of the business and are therefore very appropriate for evaluating the manager. Others focus more on the financial health or financial management of the business and would be of use to the owner in measuring the performance of her investment and also her own overall management of the business operation.

Chapter highlights

- Food service businesses have a variety of methods they can use to set menu prices, ranging from subjective pricing rules (such as competitive pricing) to objective pricing rules (such as food cost markup pricing).

- Food cost markup pricing is the most widely used pricing method in the food service industry. Prices are set according to the simple rule

  P = FoodCost/Food%.

- The food cost percentage is usually set somewhere between 28 percent and 36 percent for meals and somewhere between 15 percent and 25 percent for beverages. Even food service businesses that do not use the food cost markup pricing rule tend to have food cost percentages in these same ranges.
- Labor issues are very important in food service management as labor is usually the largest cost category and is also the category over which the manager has the most control.
- Workers who commonly receive tips can be paid a direct wage that is lower than the standard minimum wage ($2.13 versus $7.25 per hour), but the business must ensure that the worker collects enough tips so that his total hourly earnings are at or above the minimum wage. If not, the business must make up the difference.
- Tip pools are common in the restaurant industry and are legal under strict conditions. Unfortunately, restaurants often operate tip pools that violate the rules.
- Franchise restaurants offer an opportunity for people to open and operate a restaurant without needing to invent a new restaurant concept. Franchises also offer a much lower risk of failure than independent restaurants (which have a very high failure rate).
- Franchisees typically pay an upfront franchise fee and then ongoing royalty payments equal to some specified amount of gross sales. The royalty payments partly represent a licensing fee for the use of the restaurant concept and a part usually goes into a pool used to pay for advertising.
- Food service businesses can be evaluated by a number of different metrics. Some measure financial management, some daily operations management, and others track various facets of the business so that the business owner or manager can continually track the performance and the efficiency of the business.

Practice problems

Use the following restaurant details to answer these questions:

- The restaurant can seat 50 people at a time.
- Fixed costs for salaries, rent, some utilities, property tax, and advertising run $5,000 per month.
- Variable costs other than food (linens, hourly labor, dishes, and disposable supplies) run $3 per customer on average.
- The restaurant is open Tuesday–Saturday for dinner only.

152   The food service industry

1. If the restaurant wants to keep the food cost at 32 percent, what price does the restaurant have to charge for a meal with $3.50 in food ingredients?
2. If the average ticket runs $10 per customer with a food cost of 35 percent, how many meals must be served before the restaurant breaks even?
3. If you want to make a profit of $5,000 per month, how many turns (customers per seat per night) do you need to average?
4. If the best realistic estimate of turns is 1.5 for your restaurant and you keep food cost to 35 percent, what average ticket price do you need to hit your profit goal?

13 Food retailers

Food retailing has been the fastest-changing part of the food industry over the past 50 years, especially when a global perspective is taken. In pretty much the entire world except the United States, supermarkets were essentially unknown 30 years ago. Food retailers were small and often specialized. In England, 30 years ago, small, general markets existed that one could shop at for a broad selection of merchandise, but most shoppers went there for dry goods, canned goods, beverages, and non-food items such as laundry detergent. The shoppers bought meat at a butcher, produce at a green grocer, cheese at a cheese shop, and bread at a bakery. This pattern held in general for most of Europe. In less developed countries, markets were even smaller, with much of food retailing occurring at market stalls with an owner selling a single or a few items. Only in the United States were supermarkets, large-format stores selling a complete portfolio of food, food-related, and household items, prevalent.

Today, supermarkets and similar wide-ranging formats are rapidly taking over the world of food retailing. Many more people world-wide do all their grocery shopping in a single place, or at least do a large share of it there. The United States is actually the one place were supermarkets are seeing a declining market share. In 1997, US supermarkets had a 72 percent share of the grocery market; today that is down to 59 percent. Supermarkets have been losing ground to supercenters and club stores (Sam's, Costco, Target, and Walmart). To see a graph of current US market shares for grocery sales and how they have been changing, see Figure 13.1.

Food retailing is an important part of the food industry, representing over $650 billion in annual sales.[1] That is, over 4 percent of the US GDP makes up roughly half of all consumer expenditures on food (with the other half being spent on food away from home, meaning restaurants, coffee shops, vending machines, etc.). This chapter will look at some of the special features that are key to the economics and management of food retailing today.

The three main formats

The three main formats for food retailing in the United States are supermarkets, club stores/supercenters, and convenience stores. While in other countries smaller, specialty shops that focus on one category (produce, cheese, meats, or

154 *Food retailers*

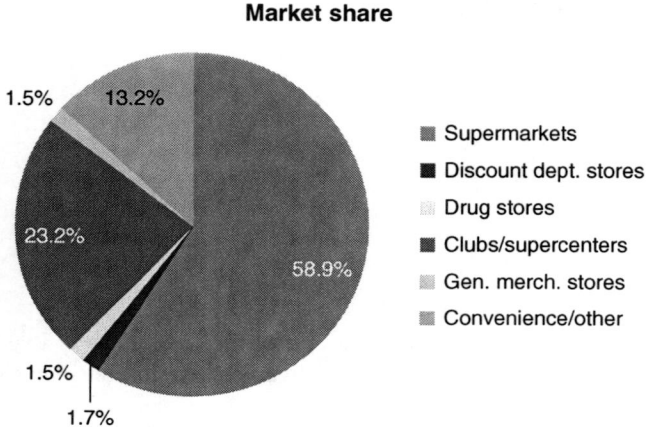

Figure 13.1 Market share pie chart.

bakery products most commonly) are fairly common, such shops represent a tiny share of the US market both overall and within their categories. The exception in the United States is the category of wine and other alcoholic beverages, where specialized liquor stores have a significant market share. Most of the growth in the food retailing industry in the United States has been in club stores and supercenters along with select supermarket chains that have found growth by clearly defining a niche within the supermarket category. In other countries, the supermarket format has been the growth format as supermarkets have become firmly established worldwide.

Supercenters and club stores focus on low prices. The club stores accomplish this by selling a limited selection of goods that they can purchase at favorable wholesale prices, by mostly selling goods in large containers, and by spending as little as possible on the store's interior. Club stores also generally charge an annual membership fee that serves to aid the stores in offering low prices. In fact, Sam's Club tries to price goods so that averaged across all goods sold, the chain breaks even; the plan is for all the profits to be from the membership fees. Supercenters, a category dominated by Walmart, also focuses on low prices but keeps its prices low through different mechanisms. Supercenters push suppliers for low wholesale prices in exchange for purchasing in large volumes and work hard to keep their overhead and logistical costs low, using that efficiency to deliver low prices to their customers. Supercenters (and club stores) also have the advantage of having non-food items represent a significant (even majority) share of their total sales. This allows their overhead to be spread over a larger dollar volume so that grocery prices can be kept a little lower.

Convenience stores, a sometimes overlooked segment of food retailing, actually represent about one-eighth of all retail food sales. These stores, often co-located with a gas station in the United States, carry a much narrower selection of goods, usually focused on beverages, snacks, and dry goods with long shelf-lives. Convenience stores get a large segment of their sales from beverages and from cigarettes, which are both typically high-profit-margin items. This allows convenience stores to offer competitive prices on beverages and even surprisingly low prices at times. Many people may not realize it, but the least expensive milk in town is often for sale at a local convenience store.

Supermarkets are the store format with the largest market share within food retailing, representing over 50 percent of all sales. Americans take supermarkets for granted (we have 35,000 of them), and residents in the rest of the world are rapidly reaching the same point where supermarkets are normal and expected, but supermarkets are a modern invention and actually quite remarkable if one stops to think about them. An average supermarket sells 50,000 different items in a store consisting of around 50,000 square feet, taking in an average of $500,000 per week in sales revenue.[2] Amazingly enough, on most days, your neighborhood supermarket will be out of fewer than 100 of those 50,000 items. And the average supermarket operates on such a narrow profit margin that it will only earn approximately $10,000 at the end of that week.

The supermarket format, however, is not generic enough these days to be treated as a single, uniform store type. Rather, supermarkets come not just in many brands, but in many flavors. There are the familiar, standard supermarkets offering a full range of products in a store likely between 50,000 and 80,000 square feet. There are value chains that focus more on low prices, usually in a smaller-format store stocked heavily with store-brand and generic items. There are high-end markets that highlight products such as organic produce, extensive deli items (ready-to-eat dishes), and high-quality seafood and meat items. These high-end markets have been at the forefront of expanding access to organic and local fruits, vegetables, seafood, meat, and dairy products. Whole Foods is the most famous of these chains, and this high-end subcategory is the fastest-growing segment of the supermarket sector; these stores are the ones helping supermarkets hold on to their market share while supercenters and club stores have been gaining market share at the expense of the standard supermarket chains.

In fact, the whole supermarket sector is moving toward one end of the format range or the other. Stores (chains) are either moving in the Whole Foods direction of high quality or in the opposite direction to identify as low-priced value chains. Store sizes are moving either toward smaller formats of perhaps 35,000 square feet or larger boxes in the neighborhood of 100,000 square feet. Supermarket executives are definitely betting on the death of the middle, segmenting customers into either the high-end, quality-motivated shoppers who are not overly price sensitive or value-motivated shoppers who care more about low prices than quality or brand selection.

The supermarket format is mostly made up of chains (Safeway, Albertson's, Publix, Kroger, etc.), but not exclusively. Approximately 20 percent of US supermarket sales come from independent stores that are not part of any large chain. These stores often are in small towns, but some independent stores exist and

Can organic and corporate coexist?

Sales of organic food products have grown rapidly to their current $30 billion per year in the United States, representing between 4 percent and 5 percent of US food retail sales. This perspective shows that while sales of organic food products has grown, they are still a small part of the total food industry. However, many of the makers and sellers of those organic products are no longer small companies.

Some of the common brands for organic products we see in our supermarkets are owned by the same companies that make the traditional products we have eaten for years. Bear Naked and Kashi brands are owned by Kellogg; Naked Juice is a Pepsi brand. As reported recently in the *New York Times*, giant food companies such as Cargill, Coca-Cola, ConAgra, Kraft, General Mills, and M&M Mars all now have organic product lines to augment their traditionally manufactured products.[5]

Along with this increase in large corporations producing both conventional and organic products has been a shift in limits of what ingredients are allowed to be used in those certified organic products. As Strom documents in her *New York Times* article, approved ingredients now include such non-natural sounding items as docosahexaenoic acid algae oil (DHA) and arachidonic acid single cell oil (ARA). Many supporters of the ideals of organics are frustrated by this move by organic manufacturers to become big business and to move away from their previous devotion to fully natural products. However, it appears to be a trend that will continue, at least until consumers begin to notice and stop buying these products.

---

survive in larger towns and cities. They might specialize in customer service, in lower prices, in local products, or just have a great location. Regardless of what the independent store does to distinguish itself, it does something to earn customer loyalty and compete in the face of the logistical and volume advantages of the large supermarket chains.

Pricing and profit margins

Price setting in a grocery store is a highly complex process, with stores trading off between their desires for high enough prices to earn profits and the reality of needing low enough prices to attract shoppers. Further adding to the difficulty is that food retailers do not have complete freedom to set prices on many of the items in their stores. Depending on the product category and even the specific manufacturer, a store may have full, partial, or no control over the retail price it will charge for a product.

At the most basic level, food retailers (and retailers in general) often begin with the simple choice of strategy for price variability: do they want to be known for everyday low prices or will they have higher regular prices with occasional sales when those prices are discounted. Retailers and marketing specialists often refer to these two strategies as EDLP and Hi-Lo. Retailers who choose the everyday low-price strategy typically target their advertising to lower-income and more value-conscious customers, emphasize their low prices in their marketing, and generally work very hard to create the perception of value among their target market. Prime examples of such a strategy in food retailing are Walmart and Bi-Lo (a supermarket chain in the southeastern United States). Stores that practice Hi-Lo pricing are both aiming for a higher-income, less price-conscious customer base and also simultaneously trying to attract new, value-conscious customers with advertised specials. If the strategy works, a store maintains a good customer base of regulars who like the specials sprinkled around the store while paying the regular prices for other items and then augments those shoppers with less regular customers who come in when a particular special sale catches their attention. Both pricing strategies can be effective, but a store generally must clearly choose one or the other.

The next step for a food retailer is to begin setting prices for individual products. This starts by considering the wholesale price paid to acquire an item, what competing retailers are selling the same item for, the price elasticity of the item, and the particular store's cost structure. For staple products with high-price visibility that stores compete with each other on, the price markup may be considerably lower than on a product with inelastic demand that figures less prominently in a customer's choice of store destination. Food retailers apply different price markups to products depending on these categories, with lower markups on some products to bring in shoppers (perhaps even planning to lose money on a product—the oft-referred-to "loss leader") and higher markups on other products that will support that pricing level and provide the profits necessary to keep a store in business.

In fact, food retailers often separate products into one of four categories, based on their sales volume and average profit margin: a support category, a destination category, a preferred category, and an ideal category.[3] Items in the support category are low-sales-volume and low-profit-margin products. A store carries these items simply because they are expected to have them in stock as a full service food retailer. A destination category product has a high sales volume, but a low profit margin. These are high-profile items such as bathroom tissue, diapers, milk, and eggs that stores use to attract shoppers to their store. Pricing on these products is designed to bring shoppers into the store more than it is designed to earn the store a profit. Preferred category products are low-sales-volume and high-profit-margin items, such as certain gourmet food products. Stores are happy to sell these products, but because the sales volume is not that high, they contribute only a limited amount to the store's profit. Finally, ideal category products are those with high sales volume and high profit margin. These products, such as brand name spaghetti sauce or premium ice cream, are everything a store could wish for, and the success of a store in selling these items largely determines its profitability. So a store puts a lot of effort into convincing shoppers—through advertising, displays, and pricing—to buy products in the ideal category (and to a lesser extent, those in the preferred category).

Food retailing is, for the most part, a very low-margin business. The average supermarket has a profit margin of around 2 percent, meaning it makes only 2 cents from every dollar of sales. Walmart, with its emphasis on low prices, appears to lose money on its grocery business (Walmart does not publicly disclose results for its grocery business). Those small profit margins mean that food retailers are always striving to improve their operating efficiency, to find ways to lower overhead costs, to convince shoppers to buy a few additional items on each shopping trip (especially some of the higher-profit-margin items in the store), or anything that can bring in new revenue.

One of the ways stores seek to increase revenue is through the use of slotting fees. Within a grocery store, the placement of a product can have an enormous impact on its sales. Items on shelves at eye level sell better than those that are higher or lower levels. The displays at the ends of aisles are also prime locations for catching the attention of shoppers. Stores capitalize on this fact by charging the food processing companies for their placement within the store; this charge is called the slotting fee. Slotting fees can be several hundred dollars per linear foot of shelf space, with better placements costing more money. In general, slotting fees are paid by branded products: soft drinks, breakfast cereals, pastas, canned soups, ice creams, canned fruits and vegetables; all the items with known name brands are likely paying for their spots in the grocery store. The exceptions have

Does Walmart lower all grocery prices?

An interesting study by Richard Volpe and Nathalie Lavoie examined the impact of Walmart supercenters on the grocery prices in a region.[6] What they found was very revealing. First, Walmart has the lowest grocery prices in the food retailing industry; they can be 14 percent–23 percent cheaper on national brands and 7 percent–18 percent lower on store brands. Second, in neighborhoods where other supermarkets have to compete with Walmart, conventional supermarkets lower the prices of their national brand products by 6 percent–7 percent and lower prices on their private label products by between 3 percent and 8 percent. The effects were found to vary by category, with big impacts on dairy product prices and no discernible impact on prices for frozen foods. Taking these prices changes and an average family's grocery spending into account, Volpe and Lavoie estimate that an average family could save $100 per year on groceries thanks to Walmart opening in town even though that family keeps shopping at a conventional supermarket.

been store-brand items, generics, most fresh produce, and the meat and seafood counter. As brands have become more prevalent in fresh produce and meats, the supermarket chains are beginning attempts to negotiate slotting fees for these products as well, expanding the list of items that pay to get stocked and to secure favorable locations within the store. Slotting fees are also more prevalent and higher for new products, with manufacturers agreeing to pay higher slotting fees to get into the stores and build a business (even up to $1 or 2 million to get in a large chain of stores).[4] If the product proves successful and sells well, slotting fees will generally decline to a lower level in order to retain it in the store and maintain a good location.

Another way that stores have strived to increase their profits is by lowering the carrying cost of their inventories. To that end, it is becoming increasingly common for items to be on the store shelves while the grocery store has not yet purchased those items. When a customer actually buys an item, the grocery store "simultaneously" buys it from the producer and only then does the grocery store owe the producer the payment for the item. This lowers the grocery store's costs because they do not need to have any working capital tied up in inventory because they collect the money from the customer before they have to send any money to their suppliers.

Grocery stores also have worked to increase profit margins by adding general merchandise to their stores. The occasional displays of folding chairs, stuffed animals, magazines, and the like, give grocery stores a chance to boost profits and move a bit in the direction of the supercenters and club stores. One might think that the increasing trend of supermarkets to have large deli sections is another step in the direction of higher-profit-margin items, but appearances are deceptive. While food retailers are definitely moving to offer more in the way of prepared (and nearly prepared) meals, along with fresh bakery products and made-to-order sandwiches, the profit earned from these deli sections is actually rather meager. While prices on these products provide good revenue per square foot, the costs in these sections are also high owing to expensive ingredients and higher labor costs.

Inventory control and automation

One of the main efforts by grocery stores to lower costs is a facet of grocery shopping that we customers are most familiar with: automation. Bar codes (technically called UPCs, for uniform product codes) were first adopted in supermarkets and were used to help automate inventory control. Before bar codes, store clerks actually had to count items on shelves to track inventory and determine what needed ordering when. Now, items can be scanned into the store's inventory as they arrive and automatically deducted from inventory as they are scanned at checkout. Food retailers were also able to save on labor hours because workers did not have to affix price stickers to all the items in the store. This has allowed supermarkets to better manage their inventory, improve their ability to have items in stock, and lower costs.

The checkout scanners, which would be impossible without the bar codes, have also made checkout go quicker and more smoothly. Further, the scanners reduce the amount of training needed for a grocery store cashier since more of the process is automated. This lowers labor costs. Self-checkout lanes lower labor costs even further and would also be impossible without the bar codes and advances in automation. But future advances in automation are going to represent even larger changes in the food-buying experience.

Supermarkets in the United States are currently testing in-store scanners in some markets that allow shoppers to scan items as they put them in their carts. A shopper is given her own scanner to take around with her cart and can keep a running tab on how much she is spending. When it is time to checkout, the items have all been scanned, so it is virtually instantaneous to pay for the groceries and head out the door. Grocery stores are also experimenting with devices and smart phone apps that can offer a shopper personalized prices and coupons based on both where the shopper is in the store and the shopper's previous shopping habits. Some stores even have software in testing that will soon allow a shopper to enter a grocery list and local store and then receive a personalized list with all their items arranged in the order they are in the store, providing information on exactly where each item is. These innovations provide shoppers with convenience, more information (which can save a shopper time), and money-saving offers on items that shoppers already like or might be interested in trying out.

Supermarket chains are cautiously testing innovations along these lines for a number of reasons. First, they want to ensure that shoppers will like them before they invest in a large-scale rollout. Second, the chains would need some expectation of increased profit from the new technology. Providing electronic coupons might increase profit since the manufacturer pays for the coupon, not the store, and shoppers may spend more in total when given the coupons. Helping shoppers move more efficiently through the store is a money-loser for a grocery store. Stores want you walking down as many aisles as possible because they hope that items not on your list will catch your eye. These "impulse" purchases can be responsible for most or all of a store's profit (remember, grocery stores only earn about a 2 percent profit margin) because they are often higher-margin products. However, chains might adopt these technologies even if they appear to be money losing on a per-trip basis if the chain believes they will make the shopper more loyal to their store and will increase the number of times per year a customer will buy groceries from them.

Loyalty programs

In addition to the above technological advances, many supermarkets have some type of loyalty program to reward their regular customers. These programs have two benefits from the store's point of view: making customers more loyal and producing a new revenue stream for the store. Loyalty reward programs can make shoppers stickier for two reasons. First, people generally prefer to build up rewards in one program rather than have them spread across multiple programs.

Second, the loyalty program rewards are perceived as similar to a discount and make the customer feel as if she is getting a better price on the product. Because people generally do not want to track more than a few reward programs, getting a shopper to participate in your store's program is definitely expected to increase the shopping frequency and total spending of that customer.

Reward programs also produce revenue for grocery stores because they allow a store to track customers over time and link their purchase history. Most grocery stores sell the checkout data from their customers to marketing firms who study consumer demand. Without an identifiable customer the data is worth something, but not as much as when it can be connected over time or even combined with demographic data. When customers sign up for a grocery store's loyalty program, they generally provide some basic demographics. Most importantly, whenever their loyalty cards are scanned, the store is able to link that purchase to all their previous purchases from that chain. This allows marketing researchers to do much more sophisticated analysis and therefore makes the data more valuable to those researchers. That means that customers who use loyalty cards are increasing the revenue stream a grocery chain can earn by selling its checkout data. In return, the customers are rewarded with discounts and whatever else the loyalty reward program promises its shoppers.

An additional benefit of loyalty reward programs is that the ability to track a customer's purchase history allows manufacturers and stores to team up to offer customized coupons. This recent development can find a shopper who always buys a particular brand of coffee or breakfast cereal receiving a special coupon for a competitor's product in the hope of enticing him to switch. Or a manufacturer might be alerted to a regular customer who has suddenly stopped purchasing its product so that the manufacturer can offer a special coupon to try to bring the customer back. In fact, with access to a customer's cell phone, stores are currently experimenting with sending special prices (essentially in-store coupons) while they are in the grocery store. Given a phone with GPS, marketers can actually pop up special offers on your phone (or in-store personal scanner device) while you are in the aisle with a particular product. How customers will respond to these new, highly targeted offers and how they will feel about different shoppers in the same store facing different prices for identical products is still being determined as these new marketing programs are still in the very early days of limited distribution.

Summary

This chapter covers some of the special aspects of the food retailing business. Food retailing is a low-profit-margin business with average grocery stores earning only around 2 percent profit as a percentage of total sales. Because of this thin operating margin, food retailers must work very hard both on their operating efficiency and to boost revenue through expanding product lines, higher prices, or alternative revenue streams such as selling transaction data.

Food retailing is separated into stores of different categories. In the United States, the main store formats are supermarkets, supercenters and club stores, and convenience stores. Supercenters and club stores have been gaining market share from supermarkets over the last few decades, although supermarkets have been doing better recently thanks to growth in higher-end, niche supermarket chains such as Whole Foods.

Price markup in the food retailing business is complicated and heavily influenced by competitors' pricing strategies. Stores generally first choose whether to pursue an everyday low-pricing strategy (like Walmart) or a Hi-Lo strategy of higher regular prices with intermittent sales on specific items (such as the strategy followed by the Kroger supermarket chain). After this choice of primary pricing approach, the store then begins to set prices on individual products taking account of manufacturer-suggested prices (when they exist), consumer demand, the store's cost structure, and the overall mix of sales in their chain. Some products are responsible for earning profit for a store, while others are priced more to bring shoppers in or keep sales volume higher.

Food retailers also earn revenues from some non-traditional sources. Slotting fees for granting prime shelf space locations to products provide one such source. Demographic and purchase data can provide another source of revenue. Club stores add membership fees as a revenue source. Sales of non-food items are another way for a food retailer to broaden its revenue base and spread overhead costs (a large advantage for supercenters that have a large base of other merchandise to sell).

Chapter highlights

- Food retailing represents a $650 billion industry in the United States, about 4 percent of the US GDP.
- Worldwide, supermarkets are rapidly gaining market share, but in the United States, supermarkets have been losing market share to supercenters and club stores as value-conscious shoppers have been switching store formats in search of the lowest possible prices.
- In fact, the supermarkets doing the best in the United States are the ones focusing on high-quality (and high-priced) products. The middle-range stores are the ones struggling the most to maintain market share.
- Most stores adopt either an everyday low price (EDLP) or Hi-Lo pricing strategy overall.
- At a product-specific level, certain staple items are priced with minimal markups to encourage shoppers to choose that store for their grocery shopping. Other, more discretionary items are then priced with higher margins in order to keep the stores in business.
- Supermarkets in the United States average only a 2 percent profit margin.
- Additional revenue streams such as slotting fees, data sales, membership fees, and sales of general merchandise are crucial to the profitability of food retailers.

Practice problems

1. Visit the websites of three food retailers from your local area, and determine if they appear to be following an everyday low pricing or a Hi-Lo pricing strategy.
2. List five products that you believe would fit in each of the categories defined by Shankar and Bolton: support, destination, preferred, and ideal categories.
3. For a supermarket with weekly sales of $500,000, weekly labor costs of $40,000, and weekly overhead of $20,000, what average price markup must the store have in order to earn a 2 percent profit?

14 Launching a new product

New product development is an important source of business growth for both food manufacturing businesses and restaurants. Food manufacturing companies can grow revenue either by increasing the sales of existing product lines or by adding new products. It is often easier to grow through new products, so businesses are usually busy with research and development of new products. Restaurants also need a constant stream of new menu items to keep their menus fresh and prevent regular customers from becoming bored with the menu. For independent restaurants, new menu items are often simply the result of the chef cooking with a different recipe, but for chain restaurants the addition of a new menu item shares many of the characteristics of a new product launch for a food manufacturing company. This chapter will focus on all the steps a business goes through from conception to sale of a new product.

Target marketing and new product development

Existing businesses do not usually decide to create a new product because they have a great idea for a product. New businesses start that way, when somebody has an idea for a new product or a skill that lets them produce a better product. After that first product, new product lines are generally added based on careful research and planning.

A food manufacturing business begins with research: what food product categories are seeing growing demand? What are the hot trends in the industry? Should the company be looking for low calorie? Low salt? High fiber? Natural? Fish? Small serving size desserts? After examining these trends, the company will look at demographics to try to find not just a business opportunity but one that has a large enough potential customer base to support enough sales to make the new product development risk worth taking. Sometimes these trends are projected into the future, so that the planning may not be for customers who already exist, but for a group of customers that the business sees emerging and expects to exist a few years in the future. This often involves what is called *target marketing*.

Target marketing means identifying a target demographic (a hypothetical customer type) and designing a product for people in that group. So if, for example, the target demographic is health-conscious females in their 40s, the company will try to design a product or products that appeal to those customers. The elderly might be a target market; or children; or singles; or dieters. Target markets can be characterized by age, by income, by health consciousness, or any other demographic characteristic that allows the company to identify a group of people with (generally) similar tastes and preferences within some product category. As a company builds this target market profile, it includes not just the personal demographics but also a profile of some product characteristics such as a price point, product category, preparation time needed, and similar broad outlines that the new product should fit within.

Essentially, this research and target marketing means that food manufacturing companies work backward when developing new products, beginning with the desires of a target customer group and then developing a product that will appeal to those customers. Businesses do not start with a product and then find a market; they find the market first and then develop a product for the targeted market. All the research and target marketing work is handed to the product development team, and it is then their job to develop new products that can fit in that box and satisfy a currently unmet demand of those target customers.

This type of market segmentation is becoming an increasingly common form of marketing. As data mining and information technology have advanced and these techniques allow marketers to learn more and more about all of us, it has become easier and easier to identify a market segment, to find people who fit in that target market, and then to reach them with a marketing campaign. With the Internet able to target ads very specifically to people based on information that has been gathered from tracking our online lives, it is now possible to target advertising spending much more precisely than it ever was in the past. Because marketers can now address a specific market segment without wasting money on people for whom the product is not designed, today it makes more sense to design products for specific market segments. Thus, new product development has evolved into not just a search for new products with broad appeal to a majority of people but also a search for products that appeal to an identifiable market segment.

New product development—the food science

Having been given a product category and some parameters by the consumer research team, the new product development team can go to work. This group will have food scientists and chefs who will begin by trying to turn the direction from consumer research into some potential new products. That means going from generic descriptions such as a frozen dessert under 200 calories per serving to an actual product idea such as chocolate mousse cups. In most cases, a number of product ideas will be generated from one target market that has been identified by the consumer research team.

After getting a list of ideas for new products, the next step is to begin to winnow down the possibilities. Each product idea must pass three tests to continue in the product development process. First, the product must be something that appears capable of being produced by a manufacturing process. Second, it must taste and look good. Third, the early estimate of cost should fall within the parameters provided by the consumer research team. The product development team will work on the product possibility list, developing recipes, adjusting recipes and taste-testing the items themselves. When the list of possible new products has been reduced to a manageable number, the testing process can move to the next stage.

Once the product development team has a set of new products that they feel are worth pursuing in more depth, they will put together some taste-testing panels. People who fit the target demographic that the products are designed for will be chosen and asked to taste both the different product under development and also (possibly) different versions of each product. The feedback received from these panels will be used to further reduce the number of possible products and also to refine the recipes for the new products that continue through the development phase. A product that makes it through development to product launch will have been through multiple taste testing panels as it gets refined and improved based on the feedback from earlier panels and also on the changes that a product goes through as it moves from the test kitchen to real production.

In the early stages of product testing, product samples are made in test kitchens with trained chefs cooking up small batches of the new product. It is these versions of the product that will be used in the first few taste tests. However, at some point in the product's development, production realities begin to enter into the picture. As the research and development team moves toward a final product, they will begin to switch from special and high-quality ingredients to ingredients that can be used in a mass production process. They will also move from special cooking techniques to using the types of techniques that will have to be used in mass production. They will likely still be making the test products in their test kitchen, but they will try to provide taste-testing panels with a more realistic version of the product (in the sense of closer to what the product will be like when it is mass produced) in order to get more realistic feedback. This process will help learn about how production realities affect the reaction to the product by consumers, both in terms of taste and appearance of the product. Eventually, after a sufficient amount of this fine tuning and testing has taken place, if the product development team still believes the product has the requisite qualities to be a successful product, they have to take the next step and move to a full-scale production test.

Regulatory issues

An important issue that enters into the new product development process at some point is ensuring that any resulting new products can pass successfully through the thicket of regulatory issues all food products must navigate. An obvious regulatory hurdle is food safety regulations. Any potential new product must be able to be produced in a manner that will meet food safety standards and regulations and then also be capable of remaining safe through distribution, sale, and consumption. To ensure a product can meet food safety standards might involve ingredient choices, the production process employed, or both. Thus, the food safety and regulatory experts in the company must be involved in the new product development process in order to check whether the proposed new products can comply with regulations or need to be modified for compliance.

Another regulatory issue food products must face are labeling and marketing claim regulations. Governments around the world have strict regulations about what information must be listed on food product labels and also on what claims can or cannot be made about a product. For example, health claims cannot generally be made unless backed up with scientific evidence. Different countries have various rules on labeling of product features, such as geographical indicators that specify where products originated (which is why California can only make sparkling wine, not champagne, which can only be made in a specified region of France). Rules on disclosing ingredients or whether a product includes anything that was genetically modified vary by jurisdiction and are rapidly changing. Product packaging and marketing campaigns need to be vetted by regulatory experts to ensure that they do not make claims that are not allowed or use words or phrases that might raise a regulatory issue. A food manufacturer needs to involve regulatory experts in the new product development process in time to recommend changes to ingredients, labeling, packaging, and marketing that will avoid later legal issues caused by running afoul of any regulations.

Production testing

No matter how well a new product does in consumer testing and when it is made in the test kitchen, even in large batches, there is no substitute for actual production testing. To really see how a product will work under factory production conditions, you have to make it in the factory. Most food manufacturers already make some similar product and can use an existing factory to run a production test. These production test runs may occur on nights or weekends to avoid slowing down production of current products, but using a real production facility is important to getting a true test of the product under real manufacturing conditions. Because reconfiguring the production facility, buying ingredients, and paying the production costs is not generally a trivial expense, only products that show real promise of being successful will reach this stage. But for those that do, this is a crucial hurdle to clear.

Some products simply cannot be produced in the factory in a satisfactory manner (at least at reasonable cost). Maybe the desired consistency cannot be reached, the appearance might be unappealing, or an ingredient might cause problems in the production process or require significant changes or additions to the normal production equipment. Sometimes, issues arise in the production test that cause the production development team to revise the recipe or even some significant aspect of the new product in order to smooth out production or achieve the desired quality. All these sorts of wrinkles get ironed out in production tests.

After settling on a formulation and production process that appears to work in production testing, the products from a production test run need to go through consumer taste-testing panels, as did the earlier versions that were made in the test kitchen. The feedback from these panels along with lessons learned in the production runs are used to revise and refine the new product until an essentially finished version is settled upon. At this stage, the food science and engineering stage is complete, and the final product launch decision will come down to economics.

Production cost and demand forecasting

While the product development team had a cost target in mind during the product development process (from the original target marketing and consumer research that was the first step in this entire product development process), now is the time when a proper estimate needs to be made. With a finished product to work with, the product development team can use the economic engineering methods covered in chapter 2 to estimate the processing, labor, and ingredient costs of the new product. The sum of these provides an estimate of the total cost of the new product. To this estimate, it is generally a good idea to add a cushion to cover unforeseen circumstances, production problems, and products that do not pass quality control. These extra costs will hopefully decline over time as the production facility gains experience with the new product, but are to be expected in the beginning of scaling up production of a new product.

This cost estimate needs to have a desired profit margin added to it, to arrive at the planned wholesale price of the product. This desired margin might be the company's average gross operating margin or a gross operating margin that the company uses for products in that product category. In many cases, a company may set a higher-than-normal profit margin on the new product to arrive at a stated, or "posted," wholesale price. This higher margin will allow the company to offer discounts in the early stages of marketing their new product in order to encourage retailers to carry the new product. Even if discounts of the posted wholesale price are not offered to retailers at the product's launch, manufacturers often have to pay high slotting fees (see chapter 13 of food retailing for a discussion of slotting fees) in order to get their new product into retailers. Slotting fees for a new product can easily be $100,000 to even over $1,000,000 to get shelf space in a major supermarket chain.[1] In order to pay slotting fees of this magnitude, the manufacturer must set the operating margin high enough to cover such fixed costs and one-time expenses as these. In order to do the math necessary to determine the operating margin that will enable the company to cover its costs, both production and marketing (such as slotting fees), the company must know how much of the new product they will sell.

A crucial part of the product launch process is to estimate the potential demand for the new product. The manufacturer can collect some information about the potential demand by putting questions to the people on the taste-testing panels about whether they would buy the product at some specified price. Using standard statistical techniques, the information gathered from these consumers, combined with data from similar products already on the market, can be employed by the company to estimate the volume of the new product consumers will buy for a range of possible prices at which it might be sold. Using these estimates, combined with an estimate of the retail markup that will be applied to their new product, the manufacturer can estimate what revenue and what profit it would earn from the new product depending on the wholesale price set (and the resulting retail price charged). With this information in hand, the manufacturer can determine a price–sales volume pair that would produce enough revenue to cover both their production costs and marketing costs such as slotting fees (if the estimated demand is sufficient to do that). If the demand forecasts are favorable, the company can select a wholesale price for the new product (which is equivalent to choosing a gross operating margin) that is at least expected to earn enough profit to make the product launch worthwhile. Alternatively, if the demand forecast suggests that the proposed product cannot reach a sales level and price combination that would earn a reasonable return on investment, sufficient to the risk being incurred in launching a new product, then the company should not launch the new product. Even though a company puts a lot of time, effort, and money into new product development, many of the products developed never get brought to market because they fail a test somewhere along the line, especially this final economic test of sufficient market demand.

Product launch

Once a new product has cleared all the hurdles and passed all the tests on the way to being introduced to the marketplace, it is time to actually launch the new product. There are four key steps to a new product launch: securing the necessary ingredients and manufacturing facility capacity, producing enough of the product to satisfy the demand, finding the retail outlets to sell the new product, and advertising the product so that consumers are aware of the new product and want to try it. The first of these three steps is often overlooked, but it is crucial. A few years ago, Wendy's restaurant chain was ready to launch a new product: a Mandarin orange chicken salad. Unfortunately, they could not secure enough supply of Mandarin oranges to launch the product on their original schedule and were forced to delay their new product launch until contracts for enough oranges could be signed and the supply was reliable enough to go ahead with the product launch. Securing ingredients before a new product launch involves not just making sure you have arrangements in place to purchase the necessary ingredients, but also that the ingredients can meet the manufacturer's quality control standards. Ingredients must be of the necessary quality and also standardized so that there are not variations in the products to a degree that consumers complain about that variability in product (in size, in taste, or any other characteristic that consumers might notice). Shortly after the Chick-fil-A restaurant chain launched their spicy chicken sandwich, they had problems with the consistency of the spice mix being used to flavor the chicken and make it spicy. Some chicken pieces were barely beyond bland, while others ended up far too fiery. Chick-fil-A had to quickly work with their spice supplier to sort out the problem and ensure a steady

Demand estimation basics

So how does a company go about estimating the demand curve for a product? There are two basic approaches a company can use, one for an existing product and one for a new product.

For an existing product, the company can build a record of price–quantity pairs. By varying the price of the product (perhaps weekly) and tracking weekly sales volume, the company can build a dataset of quantities sold at different prices. If there are any other variables that impact the level of sales for that product, perhaps prices of competing products or any special seasonal events, data on those variables should also be collected as part of the dataset. Then statistical regression techniques can be used to fit a line or curve through those points. This regression line will allow the company to estimate what their weekly sales will be at any specified price for their product.

For a new product, the company has no data to work with since nobody has previously sold the product in question. So to collect data, a company can survey people about whether or not they would purchase the new product at some specified price. The company would ask different people the same question, but with different prices offered. In this way, the company can build a data set that contains people's yes/no binary responses paired with the price that each person was offered. Combined with data on income, gender, age, and any other characteristics thought by the company to be relevant to purchase decisions for the new product, this is sufficient information to estimate the demand.

Because the data on hypothetical purchase decisions collected by the company are binary, special statistical models are needed to properly handle the statistical aspect of converting this data into an estimate of the demand curve. The most common of these models are called logit and probit models. Any standard statistical software package can handle the estimation without any difficulty. Once the model has been estimated, the company can specify a price and the demographics of any targeted customer segment and estimate the percentage of that group that would purchase the new product at the specified price. Once multiplied by the population of that demographic group, you have an estimate of the demand for the new product by the targeted group. Repeating the process for different demographic groups and/or prices allows the total demand for the new product to be predicted and for the company to choose a price that is predicted to maximize profits or meet other goals that the company has set.

Choosing a price

When a company has a finished product at the end of the product development process and is ready to enter the marketplace, it needs to set a price. In order to do that, it needs to consider three factors: the forecast of demand for the new product, the estimated cost of producing the new product, and the wholesale-to-retail markup.

The first step is to adjust the forecast of consumer demand for the wholesale-to-retail markup. If the company knows that retailers will be using an average of a 30 percent markup, then the company must take the price–quantity pairs from the estimate of consumer demand and reduce the price associated with each estimate of quantity sold to adjust for the markup. Using the 30 percent markup as an example, the wholesale price is given by

$$P_W = P_R/(1+0.30)$$

where P is price and the subscripts denote wholesale (W) and retail (R).

After adjusting the demand estimates to reflect wholesale pricing, the company can use the estimated demand curve to derive the estimated marginal revenue. Remembering that marginal revenue is the change in revenue from selling one additional unit, the company can approximate the marginal revenue by first computing total revenue at different levels of quantity sold, then subtracting the total revenues at two nearby quantities and dividing that difference by the change in quantity. This should result in a table of marginal revenues at corresponding sales levels (and each sales level corresponds to both a wholesale and retail price).

The company can then take its estimated production cost and compute the marginal cost of production. This is likely to be fairly constant once some level of production is reached, but may be high at low sales levels and decline rapidly at first as the quantity sold increases.

Using these marginal cost and marginal revenue estimates, the company can find the sales level at which they are equal. That is the profit-maximizing sales level. Then the company can set the wholesale price at the amount that is forecast to produce that sales level. In this way, the company, using the best information available to it prior to the launch of the product, attempts to maximize profits from its new product's sales.

---

supply of consistently mixed spices so that consumers knew the spiciness level that they could expect if they ordered a spicy chicken sandwich. With the quality control problem solved, the product became a huge success, and Chick-fil-A is now preparing to extend the spicy chicken product line beyond the sandwich to their chicken biscuit.

172 Launching a new product

On the production side of the product launch, the manufacturer must either retool part or all of an existing facility or build a new factory in order to have the production capacity needed to produce enough of the new product to meet the expected level of sales, or more if the product launch is more successful than expected. This part of the product launch process is generally fairly easy to manage as production test runs have already been carried out. Food scientists and engineers will design the facility and work out the kinks so that production gets running smoothly as quickly as possible. Obviously, the company must start production far enough in advance of the product launch date to build up an inventory that can be delivered to retail outlets by the date that the new product is officially put on sale. As long as the company makes sure that the production process has been tested sufficiently that the company is confident in its ability to make the new product on its planned schedule, the production side of the product launch should be the least worrisome part of the process.

If all the rest of the product development and launch process goes perfectly, consumers love the product, and the economics work, the product launch will still be a failure if the manufacturer does not have the retail outlets to actually sell the product. Some restaurant chains are essentially both manufacturer and retailer (although manufacturing may involve some outsourcing or contracting for production of ingredients or prepared food products). So, for example, Chick-fil-A did not need to find retail outlets for its spicy chicken sandwich; it is the retailer.

However, for food manufacturers that sell items in food retailers (say, Campbell's Soup or Kraft), creating a new product is not sufficient for a successful product launch; they need to get the product in enough retail outlets and get product placement within them to allow the product's sales to reach the desired or projected level. For products that are sold in grocery stores, this is likely to involve the payment of slotting fees. Initially, as mentioned above, supermarket chains may demand slotting fees that are quite high in order to add the new product to their shelves. Over time, the stores will be willing to continue carrying the product for lower slotting fees once the retailers are convinced that they will earn a fair profit from selling the product. Also, established food manufacturers can get supermarkets to carry a new product more easily because their existing products are already in the stores and have a track record and established brand name that reduces the risk of carrying the new product for the supermarket. A new manufacturer without an existing product line that is already carried in major food retailing chains has a much harder time convincing these large retailers to give them shelf space for a new, unproven product. These new manufacturers face the highest slotting fees and hardest time getting in the number of retailers necessary to build their business into a successful one. For these new companies, securing the necessary financing to pay large slotting fees is an important part of a new product launch. Planning for the expense of securing retailers is a crucial step to a successful new product.

The last part of the product launch process is the marketing campaign to attract consumers, to inform them about the new product, and to build sales volume from the product launch date as quickly as possible to a level that makes both the manufacturer and retailers a healthy profit. Advertisements need to be designed that will appeal to the target market for which the new product was designed. This book is not about how to conduct a successful marketing campaign, so interested parties need to do their own research on marketing to learn how to build a great advertising strategy. However, suffice it to say that unless the product is truly exceptional, it will be very difficult to engineer a successful product launch without a well-designed marketing campaign.

Chapter summary

This chapter has described the various steps along the road to the launch of a new product. Food manufacturers often work backward in the new product development process, beginning with consumer research that identifies a targeted customer and market niche and then designing a product to appeal to the customers who are being targeted. After a set of possible new products is created, testing begins.

First, the product development team will work to develop recipes for the products that are on the list, attempting to maximize taste and visual appeal while keeping the new product within the parameters set by the consumer research. Later, promising products move into consumer taste-testing panels. Eventually, regulatory issues will be addressed, and production tests will be conducted in order to make sure that any new product will meet all necessary legal requirements and will be able to be manufactured satisfactorily. Then retailers need to be lined up and convinced to carry the new product. The final step is to design a marketing campaign aimed at the targeted demographic in order to educate the segmented consumers and grow sales for the new product. If a company follows these steps, they are likely to have a successful product launch.

Chapter highlights

- New products are often developed not with a particular product in mind, but with a particular target market in mind. Companies work backward from the type of customer they are aiming at to the product that will appeal to that target market.
- As a product moves through the development process, it slowly moves from a conceptual product, to one made by a skilled chef in a test kitchen, to one made in a factory so that the company can see if the product can be designed for the real-world production process that will be needed when it goes to market.
- An important part of the product development process is to ensure that all ingredients used, the production process, distribution system, labeling, packaging, and marketing of any new product comply with all relevant laws and regulations that govern the production, sale, and marketing of food products. Potential new products need to be vetted and, if needed, modified to ensure compliance.

- A company preparing to launch a new product needs to secure retail outlets to sell the product, which sometimes requires paying slotting fees to supermarkets, especially if the company is a new or small manufacturer without much leverage with the supermarkets.
- A well-designed marketing campaign is also an essential part of launching a new product. Targeted consumers must be educated about the new product that they can now buy and be encouraged to go out and purchase it.

Practice problems

1. Define three possible target consumer segments by choosing an age range, gender, and marital status to identify the segment. Then use demographic data (the US Census might be a good place to start) to find out the number of people in the United States in that target market.
2. Now see if you can target those segments more precisely be adding an income range (this data is trickier to get, and you may need to make some assumptions to estimate the number of people).
3. Now (harder still), see if you can estimate the number of people left in your targeted groups if you further segment your markets to include only people who participate in some type of regular recreational activity (jogging, biking, tennis, etc.).
4. Name three food categories in which lots of new products are being introduced currently (an example would be Greek yogurt).
5. If your company is thinking of launching a new beverage, what regulatory issues would you need to be aware of and think about during the new product development process?

15 Special organizational features in the food industry

The food industry has a number of special features that play a larger role than in many other industries. This chapter will review a number of these features, including cooperatives, marketing orders, vertically integrated coordinated companies, and franchises. We will also examine the role government plays in the food industry, which involves not just price supports and crop insurance for farmers, but antitrust exemptions for producers and processors, food safety regulations, food labeling rules, governmental food purchase programs such as WIC and SNAP, laws covering advertising claims, and international trade laws that impact both imports and exports of raw agricultural commodities and processed food products. To properly manage a business in any area of the food industry, you must understand how these various special features and government rules interact with your business and the businesses that you buy from and sell to; without knowledge of the government's role in the food industry, you could miss opportunities or run afoul of the law and end up paying a fine or going to jail.

Cooperatives

Agricultural cooperatives in the United States date back to 1810 with some dairy and cheese cooperatives.[1] After the Civil War, the Grange (officially the Order of the Patrons of Husbandry) began to advocate for and help form coops. This movement gained momentum with the formation of the American Farm Bureau and the National Farmers Union in the early 1900s. Cooperatives in this early period existed particularly in the fruit and dairy industries because small farmers of these commodities could benefit from sharing basic processing facilities and from communal purchasing of inputs such as fertilizer. These efforts were enabled by state legislation and a section of the Clayton Act (1914) that tried to grant them some federal protection, but with the surer protection provided by the Capper–Volstead Act passed by Congress in 1922, they began to increasingly flourish.

Cooperatives today are somewhat more common in the Midwest and California and in fruits, nuts, and dairy products. Some are simply purchasing cooperatives, with farmers joining together to purchase inputs at volume discount prices. These are the most common type in row crops. Others are processing cooperatives, with producers sharing processing capacity and equipment. These are more common in fruit, produce, some livestock (like pork), and dairy, particularly in areas or commodities where most of the coop's members are relatively small producers who can benefit from sharing the processing facility. Finally, there are marketing cooperatives where members pool their production and market it jointly under a single name, later allocating the revenue earned among the members based on their share of production (possibly adjusted for quality). Some famous examples of marketing cooperatives are Ocean Spray (cranberries), Land O'Lakes (butter), and Blue Diamond (almonds). Many marketing cooperatives are also processing cooperatives because they first process the raw agricultural commodity and then market the processed products through the coop.

The benefits of cooperatives to farmers are often apparent without much effort. Farmers banding together through a cooperative to purchase inputs can use their joint volume to negotiate price discounts on many common farm inputs, saving all the coop members money. On the sales side, being able to market their pooled production may yield higher prices by making them an attractive seller to more potential buyers. It is not so much that the larger volume for sale leads to any market power that helps the coop secure a higher price as much as it is simply that many buyers who would not bother purchasing from individual farmers will deal with the coop because it can fill larger orders. Finally, when processing facilities are involved, the cooperative allows farmers to share the large fixed costs and overhead expenses of building and maintaining the processing plant and equipment. Individual farmers would have to spread those costs over much smaller quantities and in many cases probably could not justify the expense at their lower individual volumes. A similar argument applies to advertising. Small farmers would not pay to advertise as many of the benefits might be captured by other producers of the same commodity, but by banding together through a cooperative, they can collectively pay for advertising that benefits all coop members. This could also be accomplished through a marketing order (discussed later in this chapter), but a coop does not need to include all producers and can also build a specific brand if it so chooses. The drawbacks to cooperatives are generally the ones associated with any organization that involves people: sometimes there are management conflicts and disagreements between managers and regular members. Also, cooperatives can face difficulties caused by large swings in volume because members can choose to deliver more or less of their commodities depending on market conditions and the perceived benefits of marketing through the cooperative.

New-generation cooperatives are designed to address this drawback, along with some on the financial side of the business. New-generation cooperatives differ from traditional cooperatives in two key ways.[2] First, members are generally contractually bound to provide a specified amount (and often quality) of the commodity to the coop; no more and no less. Second, members are usually required to purchase stock in the coop in proportion to the amount of the commodity they will be selling (bringing in) to the cooperative. These stock purchases provide the working capital for the coop, which allows new-generation cooperatives to pay out a much higher rate of profits to their members than traditional coops, which often retain much of their profits to cover their capital needs. New-generation cooperatives are almost always vertically integrated, taking in the farmers' commodity and adding value through processing before selling the resulting processed product. Through this vertical integration, new-generation cooperatives seek to increase the returns to their members. Traditional cooperatives can also be involved in processing and can be vertically integrated. While this is not rare for traditional cooperatives, it is virtually universal in new-generation cooperatives.

Marketing orders and commodity commissions

A marketing order is a special organization of agricultural producers and processors who are allowed to take part in activities that are normally banned under US antitrust law. Examples of such behavior are the imposition of quality standards that apply to all producers or some set of processed product made by multiple producers, coordinated advertising campaigns, cooperative funding of joint research projects, and even quantity restrictions. The legal authority for marketing orders dates back to the 1937 Agricultural Marketing Agreement Act. In addition to sections designed to ensure the legality of earlier legislation providing price supports to agricultural commodities and other government intervention in agricultural production, this law provided specific legislative authority for exemption from the usual restrictions on separate producers coordinating their activities. After a proposed marketing order is approved by the Secretary of Agriculture, for it to be implemented producers must vote in favor of the marketing order by a 2/3 vote. This vote specifies which of the possible activities a marketing order will carry out, and to amend that list of activities later requires a new vote; thus, not all marketing orders take advantage of all of the possible behaviors. Marketing orders were conceived as a way of evening the playing field on which farmers were thought to be at a market power disadvantage to larger, concentrated wholesale purchasing and processing firms; however, marketing orders can also benefit processors since features such as generic advertising campaigns ("Got Milk?" or "Beef: It's What's for Dinner") surely increase demand for products that those processors sell.

Commodity commissions or commodity marketing boards are related to marketing orders in that they are often formed at the state or national level as part of a marketing order to oversee some or all of the marketing order's programs. They are essentially the board of directors. In particular, commodity commissions usually oversee the research programs and any advertising campaigns that are carried out. The research programs are generally funded by a check-off program whereby all producers pay some amount based on their production levels; for example, each dairy producer pays in $x per y hundred weight of milk produced. The commission overseeing the funds then allocates the money based on their research priorities and proposals received. Usually most of the money goes to researchers in the state land grant universities in the states in which the check-off funds were collected. This research is generally focused on helping producers increase productivity and profitability or on developing new products that can be produced using the commodity as an input (in order to increase demand for the commodity, thereby increasing prices).

Collective, generic advertising for a commodity and products made from that commodity are a common feature of marketing orders. Such advertising campaigns cannot steer consumers to a specific brand name, but they can promote the commodity itself. Famous campaigns under US marketing orders include those run to boost demand for milk, beef, cotton, cheese, prunes, and raisins. The aim of such a generic advertising campaign is to stimulate a demand shift, both moving it outward and also making it more inelastic. If the overall demand curve for the commodity can be shifted in this way, the increase in revenue to the industry should increase by enough to more than compensate for the cost of the campaign. If this is accomplished, then the generic advertising campaign will have been a success.

Another feature of marketing orders is the ability to impose standards and grades that apply to all producers under the marketing order (which could be a state or all producers nationwide). For example, fruit that is below some specified size can be required to be diverted to processing rather than sold in the fresh fruit market. The California olive industry defined olive sizes (small, medium, large, jumbo, and colossal) that must be used by all olive sellers.

Beyond simple standards and grades, marketing orders can also resort to the more drastic step to reduce supply through quantity restrictions. Such action can be taken through two mechanisms. Some marketing orders, such as the California almond one, can require some percentage of a year's crop to be placed into reserve for sale in a later year. Others, such as lemons and pears, impose quantity restrictions earlier in the production cycle by requiring growers to thin the fruit on the trees (sometimes called a green drop). By removing some of the fruit early in the growing season, the trees produce fewer fruit per tree, but each one will be larger and higher quality (on average). This thinning can be done by hand, actually pulling off some of the fruit, or with chemical application; which method is used depends on the crop and sometimes on grower preferences. Again, the hope in implementing such a strategy is to increase grower revenue. When demand is believed to be inelastic, growers can increase their collective revenue by reducing quantity because the increase in price more than compensates for the reduction in quantity sold. However, without a marketing order to ensure that all growers take part in such a quantity reduction, growers could not implement such a strategy since they would have an incentive to become free riders by encouraging other growers to reduce supply while they individually produced the most possible. Many marketing orders do not have the power to impose quantity restrictions, but some, mainly in the fruit and nuts categories, do have that power and often use it in order to increase industry-wide profits. For a list of marketing orders and their powers, see the application box.

Some marketing orders and commodity associations have been wildly successful in boosting demand for their commodities. The California raisin marketing

The following table lists some (not all) agricultural marketing orders, where they operate, and what powers they have authorization to employ

Fruit and vegetables marketing orders	State (if not national)	Powers
Almonds		Marketing order authorizes volume control authority in the form of reserve, but that program is not currently in effect. Almonds received by handlers are subject to quality regulations.
Apricots		Marketing order authorizes grade, size, quality, maturity, markings, pack, and container regulations for apricots.
Avocados		Marketing order authorizes grade, size, quality, maturity, container, and pack requirements for Florida avocados. It also authorizes regulations regarding the size, capacity, and weight of the containers used to ship avocados to market. Minimum grade, size, and maturity requirements established under the order also are applied to imported avocados.
Cherries (tart)		Marketing order authorizes volume controls that provide for a reserve pool in times of heavy cherry supplies. Under the order, reserve cherries may be released to handlers for free use; used in diversion programs; exported; or carried over as a hedge against a short crop the next year. Other major marketing order provisions, not currently in use, include minimum grade and size regulations and authorization for market research and development projects, including paid advertising.
Cranberries		Marketing order authorizes volume control through producer allotments and handler withholdings.
Citrus	Texas	Marketing order authorizes grade, size, container, and pack regulations for oranges and grapefruit shipped to fresh markets in the United States, Canada, and Mexico. Currently, minimum grade and size requirements established under the order for oranges also are applied to oranges imported from September through June.

(continued)

(Continued)

Fruit and vegetables marketing orders	State (if not national)	Powers
Citrus	Florida	The marketing order authorizes grade, size, maturity, quality, volume regulations, and research and promotion programs. Additionally, export regulations include size, capacity, weight, dimensions, and marking or pack of the container regulations. Grade and size requirements are in effect for citrus shipped to destinations outside of the production area. Volume regulations are authorized for specific varieties, but are not in effect. Shipping holidays are authorized during the Thanksgiving and Christmas holiday seasons. The order was promulgated in 1939 and last amended under formal rulemaking on October 9, 2009.
Dates	California	Marketing order authorizes, and currently has in effect, minimum standards for grade, size, and containers for different variety categories. The order has authority to establish volume regulations, but has not utilized that authority since 1972. Grade and size requirements established under the order are also applied to all imported dates.
Grapes		The marketing order authorizes grade, size, quality, maturity, pack, and container requirements from April 10 to July 10 each year for any or all table grape varieties except the Emperor, Calmeria, Almeria, and Ribier varieties. The order establishes limited packing holidays.
Hazelnuts	Oregon and Washington	The marketing order authorizes establishment of volume regulations in the form of free and restricted percentages for in-shell hazelnuts sold in the continental United States. Expenditures for certain kinds of advertising and promotion may be credited to a handler's promotion assessments. The order provides minimum grade and size requirements based on Oregon Grade Standards. Grade and size requirements established under the order also are applied to imported hazelnuts.

Olives	California	The marketing order authorizes minimum grade and size requirements for olives produced in California. Minimum quality and size requirements are prescribed for canned, ripe (sliced and whole) olives. Size requirements also are applied to fresh olives. Currently, minimum quality and size requirements established under the order are applied to imported olives.
Onions	Idaho and Oregon	Marketing order authorizes grade, size, and pack regulations. All of the order's authorized programs are currently active. The quality, size, and maturity requirements established under the order also are applied to imported onions from early June through early March. Shipping holidays are authorized under the order but have never been imposed.
Onions	South Texas	Grade, size, quality, and container and pack regulations are authorized under the order. Requirements are currently in effect, except for container and pack requirements. The grade, size, quality, and maturity requirements established under the order are also applied to imported onions from early March to early June.
Onions (Vidalia)	Georgia	Marketing order authorizes production research, marketing research and development, and marketing promotion programs, including paid advertising. All of these programs are active and are designed to improve the marketing, distribution, consumption, or efficient production of Vidalia onions. The order does not authorize grade, size, quality, container, or pack regulations.
Pears	Oregon and Washington	The marketing order authorizes grade, size, and quality regulations for fresh pears.
Pistachios	California	The marketing order authorizes grade, quality, size, and reporting requirements on in-shell and shelled pistachios, including testing for aflatoxin levels.
Potatoes	Oregon and California	Marketing Order authorizes establishment of grade, size, maturity, quality, and pack regulations, which are not currently in effect.

(continued)

(Continued)

Fruit and vegetables marketing orders	State (if not national)	Powers
Potatoes	Idaho and E. Oregon	Marketing order authorizes grade, size, maturity, pack, quality, and container regulations, all of which have been established and are in effect. Grade, size, quality, and maturity requirements in effect under the marketing order also are applied to imports of long-type potatoes during each month of the year.
Potatoes	Virginia and North Carolina	Marketing order authorizes the handling of all varieties of Irish potatoes grown in Virginia and North Carolina by grade, size and quality. Grade, size, quality and maturity requirements in effect under the marketing order also apply to imports of round type potatoes (excluding red-skinned) during the period of June 5 through July 31.
Raisins	California	Marketing order authorizes volume control measures in the form of free and reserve tonnage. Tonnage is released gradually through the season by preliminary, interim, and final percentages. Under the order, free raisins can be used in any market. Reserve raisins may be sold to handlers for free use; used in diversion programs; exported to authorized countries; carried over to the next crop year; sold to government agencies; or disposed to other outlets non-competitive with free raisins. All of these outlets have been used in recent years. The order also authorizes minimum grade and size regulations, and minimum requirements are currently in effect. Grade and size requirements established under the order are applied to imported raisins.
Tomatoes	Florida	The marketing order authorizes the handling of Florida fresh market tomatoes by grade, size, quality, maturity, pack, and container. The grade, size, quality and maturity requirements established under the order also apply to imported tomatoes from October 10 through June 15. The order's container and pack requirements are not applied to imported tomatoes.

Walnuts	California	Marketing order authorizes minimum grade and size regulations are authorized under the order, and are currently in effect. Volume controls in the form of free and reserve percentages are authorized but are not currently being used. Grade and size requirements established under the order also are applied to imported walnuts. Effective September 1, 2008, the order will have authority for promotion and paid advertising, in addition to research and development.
Market Orders		
Milk	Various	The Federal Orders require milk handlers in a marketing area to pay dairy farmers (producers) no less than certain minimum prices for fluid milk. The price for class 2, 3, and 4 milk is the same under all federal orders. Class 1 prices are computed each month for each marketing area based on National Agricultural Statistics Service (NASS)-released prices for milk used in manufactured products. The federal orders require that a plant's usage value for milk be combined with other plants usage value (pooled) and each producer (or cooperative) be paid on the basis of a uniform/blend/average price. This blend price represents an average of the value of milk in all uses (fluid milk, cottage cheese, ice cream, cheese, butter, etc.).

Sources: USDA AMS, Marketing Order web pages. Available online at: http://www.ams.usda.gov/AMSv1.0/ams.fetchTemplateData.do?template=TemplateN&page=FVMarketingOrderIndexPlumPrune(Washington).

order created an iconic advertising campaign with dancing clay-mation raisins (the animated raisins were molded from clay and carefully positioned to simulate motion in the video) that created increased consumer awareness of raisins and shifted the demand curve for raisins out significantly. Milk and beef both have long-running, very successful advertising campaigns financed through commodity association check-offs that serve to increase consumer demand and move tastes and preferences in favor of their commodity. The Texas citrus marketing order, which mostly supports Texas grapefruit (along with some oranges), was shown to have increased sales of Texas grapefruit by $56 million over a five-year period through the expenditure of about $2 million on various promotional programs.[3] This is clearly a very successful expenditure by farmers on a generic advertising program that managed to shift demand enough to more than recover the spending on the advertising through increased revenue to the farmers.

Vertical integration and coordination

The food industry has many examples of vertical integration and vertical coordination. Vertical integration is when a single company owns operations at multiple stages of an industry as the product moves from raw inputs to finished retail products. For example, the chicken industry is dominated by companies that start with eggs, raise the chicks until they are chickens, process those chickens into various wholesale chicken products, and sell them to food retailers. These companies are vertically integrated, owning all stages of the process except the final retail sale. Companies that own fruit plantations and then process that fruit into canned fruit products are also vertically integrated.

So what is the economic motivation for vertical integration? Firms expect being vertically integrated to bring with it three main economic benefits: higher profits, reduced profit variability, and cost savings from standardization. The easiest of these to achieve through vertical integration is the cost savings from standardization. Chicken processors control the birds that are the input (live chickens) into their processed products (various retail processed chicken products such as boneless, skinless chicken breasts) through vertical integration because doing so lets them provide all their growers identical chicks that will reach the desired weight and size on a dependable schedule. Having standardized chickens with which to begin the process of turning birds into meals allows these companies to use mechanical devices to perform many of the steps in their processing plants. If the company simply relied on a spot market for chickens when they needed to buy some, it would not be able to count on always getting a chicken with the desired size and shape. The standardization of its input and the accompanying benefits that come from that (labor savings, speedier processing) are one of the most significant contributors to the fall in chicken prices relative to beef over the last 20 or 30 years.

The higher profits come not from getting a lower price for the inputs previously purchased from a separate entity (or higher prices for products previously sold wholesale that can now be sold at the retail level) since any change like that just shifts profit from one unit of the now combined company to another. Rather, they come from cost savings realized through the combining of separate companies into one. The cost savings can be from consolidation of operations (having one set of accounts instead of two, one information technology department instead of two, etc.) or from eliminating the expense of negotiating deals with other companies that are unnecessary once a single company owns all the units within it that were previously separate entities.

Obvious examples of vertical integration in US agriculture can be found in the poultry industry. Large integrators, such as Tyson Foods, own every step of the process from laying the eggs, hatching, raising the chicks to maturity, processing the chickens, and further processing into ready-to-eat products. Tyson owns and produces the live chickens, the intermediate product of fresh chicken parts (that can be sold to grocery stores, to other companies that use the chicken as an ingredient [perhaps in chicken noodle soup], or used themselves to make additional products), and more finished products such as sliced lunch meat, pre-cooked flavored chicken tenders. General Mills is a giant company that is vertically integrated through numerous of its countless brands. A few examples: it makes flour (Gold Medal), which can be used in its baking mixes (Betty Crocker, Bisquick) and baked products (Totino's pizza), and it has vegetables (Green Giant) that can be an ingredient in its soups (Progresso).

An alternative to vertical integration is vertical coordination. Vertical coordination is when a company does not own multiple stages, but has contracts or other arrangements across levels of an industry in order to reduce risk and uncertainty about procuring inputs or having access to markets to sell its products. When tomato processing companies (like Hunt's, for example) sign contracts with tomato growers to purchase a specified amount of tomatoes for a set price for delivery on a specified date and time, that is vertical coordination. Companies practicing vertical coordination are trying to capture some of the benefits of vertical integration without actually having to buy the other companies involved in the coordination. There are many possible avenues for companies to practice vertical coordination. One is as simple as a signed agreement between two companies to cooperate in some sort of joint venture or sell/buy products between themselves. Forward contracting is a form of vertical coordination by which a processing firm contracts in advance to buy inputs (usually raw agricultural commodities). Farmers get the benefit of reduced revenue risk, while the processor reduces uncertainty over input costs and availability. In some cases where the processor needs a specific grade or variety of a commodity to use as an ingredient, vertical coordination through forward contracting may be the only way short of vertical integration to obtain the input as farmers will not be excited about growing a specialized commodity without knowing that they can sell it at a fair price. Forward contracts can involve a fixed price, but more commonly they involve some formula that bases payment on some premium above a spot or future price on the delivery date.[4]

When a food processor makes a special product under a private label (like a supermarket's own brand), that is another form of vertical coordination. Two companies are cooperating and working together, but there is no shared ownership. In fact, that is a common form of vertical coordination in the food industry, allowing a retailer to get proprietary products made without having to invest the capital in a production facility. For example, a salad dressing company that makes dressing for sale under its own label also manufactures additional dressings under a variety of private labels for supermarkets and restaurants. In fact, this company produces over 200 different salad dressings! Clearly, there are not that many varieties of dressing; most of them are slight variations of the same type (say, ranch dressing) with small changes in the amount of some ingredient used simply so that a restaurant can truthfully claim it is their "special" recipe.

Franchises

Franchises are a feature of the food industry that is concentrated in the restaurant industry, although they also play a role in some agricultural input supply businesses and in food retailing. Many of the most famous and largest restaurant chains in the United States (and the world) are made up of franchises. Franchises are also becoming common in small, local, and regional restaurant chains. Today, a restaurant that has been in business for just a few years may begin to sell franchises because so many entrepreneurs are interested in owning franchises, and restaurant owners have a difficult time raising capital for expansion.

The basic mechanics of franchising and franchise ownership begins with an existing successful business that trademarks and licenses its brand, product line, appearance, and feel. This company becomes the franchiser, which agrees to license other companies (the franchisees) to copy their business by opening other stores in different locations. In normal franchise arrangements, the franchisee pays an initial franchise fee to the franchiser in exchange for it granting the operating license and then also pays some share of gross revenues on an ongoing basis as a royalty payment to the franchiser. In most cases, the franchisee also pays a specified share of revenues to an advertising pool, that may be divided between a national pool with advertising decisions made by the franchiser and a local pool with decisions controlled by the local operators in that region. In exchange for these payments, the franchise operators are allowed to essentially duplicate an existing, successful business. They often gain access to an established supply chain that can deliver to the restaurant all the ingredients and supplies needed to run their operation. Given that small businesses often have difficulties ordering in small quantities at reasonable prices, this access to a business-specific supply chain that can offer prices available only to those ordering in large volumes (because the total volume of all franchises is large) is a large advantage gained by franchise operators. Franchisees own their own business, which they can build equity in and sell (with permission of the franchiser), but also gain the advantages of support from the franchiser and fellow franchisees so that they do not need to reinvent the wheel or develop a business concept from scratch.

While franchises are certainly not unique to the restaurant industry (you can also find them in insurance, hotels, rental cars, auto repair, printer ink cartridges, and even used clothing), they are especially prevalent in the restaurant industry. Thus, it is natural to ask why this is so. There are two key features of the restaurant industry that help make the franchise model a successful and desirable option in that sector. The first is access to capital. Borrowing money from a bank to start a restaurant is nearly impossible unless you have a long track record of success in the industry. More commonly, people who want to launch a new restaurant must either borrow money on credit cards or from friends and family in order to secure the funds needed to get started. However, a bank is much more willing to lend money to an entrepreneur who is going to operate a franchise restaurant, since then the concept's track record and average earnings can be used to gain a much better understanding of the proposed restaurant's likely ability to repay the loan.

If the franchisee has reasonable business experience and assets to pledge as collateral, a bank may approve a loan to finance a franchise restaurant.

The second reason franchises are so common in the restaurant industry is the advantage gained by familiarity in a business where many customers are not local residents. This reason also explains why so many hotels are chains of franchise operations as well. Especially in the fast food sector, where franchises are most concentrated, many customers are from out of town, perhaps just stopping for a meal while driving through, and these customers may have no local knowledge about which restaurants are worth eating at. The franchise model solves this problem by providing non-residents with information about the restaurant. If the customer has eaten at a different outlet in the same chain before, he knows exactly what to expect in this one. By reducing uncertainty, the franchise brand name educates and informs the potential customers and increases the chances that a non-local will choose to eat in that particular restaurant (in formal economic-speak, the franchise brand helps solve an asymmetric information problem).

Franchise restaurant operations range from the inexpensive to open (like Subway) to the quite expensive ($1.5 to $2 million for a stand-alone, build-from-scratch restaurant), and franchisers have widely varying standards for approving a franchisee. Some require restaurant management experience of prospective franchise operators; some are okay with basic business experience. Net worth requirements vary from $350,000 to over $1 million.

While this section has mostly referred to restaurants, franchises also exist in some farm input supply businesses (such as equipment dealers) and in food retailing in the form of convenience stores. Many gas stations are franchises and also are in the food retailing business through the food sold in the associated convenience store. The brand name of the franchise gas station confers the same benefits the franchise restaurant enjoys, so that people who are not local gain instant information about that gas station. These non-restaurant franchises play a smaller role in the food industry than restaurants, but they should not be completely ignored. For more on franchises, see the section on franchises in chapter 12.

The role of government

The federal, state, and local governments have a plethora of roles in the food industry. The federal government is heavily involved in agricultural production through production subsidies, regulations on chemical use and labor practices, research funding, extension programs, food safety and grading inspections, export subsidies, and demand-boosting programs that purchase food for lower-income people. State governments are involved in the food industry through safety inspections, establishment of state-level marketing orders, some state-specific environmental regulation of agricultural production, some state food inspections, general state regulation of businesses that applies to food manufacturers, and often some agricultural promotion programs. Local governments are involved in the food industry mainly through regulation of restaurants and food service businesses (cafeterias and caterers); this includes safety inspections, regulations on operating hours, and laws concerning the sale and service of alcoholic beverages.

The federal government plays the most roles within the food industry, part promoter and part regulator. The federal government subsidizes agriculture through a variety of direct and indirect methods: direct payments to farmers, subsidies that lower the cost of crop insurance, subsidies that help some Western farmers get water at lower cost, and federal funding of agricultural research and extension. The original rationale for these federal programs was to help family farms based on the Jeffersonian ideal of small, family farms as a key building block of a democratic society. Today, most of these subsidies go to large-scale farms that may be officially family owned but are small businesses like millions of other small businesses around the country. These subsidies continue because of the political power of farm groups in states where agricultural production is an important component of the economy and because the government values the lower food prices that all the citizens get as a result of these subsidies. Crop insurance subsidies are a particularly influential subsidy program because not only do they increase agricultural production and profits, they also have effects on what crops are planted and where crops are planted. By offering crop insurance at below-market rates, the federal government encourages farmers to take more risk, perhaps planting crops in marginal areas where they otherwise would not.

Although not a subsidy, because it does not lower costs, the federal government also boosts farm income through demand-increasing programs: the school lunch program; the supplemental nutrition assistance program (SNAP) that replaced food stamps; the women, infants, and children program (WIC); and the Food for Peace Act under which the federal government buys agricultural commodities and donates them to other countries. By creating demand for raw commodities and food products, the government helps to boost prices, increasing farm income (and perhaps saving itself some money that it might otherwise have to pay out in subsidy programs). The Food for Peace Act is a particularly successful way to boost prices as the commodities purchased are removed from domestic supply and do not reduce demand for other food products in the United States. Other demand-increasing programs do encourage recipients to purchase additional food products, but the increase in food purchases is less than the amount spent by the government to increase the demand; thus, these programs are not as effective at increasing prices as the Food for Peace Act.

The federal government also plays a role in the regulation of the food industry, thereby raising costs and lowering profits. Regulations begin on the farm, where the federal government regulates and restricts the use of chemicals used as pesticides, growth regulators, or applied for any other purpose. Chemicals must be approved for use by the government and then used in compliance with regulations that control how much may be applied and also set upper limits for the residue that may be present when the crop is harvested. Chemicals that would cause excessive environmental damage or have the potential to cause cancer or other diseases in humans are not allowed to be used at all. Farm labor practices are also subject to federal regulations that control the minimum age for workers, the pay, and worker safety practices. Regulation continues when food is processed, as the federal government controls the labor practices allowed and inspects the food and the food processing facilities to ensure a safe food supply. As the food products move to market, the government controls the information on the product label, both requiring certain information about ingredients and nutritional content and restricting claims to those that can be scientifically proven. Similar restrictions on product claims exist for advertising of food products to consumers.

State governments have a smaller, but not negligible role in the food industry. Some marketing orders are state sanctioned as opposed to federal ones, and many state departments of agriculture actively help state commodity associations that work to promote their products by sponsoring research and funding advertising campaigns. States also protect production agriculture through right-to-farm laws that help safeguard farmers from neighbors who move in nearby and complain about farm practices that generate noise, dust, or smells. State governments are more involved in the food industry once we move beyond the farm gate to the food processing and retailing industries. The general business climate, in terms of taxes and regulation, can have a large effect on the profitability and, therefore, the number of businesses in a state. Many states offer subsidies to businesses that create jobs, especially in rural areas, which can help attract food processing companies.

Local governments also play a role in the food industry, primarily through regulation of restaurants and bars. Local governments determine locations within their city or county that restaurants and bars can do business in, often control the maximum hours of operation, and control alcoholic beverage licenses. There are also often local ordinances that define what a bar is (relative to a restaurant) as the licenses and regulations often treat bars and restaurants differently. A common definition of a bar centers on the percentage of total sales from food (as opposed to beverages). If beverage sales exceed some specified percentage of total sales, then the business is a bar and is usually subject to tighter regulation. This means that some restaurants with significant bar and beverage sales need to monitor their sales carefully to make sure they stay on the right side of any local business definition. Local governments also generally are in charge of health and safety inspections of restaurants, making sure that food preparation areas are clean and sanitary, food storage meets all requirements, food temperatures are hot or cold enough, and all required labor and safety rules are being obeyed.

Chapter summary

The food industry has a number of special features that members of the industry need to be aware of in order to fully understand the business climate in which they operate. Specifically, the government is very much involved in the food industry: in production agriculture through regulation and subsidies, in food processing with regulation and demand-boosting food purchase-support programs, and in food retailing through both food-purchase-support programs and regulations of the restaurant and bar industry.

Cooperatives, marketing orders, and commodity associations give farmers and processors a chance to operate collectively in some areas in ways that can boost income through increased prices, quantity sold, or both. These special exemptions that agribusiness has been granted from US antitrust laws allow farmers and food processors to act in ways that businesses outside the food industry are not allowed to do. In particular, cooperatives can get volume discounts on input purchases by placing a single large order, can secure more favorable pricing by offering larger volumes for sale and a single sales agent, and can lower costs by sharing facilities and equipment such as packing sheds or livestock processing plants. They also can join together for advertising and other promotional activities, hopefully boosting profits.

Although not unique to the food industry, vertical integration and coordination are an increasingly important part of the industry landscape. Vertical integration is when one owner controls operations at several stages of the supply chain from the farm to our mouths. Farmers vertically integrate through cooperatives that perform value-added processing or by an individual farmer building a processing facility, whereas food processing companies get vertically integrated either by buying farming operations or production facilities at different stages of the food processing supply chain. Even restaurants are becoming vertically integrated with some now owning their own farms (perhaps growing some herbs and vegetables), and others doing their own food processing such as curing meats or making cheeses. Vertical coordination involves partnerships between firms where they contract in advance in order to act as if they were vertically integrated but without merging ownership. When a farmer agrees to plant a special variety of a crop for sale only to a specific processor, that is vertical coordination.

A final special feature of the food industry discussed here is franchises. Franchises, which in the food industry are mainly found in restaurants, provide benefits to business owners that are particularly useful to businesses with many customers that are unfamiliar with local businesses. Franchises also allow businesses to expand without having to raise the capital to fund the expansion by instead licensing their business concept and sharing the revenues with the franchisees. Owning a franchise provides an opportunity for the business owner to start and run a business without having to be completely on her own or come up with a business concept.

Chapter highlights

- The government is heavily involved in the food industry, both promoting it and restricting it.
- In the United States (and most other developed countries), the federal government provides many forms of subsidies to farmers: direct payments, water subsidies, subsidized crop insurance, federal research and extension funding, for example. The federal government also regulates farmers, controlling their labor practices, use of chemicals, and allowable pollution levels.

- The US government also has granted agricultural producers and processors a chance to be exempted from antitrust law through the mechanisms of a marketing order or commodity association. After approval by a two-thirds majority, a marketing order can restrict supply industry-wide, advertise collectively, impose quality standards, and collect money to fund research.
- Local governments also play an important role in the regulation of restaurants and bars.
- Cooperatives are another unusual feature of the food industry, with farmers using cooperatives to cost-effectively enter into food processing in order to capture addition profits.
- New-generation cooperatives are cooperatives that require their members to buy stock in the cooperative in order to join (thereby providing the cooperative with working capital) and also require the members to deliver an amount of the commodity in proportion to the shares purchased.
- Cooperatives differ from marketing orders and commodity associations because cooperatives are voluntary membership organizations, while all covered producers or processors that fall under a marketing order or commodity associations definition must participate and obey any rules or directives that are properly issued.
- Franchises are a form of business where one company licenses another to copy its business model. Franchises are present in several forms within the food industry, but are most common in the restaurant industry.

Practice problems

1. List and briefly describe five ways in which the US government subsidizes agricultural production.
2. List and briefly describe three ways in which the US government restricts agricultural practices, leading to lower production or higher production costs.
3. Find a current magazine or television ad (they are often also posted online) by a marketing order or commodity association. Does the ad seem effective? Would it make you buy more of the product?
4. For any new-generation cooperative, find the (approximate) number of members, required capital investment in the cooperative, amount of product that must then be delivered to fulfill the member's responsibility to the cooperative, and how the cooperative is adding value to the raw commodity.
5. Choose a franchise restaurant chain that is not in the table in chapter 12. Find the initial franchise fee, the royalty payments that the franchisee must pay, the net worth requirements for a franchisee, and the expected cost of opening one of their restaurants.

Notes

1 The basics of the food industry

1 See the US Bureau of Economic Analysis website for data on GDP by industry for all these sector-specific figures.

2 Cost economics for processing plants

1 The book is *Markets, Prices and Interregional Trade* (New York: Wiley, 1978) by R. G. Bressler, Jr., and R. A. King. It is out of print (and has been for quite a few years). You may be able to find a used copy or even scanned copies online. The link http://dc.aces.uiuc.edu/irwin/links_archive_book_Bressler.asp worked at the time of publication of this book. All the material in this chapter started with what I learned from that book, which I have slowly modified over the years of my own teaching.

6 Plant location and size decisions

1 For an example of a good study on this topic, see Goodwin, B. K. and Ortalo-Magné, F. (1992), "The Capitalization of Wheat Subsidies into Agricultural Land Values," *Canadian Journal of Agricultural Economics*, 40: 37–54.

9 Price discrimination

1 The case, United States v. The Borden Company, is explained in an easy-to-read manner as part of The Oyez Project at IIT Chicago-Kent College of Law. October 20, 2011. Available online at http:///www.oyez.org/cases/1960-1969/1961/1961_439/.
2 Frank, R. G., "Prescription Drug Prices: Why Do Some Pay More Than Others Do?" *Health Affairs*, 20 (March 2001), 115–128.

10 Imperfect competition and game theory

1 Cournot, A. A. "Recherches sur les principes mathematiques de la théorie des richesse" *Libraire des Sciences Politiques et Sociales* (Paris: M. Rivere, 1838).
2 Bertrand, J. "Book review of théorie mathematique de la richesse sociale and of recherches sur les principes mathematiques de la théorie des richesses," *Journal de Savants* 67 (1883), 499–508.
3 I originally learned many of the game theory concepts, particularly the way game theory can be applied to agribusiness situations, that are covered in this chapter, in a

graduate-level agricultural marketing class taught by Richard Sexton. I am indebted to him for all that he taught me about this and many other subjects.
4 Note that risk lovers and optimists are not necessarily two names for the same behavior. Optimists think good things will happen to them; risk-lovers have a utility function that values activities with random payoffs over a certain payoff with the same expected payoff. Optimists and risk-lovers are likely overlapping, but not identical sets of people. However, both could quite logically choose a maxi-max strategy. A similar logic applies to the discussion of risk-averse and pessimistic game players that follows.

11 Spatial competition

1 For an advanced look at this topic and how to solve the Hotelling location model under reasonable assumptions see, for example, Osborne, M. J., and C. Pitchik (1987), "Equilibrium in Hotelling's Model of Spatial Competition," *Econometrica* 55, 911–922.
2 Remember that a monopsonist is the only buyer of a product, the flip side of a monopolist who is the only seller.
3 This section is drawn from Mérel, P. R. and R. J. Sexton, "Models of Horizontal Product Differentiation in Food Markets," in *The Oxford Handbook of the Economics of Food Consumption and Policy*, eds. J. L. Lusk, J. Roosen, and J. Shogren (Oxford University Press, 2011). I am indebted to Rich Sexton for much advice and guidance on the direction to take in this chapter.
4 Higher relative transportation costs are analogous to more differentiated products because the distance between the two sellers is similar to the amount of differentiation between two products. Since higher transportation costs make the distance greater in a relative sense, the effect is the same as the products being more differentiated.

12 The food service industry

1 The material in this chapter on restaurant pricing and financial ratios is similar to discussions found in several chapters of an excellent book on restaurant economics: Schmidgall, R. S., D. K. Hayes, and J. D. Ninemeier, *Restaurant Financial Basics* (Hoboken, New Jersey: John Wiley & Sons, 2002). Over time, I have modified some of the rules they present based on my own discussions with restaurant owners and operators and what presentation approach seems to make sense to students. However, I still wish to acknowledge their book as being central to my knowledge on this subject.
2 For coverage of this case, see Pokorny, B. "Mario Batali Restaurants Settle Tip Pool Lawsuit For $5.25 Million" March 12, 2012, available online at http://www.jdsupra.com/post/documentViewer.aspx?fid=fb9a057a-9f11-4fa9-9660-28ed11b8b340.
3 The failure rate for restaurants is surprisingly hard to track down, and is often reported to be as high as 95 percent. However, research by Prof. H. G. Parsa when he was at Ohio State University (he is now affiliated with University of Central Florida) pinned the number down as being closer to 50 percent over a three-year period and 26 percent in the first year. Other research has suggested failure rates of around 60 percent–70 percent in five years. Some of these "failures" do not represent a loss of all invested money, but rather simply the closing of restaurants that are not earning a sufficient return to justify all the hard work involved in running it.

13 Food retailers

1 "Datapoints" Supermarketnews.com, June 25, 2012.
2 These facts about supermarkets are mostly from "Supermarkets Inc: Inside a $500 Billion Money Machine," a CNBC documentary first aired on January 27, 2011.

3 Shankar, V., and R. N. Bolton (Winter 2004), "An Empirical Analysis of Determinants of Retailer Pricing Strategy," *Marketing Science* 23(1), pp. 28–49.
4 Federal Trade Commission, (November 2003), "Slotting Allowances in the Retail Grocery Industry: Selected Case Studies in Five Product Categories." Available online at http://www.ftc.gov/os/2003/11/slottingallowancerpt031114.pdf.
5 Strom, Stephanie, "Has 'Organic' Been Oversized?" *New York Times* (July 8, 2012), Business section, p. 1.
6 Richard J. Volpe III and Nathalie Lavoie (2007). "The Effect of Wal-Mart Supercenters on Grocery Prices in New England," *Review of Agricultural Economics* 30, 4–26. This whole box is drawn from their article.

14 Launching a new product

1 Federal Trade Commission, (November 2003), "Slotting Allowances in the Retail Grocery Industry: Selected Case Studies in Five Product Categories." Available online at http://www.ftc.gov/os/2003/11/slottingallowancerpt031114.pdf.

15 Special organizational features in the food industry

1 For a good history of US agricultural cooperatives, see "Cooperatives in the U.S." by the University of Wisconsin Center for Cooperatives available online at http://www.uwcc.wisc.edu/whatisacoop/history/
2 This discussion relies on Coltrain, David, David Barton, and Michael Boland, "New Generation Cooperatives and Traditional Cooperatives," Arthur Capper Cooperative Center at Kansas State University. Feb. 1999.
3 See Williams, G. W., O. Capps, Jr., and M. Palma, "Effectiveness of Marketing Order 906 in Promoting Sales of Texas Grapefruit and Oranges," Texas Agribusiness Market Research Center Commodity Market Research Report No. CP-01-07 (February 2007) for the detailed study of the Texas Citrus marketing order's promotional efforts.
4 For more on forward contracting, see Chapter 7.

Index

Agricultural Marketing Agreement Act 177
American Farm Bureau 175
antitrust laws 102, 117, 118, 177, 190
arbitrage 2, 34, 38, 45, 47, 97
assembly costs 60, 61
autarky 35–36, 39

Bertrand, Joseph 105
Bi-Lo stores 157
Blue Diamond 176
boundaries 63–64, 68–69
break-even pricing 21–22, 28, 127

Capper-Volstead Act 175
captive supply 68
caterers 134, 187
charge sales turnover ratio 148
children's menus 140
Clayton Antitrust Act 102, 117, 175
club stores 153–155, 159
clustering, stores 124–125
collusion 106, 117, 118
commodity commissions 177–184
competitive fringe 106
conjectural variations 123–124, 127
consumer surplus 41, 91, 126
convenience stores 154–155, 187
cooperatives 175–177; new generation 176–177
Cournot, Antoine 105
cost analysis 4
cost curves 5
cost estimation 168
cost minimization 12–15
coupons 96, 113, 140, 160–161
cross-hedging 72
current ratio 148

demand forecasting 168–170
depreciation 5
derived demand 44, 81–84
derived supply 81–84
destination category 157
distribution costs 60, 96
duopoly games 106, 110–119

early-bird specials 94, 98, 99, 140
economic engineering 5
EDLP 157
everyday low prices 157
export supply 36–41, 44, 49

Federal Trade Commission Act 117
fixed costs 4, 79, 134
food-beverage sales ratio 149
Food for Peace Act 188
food processing 1, 4–31, 37, 60, 70–71
food retailing 125, 153–163, 187
food science 165
food service industry 132–152
forward contracting 70–71, 185
franchises 143–146, 186–187
futures contracts 71–72

game theory 105–121, 124; Bertrand games 111–114, 124; constant games 106; Cournot games 110–113; cooperative solutions 109; equilibrium 108; maximin objective 108; Nash equilibrium 108, 124, 129; non-constant games 106; payoffs 106; repeated games 106; rounds 106; Stackelberg games 115–116; strategies 106; time inconsistency 107; two player games 107
General Mills 185

Index

Greenhut-Ohta competition 124
government role 187–189

happy hour 140
hedging 71
Hi-Lo pricing 157
Hotelling, Harold 122
Hotelling's location model 122–123
Hotelling-Smithies competition 124

ideal category 157
import demand 36–43
import supply 37–43
increasing returns to scale 79, 84
ingredient buying pricing 24–27
interregional trade 34–46
inventories 17, 79, 133, 146, 159, 172
inventory turnover ratio 146

keystone pricing 85

labor cost function 9–10
labor cost ratio 147
labor standard 8
Land O'Lakes 176
Löschian competition 124
loss-leader pricing 135, 136, 157
loyalty cards 97, 101, 125, 160–161

managerial operating efficiency ratio 148
margin contribution pricing 138
market boundaries 63–64, 127
market segmentation 165
marketing costs 37–45, 49, 78–81, 98, 169
marketing margins 79–89, 94
marketing orders 177–183, 187, 189
McDonald's 143, 145
menu pricing 134–139
minimum pay rules 15
monopsony 125

Nash equilibrium 108, 110–114, 124, 127
National Farmers Union 175
net value 61–65; boundaries 63–64; and captive supply 68–69; choosing crops 64–65; surfaces 61–62
new product development 164–174; demand forecasting 168–170; marketing 173; price setting 171; product launch 169–173; product testing 165–168; regulatory issues 166–167

new product pricing 30–31, 171
non-tariff barriers 43–44

Ocean Spray 176
oligopoly games 106, 111, 114, 119

plant location 59–61, 65
plant size 58
preferred category 157
price discrimination 91–104; legal aspects 102
price-linkage equation 37–38, 40, 43, 47, 53–56
price risk 70–74
pricing rules: break-even 21–22; buying 24–27; everyday low prices 157; for decision making 29–30; grocery stores 157–159; Hi-Lo prices 157; ingredients 24–27; mark-up pricing 85, 136–139; new products 30–31; restaurants 134–141; target margin 22–26; target profit margin 22–26; updating 28
private label 185
producer surplus 3, 41
product categories 157, 164
product development 164–174
product testing 165–166

quasi-price discrimination 98
quotas 44, 118

regulation 188–189
restaurants 132–152; franchises 143–146, 186–187
restaurant management 132–152; common costs 132; daily specials 140; evaluation metrics 146–149; food costs 133, 137; inventories 133, 146; labor costs 133, 141–143; menu design 141; pricing 134–140
return on assets 149
return on equity 149
risk management 70–77; price risk 70–74; with forward contracts 70–71; with futures 71–73; by geographic dispersion 74–75

Sam's Club 154
seat turnover 147
Sherman Antitrust Act 102, 117
site rent 65–66
slotting fees 158–159, 162, 168, 172
SNAP 188

spatial competition 122–131
storage 47–57; costs 16, 48; economics of 47; equilibrium 48–49; in situ 54–55; monopoly 55–56; multiple period 51–54; two-period 50–51
Subway 143, 145, 187
supermarkets 153, 155–156; margins 156–159; scanners 159–160; slotting fees 158–159, 162, 168, 172
supercenters 153
Supplemental Nutrition Assistance Program 188
supply chain management 16–17, 75, 169; disruption risk 17
support category 157

target marketing 164–165, 168, 173
target profit margin pricing 22–26
tariffs 41–43
time inconsistency 107
trade 34–46; export supply 36–41, 44, 49; import demand 36–43; import supply 37–43; interregional 34; marketing costs 37–45; non-tariff barriers 43–44; quotas 44; tariffs 41–43; two region model 35; welfare impacts 41
transfer costs 45, 78
transportation costs 36, 59–62, 65, 78, 94, 126–128
Tyson Foods 184

updating pricing rules 27
utility costs 11

variable costs 4–5, 11, 13–14, 22–23, 58, 79, 134–138
vertical coordination 184–185
vertical integration 74, 177, 184–185

Walmart 153, 154, 157, 158
Wendy's 143, 145, 169
WIC 188
Women, Infants, and Children program 188
work crews 5
work capacity 8